OF ULYSSES

Rome

A

Polyphemus

I L Y

⑦

④

⑧

⑨   *Siren*

⑤

⑩

Helios

⑪

Olympus

Istanbul

②

①

Trojan horse

T U R K E Y

⑫

G R E E C E

⑬

⑯

⑭ ⑮

Athens

Minotaur

⑰

Tripoli

Poseidon

KRETZER

THE VOYAGES

With commentaries
by
PROFESSOR C. KERÉNYI
MICHEL GALL
HELLMUT SICHTERMANN

With selections from
T. E. Shaw's translation of the Odyssey
and
Ithaka, der Peloponnes und Troja
by
Heinrich Schliemann

Pictorial and Literary Index
by
Cornelia Kerényi

OF ULYSSES

A photographic interpretation of Homer's classic
by

ERICH LESSING

HERDER FREIBURG · BASLE · VIENNA

The contributions have been translated
from the original French and German by
Kevin Smyth, Paris

Text from the *Odyssey of Homer,*
translated by T. E. Shaw,
reprinted with the permission
of Oxford University Press, Inc., New York

First published in West Germany
© 1965 Herder KG
Printed in West Germany by Herder 1965

CONTENTS

PUBLISHER'S PREFACE

This is a book about the wanderings of Ulysses, the hero of the Odyssey, an epic poem by the Greek singer, Homer. It is the story of a man who lived more than three thousand years ago, or at least of a figure from those times, because we have no final proof that Ulysses was a real character at all. His adventures were strange and sometimes incredible, an astonishing and diverting mixture of myth and apparent reality, of hairbreadth flesh-and-blood escapes and hallucinating fantasy encounters with gods and monsters, with storms and seductive maidens. Just as a story Ulysses' adventures will never die. Yet Ulysses has taken on symbolic meaning over the ages until he has become, in fact, the classic symbol of man's endurance and man's ingenuity. Behind the mythic story of Ulysses' distracted and tormented travels, of the heart now dulled and despairing, now bewitched and forgetful, lies the story of every man's own longing for his home.

As man and symbol Ulysses and his ten year voyage around the Mediterranean world and finally home to Ithaca has inspired the craftsmanship of painters and sculptors as well as the artistry of poets for centuries. Ever since Homer the word "Odyssey" has been used to speak metaphorically of dangerous journeys into the unknown. In the *Divine Comedy* Dante invokes Ulysses, unkindly placing him in hell. James Joyce, one of the fathers of modern literature, was so conscious of the timelessness of the Greek hero's longing for home that he gave his story of Leopold Bloom the title *Ulysses*.

But how are we to picture this immortal hero? What did the places look like that he visited on his travels? And where, exactly, did he go? This book is an answer to such questions. It is a picture book done in a new way. In the past, of course, there have been Odyssey books, for the most part assemblages of unconnected places and objects. But here for the first time is an effort to use both landscapes and works of art to tell an informed and coherent story of the past. This pictorial technique which Erich Lessing calls "evokation" is quite simply an intellectually sound and imaginative choice of images and words to create an organic impression of a man and an age — to bring the figure of Ulysses and the spirit of his world to life.

Habent sua fata libelli — books, too, have their history and their destinies. The truth of this saying of Terentianus Maurus (end of the 3rd Century A.D.) is clearly displayed in the story of how this book came into being. It began in Vienna with a conversation between photographer Erich Lessing, who had just finished a book for us called *Imago Austriae,* and Dr. Wolf Stadler, an editor of this publishing house. Somehow the conversation came around to Ulysses and various images of him. "That would make a marvelous book," Lessing said, and the next time the two men met, Lessing brought along a couple of books which he had picked up second-hand in Paris. They were the works of the French scholar Victor Bérard, who was convinced that real geographic and nautical facts must lie behind the wanderings of Ulysses, and who had spent years studying and sailing in the Mediterranean trying to reconstruct the exact path of Ulysses' journeys. Bérard even took a photographer with him and had made pictorial records of the places named in the Odyssey. But all that was many years ago. Just the same Bérard's book and its deficiencies provided the final impulse for this present volume. With the help of modern photography and research we decided we would be able to do something different, more definitive, and, with luck, delightful.

France's André Malraux coined the phrase "the imaginary museum". By this he meant a book or the mind of man in which are brought together works of art that in reality are scattered in the most diverse museums all over the world. When Johann Wolfgang von Goethe travelled to Italy in 1786, he created a private imaginary museum. He saw only the Italy of antiquity. He travelled so to speak in blinders and paid attention neither to the magnificent works of the Italian Renaissance or of baroque, nor to the Romanesque of the middle ages or even the Byzantine mosaics. He travelled to Italy to admire the works of classical antiquity, and that is all he saw. But he looked at it well and fixed an indelible picture of it in his mind.

Our imaginary museum tries to do something similar. It avoids the confusing multitude of impressions which museums or cities visited by a traveller leave upon him. Instead we are trying here to bring out in full clarity the picture (and the spirit) of Ulysses and the Odyssey so that it can become, in a new way, an imperishable spiritual possession. Anyone who has ever travelled to Greece, Italy, Spain, or France, knows how many different impressions crowd in upon him. And he knows how often one tires of all the sights and really goes on only because he has paid good money for the trip and the programme. Any cultural traveller has suffered from this kind of cultural indigestion.

The museum of the imagination is a preventative against cultural indigestion. It is a museum without director, keepers, or barriers. One can look at things as long as one likes. There is no supervisor to insist that we move on to the next treasure. This was the sort of museum that Verlag Herder and Erich Lessing decided to create around the Odyssey that evening in Vienna. The work of preparing it was enormous. The views and works of art to be used in the book, as we envisaged it, were scattered all over the world. Lessing travelled over 16,000 miles by car, train, airplane, and ship to gather all the material. His travels on the track of Ulysses and his omnivorous reading in scholarly works on the subject turned out to be another journey into the unknown, often full of frustrations, small clues and mysteries. Once Lessing was in East Berlin, photographing the tiny cameo of Ulysses mourning which appears in this book as Plate 30. A young student told him that a text had just been published for the first time describing a Greek vase in Amiens with a picture of the Phaeacians' ship landing Ulysses on Ithaca. Lessing drove from Berlin to Amiens, found the vase and proudly took several pictures of it. Then he went on to Rome, and learned to his dismay from Dr. Hellmut Sichtermann, the expert who discusses the archaeological sources of the Odyssey on pages 199 to 228, that his drive and film had been wasted! What he had seen in Amiens was only an extremely clever forgery!

The pictures in this book could not have been assembled without patient advice and the generous help of museum officials and directors all over the world. Often enough Lessing would turn up at a museum as he did at the

Louvre and say something like: "I have a scientific work citing a statue, vase, or bronze illustrating the Odyssey which should be in your museum." Sometimes, as at the Louvre, no one knew where the piece was to be found. The searches often lasted for days and were not always as successful as they were at the Louvre. There, thanks to the tireless efforts of one of the curators, the relief showing Ulysses' ship passing the Sirens (Plate 84) was found at last, covered with dust, on top of a 12 foot high chest. It might have stayed there for a long time if it had not been wanted so urgently for this book. Another similar and apparently hopeless search was undertaken at Lessing's request by the Kunsthistorisches Museum in Vienna. Lessing wanted to find a bronze statuette of Ulysses, only $1/4$ inches high. The only clue was a reference in an old German book on the Odyssey, describing a statuette (which appears as Plate 2 of this book) in the Bibliothèque Nationale in Paris. The reference simply said that a similar statuette existed in Vienna. The Vienna museum has over 4,000 ancient small bronzes. None are catalogued! All the same, the devoted curator found the bronze Lessing was looking for. It wound up as Plate 102. So let us take this occasion to thank all the directors, scholars, and keepers in museums everywhere we went for everything they have done to make this book possible.

The hunt for the places around the Mediterranean which Ulysses visited (or was supposed by specialists to have visited) was no easier! Lessing travelled for months on the track of Ulysses. His first guide was Homer's Odyssey to which he added the works of Bérard and Ernle Bradfords *Ulysses Found,* an account of Ulysses' travels written from the viewpoint of a veteran sailor. And, as with Heinrich Schliemann who found Troy by digging, not where experts of his time suggested, but by studying Homer's text in the Iliad, it often happened with Erich Lessing that the descriptions of places given by Homer were so precise, when read correctly, that there could be no doubt about fixing the spot. Homer, for instance, describes the land of the Phaeacians and the stream where Nausicaa brought her laundry (Plate 40) so exactly, that Lessing, like Bérard fifty years before, could find and photograph the stream which turned out to be the only freshwater stream entering the sea on that side of the island of Corfu. Other places were too vague to locate exactly. The isle of Calypso, for example, which has been identified with Malta by many scholars, or placed even beyond Gibraltar, was not photographed at all by Lessing because he came to the conclusion that this place, which Homer calls "the navel of the earth" could only have been a mythical site. It was everywhere and nowhere.

Perhaps it is necessary to say a word here to explain why this book shows no shrine of Apollo in Delphi, no acropolis of Athens, none of the sights, in fact, which are to be seen elsewhere in books about Greece and even in books which claim to follow in the path of Ulysses. We did not use these classic structures of Greece, because in Ulysses' time they did not yet exist. However, what we do use, the palaces of Cnossos (Plate 15) and of Mycene (Plate 16) and sandy Pylos itself (Plate 20), all existed in the age of Ulysses, roughly 600 years before Athenians raised the marble temples of the acropolis. The ancient palaces, with their masonry that seems to have been piled up by giants (still called "cyclopean" masonry, in memory of the monstrous Cyclops of the Odyssey), speak the same language as Homer's epics of Ulysses and the Trojan War. They speak of men who acted like gods, and gods who acted like men, and recall a pre-history already grown mythical in Homer's time. It was to this spirit that we have tried to be true.

The pictures, of course, were not enough. They needed words to accompany them — inevitably, the words of the poet. Accordingly, we have put Homer's verses immediately beside the pictures. These, with summary narrative passages to link them, tell the eventful story of wily Ulysses during his ten year's wandering. Even this was not enough. For the book, to be a really complete imaginary museum and give a full picture of the age of the Odyssey and its brilliance, would need the commentary of scholars and writers.

Accordingly, Lessing called a friend in Paris, Michel Gall, a journalist who has spent years studying various accounts of Ulysses' route. The result became our introductory text (pages 13 to 38). Combining his own experiences with the findings of experts who have devoted their lives to sailing about the Mediterranean, Gall consulted old texts as well as the Odyssey itself to establish just where Ulysses sailed. His text provides a fine guide to past adventure and present geography, and is probably the best way of getting into the book.

Because the pictures of Ulysses — from statuary and primitive vases and frescoes — reflect not only the spirit of Homer's hero but document the development of artistic attitudes through nearly 700 years of classical art, we needed another sort of expert to tell about them. Dr. Hellmut Sichtermann, a well-known German archaeologist and art historian turned out to be our man. On pages 199 to 228 you will find his absorbing essay which traces representations of Ulysses as they developed from 600 B.C. to 100 A.D.

The most remarkable commentary in the book, however, was done by Professor C. Kerényi. A disciple of Jung and world famous classical scholar, who has devoted his life to Greek mythology and religion. Kerényi (on pages 233 to 261) traces the origins and significance of the Ulysses figure, showing how the Odyssey portrait of Ulysses is a strange mixture of poetry and reality, how much it owes to myths more ancient than itself, to history, and, surprisingly enough, to plain seafarers' tales handed down from generation to generation. To help with the project Professor Kerényi's daughter Cornelia, herself a student of archaeology, painstakingly prepared an index to all the pictures which tells exactly where they can be found, when they date from, and what literature there is to describe them.

These are the ways, the many images and many voices, which we have used to lay hands on the reality and spirit of the world's most famous traveller. Readers can approach the subject by any and all of them. Some will begin with the poetry and the pictures. Others (the most faithful and meticulous) will begin with this preface. A few will turn to the back and find a special, historic description of Ithaca, Ulysses' home island, as it appeared around 1870 to Heinrich Schliemann, a sales clerk turned archaeologist, who found the ruins of Troy by ignoring what experts believed and digging at the place which best fitted

Homer's description in the Iliad. But wherever he starts we believe that the reader will return to this book again and again, from many different angles. Because the greatness of the subject, the beauty of the ancient world, and the heroic vision which inspired Homer have depths of delight which require long contemplation.

When Erich Lessing said good-bye to Professor Kerényi after showing him the pictures and a plan for the book and asking him to contribute an article, the Professor paid him a compliment and offered him a warning. "Take great care when you make this book," he said, "because a book like this will not be done soon again and generations of men all over the world will be seeing the figure of Ulysses as you see him and as you show him." We hope this book has lived up to his high expectations and to our own.

THE VOYAGES OF ULYSSES
by
MICHEL GALL

MICHEL GALL was born on July 29, 1932 in Metz. He worked on films before devoting himself entirely to journalism. Among other things he produced a documentary film on the art of the high period of the Columbian culture. After retiring from the film world he acted as film critic for several French newspapers before becoming chief editor of a television magazine. For the last five years Gall has been chief reporter for the "Paris Match", concentrating on literature and art.

Besides his occupation as chief reporter Gall has written six novels which he intends to publish as soon as he has written his tenth. In spite of being forced by the demands of his job to pay special attention to daily world events he has always been fascinated by the truth lying behind the great epics of the past. At the moment he is working on an extensive essay on the historical reality behind the "Arabian Nights".

It was only ten years ago that I first began to wonder about certain questions raised by Ulysses' voyage round the western seas. Up till then I had known what everyone knows: that Ulysses, returning from Troy, had wandered nine years before reaching his island home, Ithaca.

I also knew that Troy was in Asia Minor, west of what is now Turkey, and that Ithaca was a Greek island. Today, a steamship makes the trip from Troy to Ithaca in one day. Ulysses' wanderings lasted nine years, and this means that his voyage took him to almost every country that borders on the Mediterranean.

At the time I was in Naples. It was summer and for our holidays at Anacapri my family and I had rented the house of film-producer Alberto Cavalcanti; a set of terraces overlooked one of the most beautiful straits in the world. When I landed on the island of Capri all I knew was that it boasted a marvellous blue cave, had been used as a residence by Tiberius, Axel Munthe, Oscar Wilde, and Krupp, and also that it was known all over the world as "the isle of the Sirens". My children were not old enough to read the plays of Wilde, so I had brought with me, for their bed-time reading, a copy of the Odyssey.

They read it rather indifferently at first, then later passionately. Finally, using their inflatable boat, they began to play at being Ulysses in the bays of the island. Little by little the questions began : "Why is Capri called the isle of the Sirens? What did Ulysses do here? Where are the Sirens? There aren't any Sirens here!" I found it impossible, and still do, to give a satisfactory answer to these questions. This embarrassed me considerably at the time, and still does. However, in my own way — even though

it is not really my department, for I am a journalist — I have become something of a specialist on Ulysses. I have read Homer many times, as well as all the commentators I have run across. For ten years I have taken great pleasure in comparing the original text with the various interpretations which have been made of it.

The official Odyssey specialists, for their part, do not place the isle of the Sirens at Capri. The Sirens of Capri are part of the fairy-tales told by guides and publicized in travel leaflets. Scholarly students of Homer place the isle of the Sirens several sea-miles away from Capri, in the archipelago of the Galli (Plate 85). But most tourists never hear this. The *Guide Bleu, Nagel, Baedeker,* and above all the weight of local tradition all name Capri the island of the Sirens. The man who hired out deck-chairs on the beach where we swam introduced himself as Ulysses. He rowed me out to sea and painstakingly pointed out that two adjoining rocks, the Faraglioni, had the shape of women with robust breasts and the underpart of the bodies like a fish-tail. This explanation, he said, had been handed down from father to son in his family for generations. I do not have much faith in the value of oral tradition where the adventures of Ulysses are concerned. I shall come back to this later on. The fact that in Italy, Corsica, and Sardinia, there are some thirty caves traditionally called "the cave of Polyphemus" seems to me, at least, to cast suspicion on the value of oral tradition.

In the archipelago of the Galli, almost equidistant from the tourist port of Sorrento and the fashionable beach of Positano where Jacqueline Kennedy, following the example of certain European heads of state, likes to come for a rest, are two islands which are, or have been, inhabited. Dancer Léonide Massine lives on one of the islands every summer; the other was once occupied by an eccentric dwarf, who built a tower with doors not more than three feet high so that his guests involuntarily curtsied to the master of the house every time they entered. Neither the correspondence of the strange dwarf, nor the conversation of Massine has ever been able to cast the least light on a possible connexion between Ulysses' Sirens and the respective properties of these two.

None of the islands in the Galli stand out in any particular relief, and as landmarks for sailors they are much less important than Capri. Have they a special charm? A special beauty? Not really. They are only dry, rocky islands. Except that some of them vaguely resemble a half-submerged camel, their shape is rather nondescript. After nightfall, when flooded by moonlight, they do look beautiful to anyone cruising around them in a sailboat, but the entire coast of southern Italy looks beautiful under the moon.

Take one look at the Lorelei rock on the Rhine and you instantly understand the legend which has grown up about it. If that legend did not exist it would have to be invented; the Rhine landscape invites the creation of legends. But as for the Galli islands, one could cruise around them a hundred times, climb them, camp on them, and never think of attaching a legend to them.

Mr Ernle Bradford, who is an authority on Homer — his book, *Ulysses Found,* was published in 1963 in the United States — is perfectly aware of this. He has resorted to wild conjecture in order to justify his identification of the Isle of the Sirens with the Galli islands. Bradford is an energetic, sea-going professor of Greek, with a blond, pointed beard who looks, in his photographs, rather like Kirk Douglas playing Ulysses. He records that in 1944, while standing watch on board a warship cruising off the Galli out of Naples, a strange and sudden music reached his ears.

I will let him speak for himself, for even the least imaginative reader may find a certain magic in his words:

". . . I suddenly heard something that sounded like a song. I cannot describe it exactly, but it was low and far away. It resembled the waves and the wind. Yet it certainly was not produced by either of them because it had a human quality, disturbing and evocative . . . and for some reason that I cannot explain, I felt afraid . . . Our boat came as close as it could to the reef (probably Gallo Grande but I cannot remember), and we cut our motors . . . Suddenly the song started again. It seemed to come from another direction. A moment before, I could have sworn it came from the shelf off which we were lying, but now it seemed to come from beyond it and to be muted by it. At the beginning, as I have said, it sounded indistinct, like the wind being swallowed up in a cavern. But little by little, as I listened, it became more vocal and human. I know it was essentially feminine, because no male throat could have produced a sound so sweet and low."

Bradford then alerted the crew. "Listen! Don't you hear it? Could it be the survivors of a wreck? If not, what or who is it." Everyone was frightened, of course. The island was deserted. But the sea in that area was calm and *there was no wind.*

This childish story takes up five pages of *Ulysses Found*. The passage ends with Mr Bradford's last visit to the Galli some years later. But this time the mysterious voice is no longer heard. Why? Probably, writes Bradford, humorously but not very impressively, "because this time I had brought my wife along. And who ever heard of Sirens who sang to a ship with a woman aboard?"

I sailed out with my children one night, close to the Galli. Needless to say, though they are all boys, none of us heard even the echo of a song.

Jean Bérard, the son of that remarkable scholar, Victor Bérard, who spent most of his life trying to trace the voyage of Ulysses, also attempts to localize the Sirens. The great merit of his thesis is that it is perfectly logical. In a marginal note to his father's admirable French translation of the Odyssey, he writes:

"Now in this place (the promontory of Molpe, near Cape Palinuro, not far from the Galli) there is a cave which is only visible from the sea, where incredible masses of fossilized bones are piled up. Their off-white brilliance stands out against the darker gap of the cave in a rocky wall. It makes one think that even a detail like the whitening bones on the Sirens' strand is not poetic licence contrary to what one might have supposed." (This suggestion is based on *Les Mélanges d'archéologie et d'histoire de l'École française de Rome,* published in 1954.)

Unfortunately, only archaeologists seem to be able to see these heaps of bones. When the French School at Rome published their findings, I offered to photograph the "cliff of the dead" for a magazine. It seemed to me that a photograph of the bones would have a certain success in a popular weekly. The Italian correspondents of the magazine made inquiries. The place which had been indicated turned out to be hard to identify exactly and quite impossible to photograph. The sea dashes up against the cliff and the famous skeletons are perpetually buried in foam.

At all events, it seems to me regrettably evident at the moment that even if we found what might be the cave of the Sirens, the mystery of their song would still have to be cleared up.

But if the Sirens of the Galli remain an enigma to me, I am nevertheless convinced that for twenty-eight hundred years the Odyssey has been a real lesson in living geography. It is a continuing proof that in spite of the divergent opinions of modern commentators, pure poetry and exact information are not incompatible.

SOURCES FOR THE MODERN INTERPRETATION OF THE ODYSSEY

I have continually tried to answer the question: "Apart from the Odyssey text itself, where do we find the little information that we do have when we set out to trace Ulysses' voyage?" Here is what I have found:

At the beginning of the fourth century B.C., Thucydides, the famous historian, then serving as captain of a Greek squadron, was defeated off the coast of Thrace. His fellow-citizens promptly sent him into exile. Forbidden warlike activities, he spent his time visiting the countries which were the theatre of the events whose history he wished to write. The Odyssey was given its final form probably more than four centuries before the History of Thucydides, and yet, to the former naval officer, the strange voyage of the Achaean sailor Ulysses was still full of valid information, so much so that he gave almost complete commentaries on it, replacing legendary names by the real names of real places. It is to Thucydides that we owe the first definite identifications of Ulysses' ports of call.

Much later, almost as late as the birth of Christ, another Greek historian, Strabo, made a tour of most of the Roman empire. Drawing on his own experiences and on the works of Eratosthenes and Hipparchus, and still more on Ephorus, Polybius, and Posidonius, he wrote a geography in seventeen volumes. It is the most important work in this field which has survived from antiquity. The *Geography* of Strabo frequently quotes the Odyssey, giving the voyage of Ulysses a definite framework.

But the most important text for the understanding of the Odyssey is a periplus (literally "round trip") of the fourth century A.D. Its text comes so close to that of the Odyssey that at times it almost seems to be a popular edition of Homer's poem.

Such peripli have no doubt existed as long as sailors have sailed and men have known how to write. During the twenty-five centuries of Mediterranean history known to us, sailors have swapped or stolen these mariners' charts composed of maps and descriptions. The *periploi* were modified and enriched unceasingly in the course of centuries, but the oldest source in them we can reach is the periplus made by the Carthaginian navigator named Hanno who sailed in the fifth century B.C., along the Atlantic coast of Africa as far as Rio del Oro. This and the Odyssey. In fact, Ulysses, in line 259 of Book XII, is definitely presented as a great explorer of "the by-ways of the deep" in the western seas.

Over the centuries, peripli were given different titles. But in fact they were always based on the same periplus, only made a little more definite with each new edition. In the fourth century after Christ, Scylax of Caryanda rechristened them "the Sailors' Handbooks"; later on they became known as "Portulans", then as "Mirrors of the Sea". Finally they appeared in our own day as *Instructions nautiques* and *Admiralty Pilots*.

It is here that we must look for precise clues to Ulysses' real itinerary. If we compare the text of the Odyssey and the *Instructions nautiques*, they will often be found to coincide.

All modern commentators of the Odyssey have the *Instructions nautiques* or the *Admiralty Pilots* on their desks. The four most important commentators are: Samuel Butler, who lived at the end of the last century; Victor Bérard, who, with photographer Fred Boissonas, made the same voyage as Erich Lessing, the creator of this book; Jean Bérard, and Ernle Bradford, both of whom we have already mentioned. All of them used these official handbooks as the basis for their studies. It was very often by following such handbooks that archaeologists decided where to dig. Some of the excavations, like the famous discoveries of Heinrich Schliemann at Troy and more recently Carl Blegen's discoveries at "sandy Pylos" seem to have furnished the only unquestionable indications of the geographical reality behind the Homeric poems.

THE LAND OF THE LOTOS-EATERS

The first stop made by Ulysses and his companions in a really unknown land is in "the land of the Lotos-eaters, men who browse on a food of flowers". (In English "lotus" is the usual form in which the Greek word has come down to us.) There, as soon as one of the sailors has tasted of "this honey-sweet plant, the wish to bring news or return grows faint in him". It is only by using force, by tying them up, in fact, that Ulysses succeeds in re-embarking three of his men who have tasted the fruit.

Herodotus and Scylax of Caryanda place the country of the Lotos-eaters on the coast of Tripoli and southern Tunisia. Strabo is more definite: "It is the island of Djerba" (Plate 53). Bérard and Bradford agree. The Encyclopaedia Britannica (1963) is alone in writing: "It should be plain enough that the Lotus-eaters and their country are situated in fairyland . . . many ancient scholars amused themselves by trying to identify them with some people of northern Africa . . . This foolishness has been imitated by some moderns."

We are quite ready to take responsibility for this "foolishness", especially since Bradford proved that in nine days and nine nights (the round number given by Homer) Ulysses' "cruiser" with a good following east wind could, in fact, have sailed six hundred and forty-eight miles. Djerba is situated six hundred and fifty miles from Ulysses' starting-point, which was half-way between Cape Maleia and Cythera, in the extreme south of Greece. Studying all this I came to accept that Djerba was the land of the Lotos-eaters.

Under the name "lotos" the ancients ranged several different plants (Plate 54). The lotos of Egypt was a water-lily. The lotos of the Odyssey, according to Herodotus and Polybius, was the nettle-tree *(Celtis australis),* rather than the jujube-tree *(Zizyphus lotus).* Bérard says it was the date-palm.

As far as I know, neither the dates of the palm-tree nor the fruit of the nettle-tree have ever created forgetfulness in anybody. Bérard explains skilfully that the story is based on a play on the words lotos and *lethe* (forgetfulness) which is found in line 102 in Book IX of the Odyssey. But I find it almost an insult to Homer's talent to suggest that he made this colour the whole passage, which would be a type of heavy-handedness quite out of keeping with the rest of the poem.

Bradford contents himself with simply pointing out that the "lethargic" climate of northern Africa is well known. I am quite sure that the climate of Greece is every bit as lethargic, and that the temperature at Djerba cannot have come as a surprise to anyone who had just spent ten years at Troy in Asia Minor.

I note on the other hand that Ulysses' three comrades who tasted the lotos seemed to live in a dream. Their condition was so critical that they had to be tied up under the thwarts of the ship. They wept for the lost lotos, and their intoxication lasted for days. There is only one plant, to my knowledge, whose withdrawal causes addicts to weep for it. It still has, in our time, the same effect on its users as on Ulysses' companions. I cannot see why we should not simply identify the "lotos" with hashish.

There were probably no more smokers of Indian hemp at Djerba than anywhere else at the time, but no doubt Homer wanted Ulysses' voyage to begin with a general warning to sailors, urging them to be on their guard against the insidious dangers of their ports of call. The adventure of the Lotos-eaters is nothing but a "cautionary tale" such as can also be found at the beginning of many "Naval Handbooks".

POLYPHEMUS
AND THE LITTLE ISLAND

Ulysses, driven by a wind and current encountered off Cape Maleia, much against his will reached the land of the Lotos-eaters. From there he tried to head back. He must have lost his way because, suddenly — Homer does not say how long afterwards so anybody's guess is good —

he came to the "Land of the Round Eyes" where the Cyclops Polyphemus lived.

Samuel Butler, author of *The Way of All Flesh,* was also fascinated by the Ulysses legend. Throughout his life he studied all the possible interpretations of Ulysses' voyages and he places Polyphemus' cave at the foot of Mount Eryx. The cave may still be visited today. Like most Sicilian caves, it is used as a sheep-fold. The natives call it "la grotta di Polifemo".

Ernle Bradford, careful for once, writes: "It would be very strange if an oral tradition had been preserved unchanged for three thousand years through all the vicissitudes of Sicilian history." It would indeed!

Bradford, without situating the cave precisely, still keeps it in the region of Trapani, a town in the extreme west of Sicily. "The caves of this region have always been famous", he writes. "On Levanzo, an island which is a few miles away from Trapani, with which it was probably linked earlier by an isthmus, there is to be found one of the most remarkable of prehistoric caves. Its wall-paintings rival those of Lascaux and Altamira." The truth probably is that he, and others, picked the region of Trapani because it is not very far from Djerba, and is logically the first point at which the Achaeans would have landed on their way to Greece.

That is also why most ancient commentators place the land of the Cyclops in Sicily. According to Bradford, there is only one point in Sicily which can correspond to the description given in the Odyssey. Homer says that Ulysses and his companions, before disembarking on the territory of Polyphemus, landed on a tree-clad isle, on which an extraordinary number of goats were grazing. "Its haven is a natural port requiring no such gear as anchors or warps . . ."

This isle is Favignana, which lies four miles off the west coast of Sicily, opposite Trapani. It has a very sheltered harbour. In classical times it was called Aegusa, "the island of goats", which need be no more than a coincidence. It is situated not far from a volcano, Mount Eryx, and all antiquity recognized that Polyphemus was a volcano. According to Homer, Polyphemus is "like a tree-grown crag", belching and vomiting and hurling stones.

The ancients went even farther afield. From Thucydides to Virgil, they identified Polyphemus with Mount Etna, and even in ancient times some rocks on the eastern side of Sicily, not far from Catania, were called the rocks of the Cyclopes.

Obviously there is no lack of candidates for the land of Polyphemus. And every commentator upholds his point of view with arguments which are very strange at times. Samuel Butler, for instance, who maintains, along with his disciple Robert Graves, that Homer was a woman, has gone on at considerable length about the thick fogs which are not unusual in the region of Trapani. "Homer", he says, "notes very precisely that Ulysses arrives in the land of the Cyclopes in the middle of a thick fog. He can only mean the fogs of Trapani, which are particularly frequent." Butler even goes so far as to insist that Homer wrote the whole of the Odyssey at Trapani itself.

It came like a bombshell to the world of Homeric scholarship when Victor Bérard boldly announced at the beginning of the century that the land of the Cyclopes was not to be looked for in Sicily at all, but in another volcanic zone of southern Italy, in the gulf of Naples (Plate 55).

"That's much too far from Djerba! And how could Ulysses have sailed round Sicily without seeing it?" was the rejoinder of his opponents. "Come and have a look", was Bérard's answer. "Point by point I have rediscovered the country described by Homer. The resemblance is amazing." There it was that Erich Lessing went; and in 1964 he actually photographed the "round eyes" (Plate 56).

In fact, Bérard's idea was to identify Polyphemus not with Vesuvius, which was inactive during the entire pre-Christian era, but with the Phlegraean Fields and Solfatara, which is only semi-active today. There, ground-level craters irresistibly suggest Homer's "round eyes".

Opposite this strange countryside — one of the strangest in the Mediterranean, so that it is not surprising if the Polyphemus episode is the most extraordinary in the Odyssey — lies an island called Nisida. The name comes from an ancient Greek word meaning "little island". This is the name by which Homer several times mentions the island where Ulysses and his companions debarked.

As for the island where I began to ask myself questions about the Odyssey, it is quite close by. Its name Capri can be translated as "the island of goats". It is very likely that the periplus which Homer had before his eyes mentioned the "isle of goats" and the "little isle". The author probably combined the two into one.

Nisida is the summit of a submerged volcano. The sea has penetrated into its crater through a narrow breach. The island is a broken circle of land surrounding a sheltered basin called Porto Pavone, one of the safest harbours in the Mediterranean.

Opposite Nisida, on the slopes of Mount Posillipo, we can see the gaping jaws of an immense cavern with features which are still startlingly similar to those mentioned in the Odyssey. "As we came to the nearest point of land we could see a cave at its seaward extremity — a lofty cave embowered in laurels . . . Round the cave-mouth a strong-walled yard had been contrived of rocks deeply embedded with a fence of logs from tall pines and spreading oaks." If you look at the photograph taken by Erich Lessing (Plate 62) you will see the pink oleanders, the embedded rocks and above all the tall pines which you would seek in vain in Sicily. It may well be, however, that this cave is of more recent origin than Bérard suggests.

At each end of the little isle, to the east and west, there are sharp rock needles which could be the two rocks which Polyphemus threw at Ulysses' ship. "He tore the crest from a great mountain and flung it at the black-prowed ship, but overcast by a hair's breadth."

I took long walks on Posillipo, from the cave of Polyphemus to the still more spectacular cave of the Sibyl at Cumae. I wandered round the Phlegraean Fields, and into the eroded crater of Solfatara. At midday, with not a breath of air stirring and the only noise the simmering of the two great round eyes of burning mud bubbling away at ground level, it is one of the most impressive and sinister places in the world (Plate 56). It makes a perfect setting for the cruellest episode in the Odyssey. The periplus which Homer followed probably spoke of these horrifying details. Even today the air is still sometimes darkened by the emanations from the ground. Perhaps we should see in these smoke-holes, which must once have given out thick clouds of smoke, the origin of the fog mentioned by Homer and so dear to the hearts of Butler and Bradford.

THE ISLAND OF AEOLUS

"So we came to the Aeolian island. In that sea-cradled fastness, within a *bulwark of invincible bronze* from which the cliff falls sheer, lived Aeolus son of Hippotas, a friend of the eternal Gods." This is Ulysses' second stop in the western seas.

From remotest antiquity, the home of Aeolus has been identified with a cluster of islands known as the Lipari. Virgil places it very precisely on the island of Stromboli (Plate 64), which in his time must have been the most important of the group. Bradford rejects this idea. "Homer speaks of a single island", he says, "he does not speak of an archipelago!" So he assigns to the lord of the winds a very isolated island off Sicily, the island of Ustica, which is dominated by Mount Guardi, a peak some nine hundred feet high. "Ustica", he says, "certainly lies on Ulysses' homeward route, and all the winds of the Mediterranean converge on it." (See the map inside the cover of the book.)

But there is nothing resembling a "bulwark of bronze" about the flanks of Mount Guardi, whereas those of Stromboli cannot fail to remind us of a construction of polished metal (Plate 65), at least the home of some fabulous Atlantes, if not of a god.

The slopes of Stromboli, composed in part of a very hard obsidian called liparite, were exploited very actively for centuries, as the heaps of debris which have been found there indicate. This kind of mining would explain the riches attributed to Aeolus by the Odyssey.

T. E. Shaw calls the island of Aeolus "a sea-cradled fastness". Bérard gives a very satisfactory explanation of Homer's term if we accept the more familiar translation "floating island". He writes: "The crater of Stromboli throws out very light pieces of pumicestone, which float on the water and can be carried great distances by the winds and currents, sometimes as far as the coasts of Corsica or Provence. This, it would seem, is the origin of the legend of the floating isle which Aeolus was supposed to inhabit."

Finally, we have recently learned of a new argument in favour of identifying Stromboli as the home of Aeolus. In 1949, potsherds (bits of pottery) were found at Stromboli unquestionably dating from the early Mycenaean age. It was the first time that traces left by the Greeks of the twelfth century B.C. had been found at one of Ulysses' possible ports of call. The discovery allows us to affirm that the basis of the Odyssey is to be sought in the con-

tacts made by the Achaeans of the heroic age with the western basin of the Mediterranean.

THE LAESTRYGONIANS

While Ulysses slept, his companions foolishly opened the leather bottle containing the winds entrusted to them by Aeolus. The unfavourable winds now let loose drove the ship, which had almost reached Greece, back to Stromboli. Cursed by Aeolus, the Greek hero sets another course and sails away to Laestrygonia, where he lands: "Its harbour is good, for an unbroken wall of rock shelters it from side to side; while parallel headlands jut forth to mask the entrance which is rather narrow."

Once the ship is moored, Ulysses sends three of his men towards the town. They come to a fountain where they meet a giantess, the daughter of a king, drawing water. She takes them to the palace where the king without any ado "seized hold of the first and proceeded to eat him for his dinner out of hand". Other Laestrygonians hurl boulders at Ulysses' fleet and shatter some of the ships, then harpoon the swimming Achaeans like tuna-fish and make a horrible feast of them.

I find this one of the feeblest stories narrated in the palace of Alcinous. It comes too close to the story of Polyphemus, another giant who is also a cannibal, and adds practically nothing to it. None the less, the episode has aroused passionate interest among Homeric scholars, for the location of Laestrygonia is the subject most hotly debated.

Here are four theories among many others now put forward:

1) Telephylus (Tall-tower), the name given by Homer to the city of the Laestrygonians, may be Leontini in eastern Sicily. This is the opinion of the most ancient Greek commentators. But Leontini lies five miles inland and was never a port. And no point on the adjoining coast corresponds to the description given in the Odyssey.

2) Telephylus may be Formia on the Gulf of Gaeta on the west coast of Italy. This was the opinion of Cicero and Horace. But the harbour at Formia, like that of Gaeta, is artificial. This strip of coast likewise contains no harbours corresponding to the description in Homer.

3) Telephylus may be Porto Pozzo, on the Sardinian side of the straits between Corsica and Sardinia. So says Victor Bérard. Porto Pozzo is a deep and narrow gulf which does not correspond exactly to Homer's description, but was chosen by Bérard for two philological reasons. The headland on the way to it is called the Cape of the Bear, because when seen from the sea it looks like that animal. And Homer actually mentions a Spring of the Bear in the land of the Laestrygonians. Also, a certain rock now called Colombo rock, formerly Lais Trygonia, is still used as a landmark by navigators to locate the entrance of Porto Pozzo among the granite masses of the neighbouring headlands. The name, Lais Trygonia, sounds very much like that of the Laestrygonians.

4) Telephylus may be Bonifacio in Corsica, on the other side of the straits. This time the environs of the port and the description of it given by the *Instructions nautiques* are perfectly in accord. This is what Erich Lessing found, following Bradford (Plate 86).

It must be noticed that even if the Laestrygonian adventure is of little importance in the poetic framework of the stories told to Alcinous, it must have been of major significance in the periplus which Homer used. The straits between Corsica and Sardinia are in fact among the most important in the Mediterranean. From Homer's point of view it would indeed have been a pity if Ulysses, "explorer of the by-ways of the deep", had not come upon them.

THE CIRCE EPISODE

"In very disheartened mood, having lost every one of our dear comrades (yet with the consolation that we were still alive", Ulysses and his companions now reach "Æava, where lived a formidable Goddess — though she spoke our speech — Circe of the luxuriant tresses".

Strabo writes: "Since Mount Circe is surrounded by marshes and the sea, one could say that properly speaking it is an island." From time immemorial it has been held that Mount Circe, on the Italian coast between Rome and Naples, is the place to situate the Circe episode, and the various naval instructions still echo the early words of Strabo: "Situated at the extreme south of the Pontine Marshes, this mountain looks like an island when seen from a distance" (Plate 67).

Among ancients and moderns alike, only one commentator has ever tried to look elsewhere for the castle of smooth stones where the sorceress and her servants lived. Dante makes Ulysses say, in *The Divine Comedy:* "This Circe, who held me for a year by Gaeta . . ." Gaeta is where Cicero and Horace placed the land of the Laestrygonians. Dante has only taken over an erroneous tradition which made Gaeta one of the high points of the Odyssey.

At Mount Circe (or Monte Circeo in Italian) Erich Lessing found unchanged the country and sites described by Homer (Plates 68, 72): the bay where Ulysses moored his vessel (at the grotto called "the cave of goats" rather than at the cave of San Felice which is about two hundred yards away and is erroneously mentioned in many guide books), the "crow's nest" to which he climbed (the peak of Belvedere, nineteen hundred feet high, is today crowned by a watch-tower in ruins), the marshy plain, which can be seen, from there (the Pontine Marshes) and which once bore the enchantress' house from which deadly fumes rose. Finally, Erich Lessing found growing there in abundance a strange flower (Plate 73) which might be that magic "moly" given by Hermes to Ulysses to ward off Circe's evil spells. Homer narrates Hermes' instructions, and then: "Upon such explanation the Slayer of Argus plucked from the ground the herb he promised me. The Gods call it Moly, and he showed me its nature, to be black at the root with a flower like milk." This description

as you can see by looking at Lessing's picture, is very close. Bradford makes an interesting remark about this. From classical times the name "moly" has been applied to a species of garlic *(Allium moly)*. Now in the fourteenth century sailors thought that garlic had the uncanny power of being able to neutralize — or "bewitch" — the needle on a compass. This maritime tradition may be a distant memory of Hermes' magic herb and the discoveries of Ulysses.

Bérard locates the exact site of Circe's house in a valley today called Val San Benedetto at the foot of the Lepini mountains, the last bastion of the Appenines, where building stone is abundant. (Homer stresses the fact that Circe's house was "a noble house of dressed stone".) In Val San Benedetto there was a cult, which survived until Roman times, of a goddess of wild beasts called Feronia, whose temple was surrounded by animals in stone and in the flesh, just as Circe's house was.

But the valley of San Benedetto is rather far away from Mount Circe and Erich Lessing has preferred to situate the sorceress's manor at the very foot of this mountain, about two miles from the sea.

The house of smooth stones is no more. But I dream of the day when excavations by archaeologists in this still little-explored region may perhaps unearth the traces of the undoubtedly strange house inhabited by the heroine to whom Homer consecrated the largest number of verses in the Odyssey, the lady who according to post-Homeric tradition, bore Ulysses a son, Telegonus.

IN THE LAND OF SHADES

"We tarried day by day till an entire year had lapsed, sitting to table and delighting in untold wealth of flesh and mellow wine. Slowly the year fulfilled itself, as the seasons turned about and the months died, bringing down the long days once more. Then my men took me aside, saying: — Master, it is time you called to memory your native land."

Ulysses, who had found Circe a delightful companion, at last made up his mind to leave. He said good-bye to the sorceress, who kept her promise and let him go. But before his departure, she organized for him — out of love, or out of a desire to display her magical powers — an interview with Teiresias, the seer of Thebes. Teiresias was to give these enduring heroes the best advice on navigation. "But who, O Circe, can guide us by this way? No human being ever reached Hades in one of our black ships", wonders Ulysses. Circe answers: "Let not the need of a pilot for the ship concern you at all. Set mast, hoist sail, and then sit quietly. The northern airs will bring you thither."

Circe gives him to understand that it will be a short trip. And true enough, having sailed from Mount Circe in the early morning, Ulysses reached the entrance to Hades by evening. This might lead us to the conclusion that the entrance to Hades is only about forty sea-miles, at most, from Mount Circe, since Ulysses' ship could at most have covered that distance in twelve hours.

That is why, like Virgil in the *Aeneid*, Strabo and Dio-dorus Siculus, basing their opinions on information offered by the historian Ephorus, place the Hades of Ulysses near Lake Averno, a small lake beside the Phlegraean Fields in the land of Polyphemus.

Obvious as this site is, the question of Hades is not as simple as all that. Ancient writers had several alternatives to offer for the entrance to Hell. The most famous was at Cape Taenarus, the most southerly point of Greece. Another was near Enna in Sicily. But Circe herself is very specific: "There Pyriphlegethon (with Cocytus a tributary of the water of Styx) runs into Acheron." These rivers still exist and they still flow into the Ionian Sea at Phanari on the west coast of Greece. The German historian, Ivar Lissner, in 1962, found that where they flow together Homer's description fitted exactly. It seems that at this point Homer combined information based on several different sources. His description of the two entrances to Hell is a composite: it is made up of the description of Lake Averno given in the periplus which he was probably using mixed with traditional Achaean tales.

Unquestionably, in the Odyssey, the visit to Hell has a different ring from the rest of the work. Here we see Ulysses, the enduring hero, in a very strange light. When Circe tells him that he must go and visit the sinister blind seer Teiresias, he behaves like a common coward. "She ceased," he tells Alcinous, "and again my loving heart gave way. I wept as I sat there on her bed, nor did my soul any longer desire to feel or see the shining of the sun: till I had wept and wallowed myself impotent." A likelier explanation for this odd behaviour is that he is afraid that the sorceress, angry at his departure, has decided to play a trick on him to avenge herself. At this point, in any case, interpretation is difficult, for we are dealing with magic.

That is why Ernle Bradford makes use of this episode to justify a fantastic theory of just where Hades is. He suggests it should be in the straits of Gibraltar, bounded by the pillars of Hercules! If Ulysses and his companions took only a day to reach it, well that was merely because their entire voyage had been thoroughly bewitched from the start!

Unlike many critics I do not believe that Circe, seeing Ulysses about to leave her, tries to hold his attention by any magical trick. It seems to me, on the contrary, very much in keeping with this strange woman's temperament to tell the truth just at this moment. She knows that her magic can no longer surprise Ulysses. The only thing left, in fact, to startle her lover would be to tell the truth. And so she does. Hades, she says, in Bérard's translation, is a day's sail from her home. Ulysses does not believe her. It is love that makes her reveal one of her secrets for the first time, just before they part.

After a day's sailing, Ulysses nears Lake Averno (Plate 76). Circe had counselled him to take his sword and dig a hole one cubit square, and then make libations. He was now in the land of the Cimmerians, a people for whom "no flashing Sun-God shines down a living light, not in the morning when he climbs through the starry sky, nor yet at day's end when he rolls down from heaven behind the land. Instead an endless deathful night is spread over its melancholy people."

Ephorus, as Strabo reports, thought that these Cimme-

rians who lived in the night were the troglodytes who lived in the gloomy caves of the Phlegraean Fields. This assertion seems highly unlikely to me. The climate at Naples is so mild that the troglodytes would have been able to spend most of their time out of doors. I believe, instead, that the "night" of which Homer speaks is something quite different.

Lake Averno (motionless and unreal, as Bérard correctly describes it) is profoundly dramatic in character. A light mist often shrouds it. It is a beautiful place, but somehow far too sad for anyone to want to live there. The night Homer speaks of must be, I think, only a metaphor for the depressing atmosphere of the place. Between sadness and night is only, after all, a step; and a step which poets through the ages have often taken.

For a modern Hell, with its flames, roasting pits and devils, the entrance would have to be sought somewhere in the Sahara. But I imagine the entrance to Homer's Hell as lying near a lovely dead lake, with insidious still waters that freeze the soul and the blood.

THE SIRENS, SCYLLA AND CHARYBDIS

Teiresias does not give Ulysses any precise geographical indications about the route he is to follow. He contents himself with beseeching Ulysses to leave unhurt "the oxen and wonderful sheep of Helios our Sun" on the isle of the Trident. Ulysses is therefore supposed to pass by Thrinacia, "the isle of the Trident", as he makes his way home to Greece.

From remotest antiquity, Sicily has been recognized as the isle of the Trident. Only a few modern commentators, among whom are Bradford and Bérard, express doubt. They maintain stoutly that Sicily does not resemble a trident but a triangle. I readily agree that it is shaped neither like a fishing-trident nor like a trident of Neptune. But it has got three enormous teeth, the three giant capes which mark out its shape. Faced with this geographical fact the commentators in question reply that Sicily only seems to have three teeth when seen from above, but that the Phoenicians were looking at it from the sea. I fail to understand these arguments. It seems to me that if the Phoenician whose periplus Homer was following had sailed around Sicily he would have been perfectly able to ascertain from sea level, as early map-makers had to do, that this great island had the shape of a three-pointed star, a star with three teeth.

I have discussed this problem because both Bradford and Bérard devote many lines and pages to it. But I regard their reflections as largely academic. When anyone seriously wants to find a location for the pastures of the Sun he will find himself forced to choose Sicily. As I think will be clear later on.

Circe, once Ulysses returns from his visit to Teiresias, tells him how to go to the isle of the Trident; she certainly knew the danger on that island but she had sent Ulysses to see Teiresias in order to keep him with her a little longer, to make their separation less brutal and to keep him in her arms one more night.

And the lady is a fine guide for the best route to the straits of Messina. She explains to Ulysses that he will have to sail past the bay of Naples, where he will meet — at Capri? — at the Galli? — the famous Sirens. After that, he will have to choose between two routes, one long and venturesome which goes around Sicily, the other short but dangerous which passed through the straits of Messina, between one of the teeth of Sicily and the toe-cap of the Italian boot.

"On the other side", says Circe, "stand two huge crags." These are the two most famous crags in the world. They are called Scylla and Charybdis. All commentators have placed them at the same spot, on either side of the straits of Messina. On mariners' charts they still go by the same name.

The straits of Messina are still particularly dangerous today. The *Admiralty Pilots* say this about them: "Their currents and whirlpools call for extreme prudence in navigating inside the straits; further, from the direction of the land, ships are exposed to violent gusts of wind which blow down the valleys with such force that they sometimes render navigation difficult even for steamships." And as early as Thucydides, we get an explanation of the origin of the whirlpool called Charybdis: "This current", he says, "is created by the Tyrrhenian sea, where it pours into the Ionian."

Bradford sums up all these details by explaining that the current in the straits is created by a noticeable difference in the saline content of the two seas. But the straits are also one of the few places in the Mediterranean subject to tidal action. These tides which, for the Greeks of the eighth century, limited to the basically tideless Mediterranean, were a legendary curiosity and almost an absurdity.

The *Admiralty Pilots* account goes on to say: "Twice a day, throughout the straits, the level of the water takes on a slope in the northern direction, and twice a day in the southern direction. The current created by these slopes is at its strongest where the straits are narrowest, between Punta Pezzo and Ganzini."

Punta Pezzo lies very close to the Italian village which today still bears the name of Scilla, and near which stands the famous rock (Plates 87, 95). Today it is lower — barely ninety feet — than Homer seems to suggest: "Into heaven", says the poet, "it thrusts it sharp peak which yet is covered always by a sombre cloudcap. No mortal man could scale that height or ever keep his footing there — not with twenty hands and feet."

Bradford maintains that in ancient times the Scylla was much higher. He thinks that since the eighth century erosion must have been at work on this rock with particularly grave effects. But the only proof he has to offer is an account by a Dutchman of the eighteenth century, who writes, in describing a contemporary picture of Scylla: "This rock has the shape of a woman; it contains large fissures and deep caves where the winds and the waves set up a horrible whine." It seems to me that this argument is glaringly improbable. It shows how anxiety to make all the details of Homer's text appear to match reality can make a commentator lose his head. I find it quite sufficient to note that Scylla is still called Scylla, that it is still dangerous for sailors and that it is directly on Ulysses' route. After which, I leave to Homer, the poet, the heights of fancy in the words, "thrusts into heaven its sharp peak".

In fact it is extraordinary how precise Homer is when he says that Scylla is inhabited by a frightful monster with six huge necks, twelve feet and many horrible jaws. Everybody can recognize in this description that the monster is an octopus. Thus the passage of the Odyssey which deals with Scylla has found more commentators than any other. The zoologists join the geographers and the men of letters. Indeed they have always been fascinated by the "sea-monsters" or giant squids which liked to capsize boats in past centuries. According to them, there is no doubt that a sea-monster once haunted the straits of Messina and the periplus of Homer faithfully recorded its existence.

Sea-monsters are certainly long-lived. But in thirty centuries Scylla the sea-monster has had plenty of time to die. Her offspring, too, although the "region of Messina is still known today for the great number of squid, octopus and jelly-fish which inhabit it". But nothing will persuade me that a "sea-monster" did not prowl about these straits long ago.

Hence I admire the courage of Ulysses who seizes two long pikes and takes his stance on the fore-castle. But he could see nothing though he "stared his eyes bleary with trying to pierce the shadows of the gloomy cliffs". Bérard has noted that the stance of the lookout-man on the forecastle, armed with two long spears, is still used by present-day harpooners hunting tuna or sword-fish in the straits. There is at any rate no other clear reason why Italian fishermen of today should hold two spears in this special way. They might as well hold a single, longer spear at the stern of the ship. I like to think that their stance is a custom handed down for centuries — thirty centuries in fact — from Ulysses' time to our own.

The episode of Scylla and Charybdis is one of the most human in the Odyssey. It is the only one whose geographical location is not contested at all. All arguments, no matter from where they come, move in the same direction: Charybdis exists, Scylla also exists, the sea-monster could have existed, the stance of Ulysses is that of the fishermen in the straits of Messina. Here, every line of the Odyssey seems satisfyingly to coincide with today's reality. I personally wish we could say the same thing about the seductive Sirens!

THE OXEN OF THE SUN

"Now we were through the dangers of the Skurries and of Scylla and Charybdis. We neared the God's good island where Helios Hyperion kept his broad-browed splendid cattle (Plate 93) and many flocks of fat sheep... We brought our staunch ship to rest in the sheltered haven by a spring of fresh water."

This landing was disastrous for Ulysses. The sirocco kept him at anchor for a month, and his companions, dying of hunger, defy the counsels of Teiresias and sacrifice the oxen of the Sun. Six days later, Zeus, to avenge the Sun who was threatening "to quit for Hades and shine his light there upon the dead", shattered the dark ship with a thunderbolt.

Where are the pastures of the Sun? Bérard puts them at Messina itself, where the harbour is sheltered by a long natural breakwater in the form of a sickle. Bradford, for his part, notes that the ancient name of Taormina, which is twenty-six sea-miles away from Messina, was Tauromenion. Taurus means a bull. Hence it might be that great herds of cattle grazed at Taormina long ago.

Unhappily for this theory, Taormina represents a slight detour for Ulysses, who is hurrying back to Greece. And Teiresias, as well as Circe, has clearly indicated that Ulysses has no choice but to pass by the famous pastures. Erich Lessing was unable to decide whether Bradford or Bérard is right. I am convinced the herds of the Sun were grazing somewhere on the coast of Sicily or Calabria, close to the straits — but exactly where? Like Lessing, I don't know. One thing is certain, however; the exact location cannot be decided on the basis of local geography.

CALYPSO

When his boat is shattered by Zeus's lightening, Ulysses ties together the mast and keel as an improvised raft and lets himself be carried off by the waves. The current brings him back to Charybdis. The whirlpool engulfs the raft, while Ulysses hangs by his arms from the branches of a providential fig-tree whose vast branches are "shading all Charybdis". He waits for twelve full hours until the tide returns his raft to him. "Then," says Ulysses, "I let go and dropped with sprawling hands and feet, to splash heavily into the water on the lee side of these great beams. Across them I sat and paddled hard with my hands. So I drifted for nine days. In the tenth darkness the Gods cast me ashore on Ogygia, where lives Calypso, the high but humane Goddess who greeted me kindly and tended me."

The Greeks of classical times no longer thought they knew where to place the isle of Calypso. They guessed it lay in Italian waters, near the gulf of Tarentum. Samuel Butler locates it at Pantellaria. Bradford makes it Malta. In fact the location of Malta, at the centre of the Mediterranean, corresponds to the comparison made by Homer, who describes the isle of Calypso as the "navel of the seas". (T. E. Shaw with typical Anglo-Saxon sang-froid translates "a speck in the belly of the sea".)

But C. Kerényi, believes — (see his text on page 233) — that Calypso's isle is a myth. His opinion is in direct contradiction to Bérard's who places it on the Moroccan coast at Centa, at the foot of the Atlas Mountains, directly across from Gibraltar. In 1912 he discovered several sites there which exactly match Homer's description: among others, the cave of Calypso with its four springs which rise from the base of the rock.

Here again it is difficult for me to make up my mind. Erich Lessing accepts Kerényi's theory that Homer's four springs are only a poetic image to describe the four points of the compass. It is a pity that this place cannot be definitely identified, because according to the Odyssey Ulysses made the longest stay of his entire voyage with Calypso. It lasted seven years, and, according to the post-Homeric poets,. gave Calypso time to bear him three children: Hausithous, Nausinous, and Latinus. Yet every day found Ulysses sitting on the shore "his eyes as ever dewed with tears at this ebbing of his precious life". So, at the intercession of Hermes, Calypso at last provides Ulysses with the means of returning: a new ship.

It was a boat, not a raft as most translators write it. The word used by Homer, σχεδίη, was translated in Latin as *ratis*. But *ratis* is a very general poetic term which can mean a swift sailing-ship as well as a raft.

The vessel which Ulysses built with his own hands, using timber from twenty trees and following the instructions of Calypso who had given him a set of carpenter's tools, has a strange resemblance to the sharpie, a square-bodied coastal lugger, which was for decades the traditional boat of the New Haven oyster fishermen and was introduced into Europe at the end of the last century.

This is how Georges Paul Thierry, vice-president of the French sailing-yacht club, in his book *A Century of French Sailboat Racing,* describes Ulysses' work.

"First of all, Ulysses built a number of well-assembled frames, arranged on a line between two beams with their ends in the sea so as to make the launching easier. The frames, through which holes had been pierced beforehand, were then bolted together, and the work was completed by fitting cross-pieces fore and aft to make a sort of planking."

Having put together the necessary spars and a rudder, stayed his masts, ballasted his ship and provided it with a cockpit, Ulysses is given cloth by Calypso to make a sail.

This square-bodied lugger moving under sail — is it not quite simply the first sharpie? The Odyssey goes on: "As broad as a skilled shipwright would design and lay down the floor of a roomy merchantship, just so full in beam did Ulysses make his (c)raft. To carry his upper deck he set up many ribs, closely kneed and fitted, and he united the heads of these with long rubbing strakes, for gunwhales. He put a mast into his craft with a yard in proportion: also a stern sweep with which to steer her. To defend himself from breaching seas he fenced in the sides of the (c)raft with wicker work, wattling it cunningly all of osiers like a basket and adding a lavish reinforcement of stanchions. Calypso came again with a bolt of cloth for sails, which he stitched strongly. Then he set up stays and sheets and halyards, and at last with levers he worked the (c)raft down into the sacred sea." It all reads like a description of how to build your own thirty-foot sharpie.

I have dwelt on the building of this boat to show once more how precise and accurate the poet can be. Perhaps we ought to believe that Polyphemus is a volcano, that Scylla is a crag and a sea-monster, that the home of Aeolus is Stromboli, because Calypso's raft is really an excellent thirty-foot sharpie.

THE PHAEACIA OF NAUSICAA

Ulysses was at sea seventeen days. But the moment he approaches land, Poseidon destroys his sharpie. Ulysses finds himself swimming in front of a terrible cliff. "Woe is me!" he groans, "Has Zeus let me behold this land only to make me despair? See, I have won my way from the depths of the tide, to find that there is no escape out of the foaming waters. There face me walls of sheer cliff, about which tumultuous seas clash loudly; and smooth the rocks run up, steep-to, so that nowhere is there lodging for my feet to bear me free from disaster."

Although this description seems to resemble any number of romantic storm scenes from literature of the nineteenth century, in fact this first glimpse of the land of Phaeacia perfectly suits the west coast of Corfu, a cliff of gashed rock against which the sea dashes furiously in stormy weather. All commentators, ancient and modern, have recognized this. All the legends about Phaeacia also give it the same name as Homer does — "Scheria", which, according to Bradford, means "the cliff". The modern name of the island, Corfu, is said to be derived from the word for "cruiser", used in the Odyssey to describe a fast ship. Bérard holds, in fact, that the island was formerly called Kerkyra or Korkyra, a word which meant "cruiser" to Herodotus. (The Hebrew word for female racing camels is likewise kerkera.)

Modern critics, however, disagree about which points of the island correspond to Homer's descriptions. The *Guide Bleu,* for instance, says: "Some people even reject all identifications, and consider the descriptions given by Homer to be pure imagination."

Bradford and Bérard are for once in agreement in identifying the strand at the estuary of a river as the place where Ulysses finally found a foothold. According to them it can only be the bay of Ernones, the only bay on the coast (Plate 36), while the rapids of the Ernones River correspond neatly to the basins where Nausicaa washes her laundry: "Within which from beneath there bubbled up such abundance of clear water that its force was sufficient to clean the very dirtiest things."

Nausicaa left home very early in the morning to reach these basins. Like those of our grandmother, the Phaeacians' linen-chests held so much that the washing was done only at infrequent intervals, but then it had to be done in hard-running water. The Ernones basins were ideal for the laundry of the palace of Alcinous. The most elaborate photographs in washing-machine advertisements can never evoke the idea of fragile perfection and purity which is suggested by Erich Lessing's photograph of the rapids (Plate 40).

In ancient times, however, Phaeacia was not always associated with the idea of cleanliness and purity. Alcinous and his wife Arete are brother and sister; an incestuous union which the Achaeans judged to be the height of infamy.

Everything connected with the Phaeacians has to do with the sea. Homer says that they are a "people of navigators". That is why Bérard attaches such great importance to a rocky point situated on the north-west coast of Corfu, which is now called Karavi, or "the boat". This would be the Phaeacians' cruiser, transformed by Poseidon, after their return from Ithaca where they had gone to escort Ulysses. "Smite this good ship", counsels Zeus, "into a rock of her own size and shape quite near the shore, while the whole population gaze from the quays upon her arrival. So will every man be wonder-struck."

"Where the boat is, there must be the city", was Bérard's idea, and he tried to place the city of the Phaeacians at a point from which the islet could be seen. He did not succeed, and he was obliged to situate it much farther away, at Paleocastrizza. This is a headland with a bay on either side corresponding to the two ports which Homer mentions as serving Alcinous' city. Unfortunately neither a trace nor a memory of any ancient city has ever been found there.

What a city it must have been, though, if we can judge from the description of one of its buildings alone, the palace of Alcinous. "The brilliance within the high-ceiled rooms of noble Alcinous was like the sheen of sun and moon: for the inner walls were copper-plated in sections, from the entering in to the furthest recesses of the house; and the cornice which ran around them was glazed in blue. Gates of gold closed the great house: the door posts which stood up from the brazen threshold were of silver, and silver, too, was the lintel overhead: while the handle of the door was gold."

This passage, taken by itself, might make us doubt the existence of the Phaeacians. Outside the Odyssey there has never been any mention of this dwelling-place and it is easy to consider it the home of some mythical beings. Erich Lessing thinks so, and he likewise refuses to follow the opinion of Bradford who, accepting a local tradition, locates the city at Garitsa, a suburb of present-day Corfu. There is in fact another rock in front of Garitsa in the form of a petrified boat. Today it is still called the "isle of Ulysses". But the muddy lagoons surrounding Garitsa could never have been used as harbours, and only the local pride of the modern inhabitants of Corfu could insist on placing Alcinous' city there. So says Bérard, at any rate.

We may take it that Alcinous' palace was not mentioned in the periplus which Homer followed, because it probably never existed. No more than those navigators existed who took Ulysses on a ship, "which unfalteringly sped forward in her race, lighter than the circling hawk, though that is swiftest of the things that fly", and left him asleep on the beach at Ithaca.

But the wood of Athene, where Nausicaa advised Ulysses to wait for a while before going to introduce himself to her father, is still there (Plate 43) where the periplus undoubtedly placed it, between Paleocastrizza and the plain of Ropas. It is still just as it was described by the young maiden: "A grove of black poplars. Within it is an eye of water: and about it meadows. That is an estate of my father's and his abundant garden . . ."

ITHACA

For more than three thousand years a Greek island has born the same name: Ithaki. (The word in Greek means "sharply sloped".) And we can read of Ithaca in the Odyssey: "Rugged it may be and unfit for wheels, but no sorry place for all that it is straitened . . . Goats find plenteous grazing and cattle pasture."

The Ithaki (or Thiaki) that we know today is fifteen miles long, four miles wide. A rocky isthmus not much more than half a mile wide divides it into two mountainous masses, to which Homer gave the names Neion and Neriton.

Commentators have been found, however, who deny that this island was Ulysses' homeland. The German Wilhelm Doerpfeld, an assistant to Schliemann, maintains that the Ithaca of Ulysses is Leucas, an island not far from present-day Ithaki.

I am not surprised at these contradictions. We have already met others like them. The fact is that the Odyssey is one of the most personal pieces of literature in all history, and this extremely personal quality is contagious for those who study it. Ulysses is above all a man *on his own,* alone in face of one of the wildest adventures we have ever heard of. While they are alone, far from their homeland, in territory more than foreign, heroes like Siegfried and Roland remain strictly national products. They behave like Frenchmen or Germans of their time and station and they are, in a way, the epitome of certain national values. Ulysses' personality, on the other hand, is that of a man who is cut off from his homeland. He has no other resources than himself and his gods. He is in search of nothing and cares nothing for his wife, whom he betrays with wild abandon. Has he any ideal? No. The fact that he wants to return home at all costs is not strictly speaking an ideal. It is an instinctive need which he himself would have found difficult to explain. I find that Ulysses and Kafka's Joseph K., struggling to understand an inhuman society so that he could determine his place in it, are very much akin. James Joyce understood that admirably.

The example set by Joseph K. is particularly contagious; I know a large number of men who have fancied they were he. I think that most commentators, whether they know it or not, are inclined to take themselves for Ulysses. They travel once more, in their minds, as we have just done, the route taken by Ulysses, and they are tempted to do it alone. Even the most serious scholars are tempted to be a law unto themselves as they retrace the way.

If one devotes one's life to the study of the most original of heroes, one is perhaps tempted to try to be original oneself. So Doerpfeld, in 1927, must have felt a sort of heroic tremor, when he asserted in spite of everything and everybody, that Ulysses' Ithaca was Leucas. He even went to the very spot and sifted every square yard of the island in order to find evidence to support his theory.

His theory was based on the excavations which had revealed Mycenaean tombs and ruins on Leucas. But since then, more numerous traces of the Mycenaeans have been discovered at Ithaca. Doerpfeld's theory has collapsed.

Excavations on Ithaca, however, are not at all satisfactory either. As on Corfu, no traces of the city in which the lords of the island lived have turned up. Only two palaces of Achaean heroes have been found and tentatively identified: Agamemnon's establishment at Mycenae and Nestor's palace at sandy Pylos.

Still undiscovered is Ulysses' manor, described in the Odyssey as having fireplaces, pillars against which the weapons of Penelope's suitors were shattered, and, holy of holies, a circular bedroom where a growing olive-tree did duty not only as one of the bed-posts but as a supporting pillar for the whole house. But let us not despair: the "palace of Nestor" was found only seven years ago.

Meanwhile let us make a tour of Ithaca. It is not large. A good walker could discover all its secrets in two days. Let us retrace the path of Ulysses as he comes back to his home.

The Phaeacians leave him, asleep, in a safe harbour. Nearby is "a cave set apart for those nymphs they call Naiads; a charming shadowy place containing store-bowls and jars of stone in which the honey-bees hive and lay up their sweetness. There on great long looms of rock the nymphs weave sea-purple robes, marvellously beautiful; and its springs of water never fail."

The harbour is easily identifiable as the huge but narrow roadstead at Port Vathy (the "deep harbour") at the end of which is the modern capital of the island (Plate 96). But in order to find the nymphs' cave we must go further — an hour's walk — which is a little more than the poem seems to suggest.

The cave entrance is tiny (three feet by two), which

explains how Athene, after having deposited the treasures presented to Ulysses by the Phaeacians, was able to close it with a large stone. The interior, which still contains an ancient altar and bright-hued stalactites and stalagmites, perfectly suggests the mysterious workshop of some divine weaver. An uncanny light streams from the roof of the cave, where there is a second entrance. Is it the doorway of the gods? (Plate 99).

Once his treasures are secured in the cave of the nymphs, Ulysses, whom Athene has conveniently given the appearance of an old man with rheumy eyes, takes "the hill-path that climbed straight from the timbered plains into the highlands" to reach the domain of Eumaeus, the honest swineherd.

"You will find him", Athene says, "watching his beasts grubbing round the Raven's Crag and Arethusa's fountain." It is still up a rocky and difficult road that leads from Vathy to the plateau of Marathia — about an hour and a half's walk (Plate 100). At the edge of the plateau is the spring called Perapigadi and behind it a cliff rises one hundred and twenty feet which corresponds to the Raven's Crag. This spring would be the famous "fountain Arethusa" — a name melodious enough to be used today for a great building, the Résidence Arethuse, just beside the Concorde bridge in Paris, but still a mystery for philologists. According to Bérard this spring was used as a watering-place by foreign sailors, in spite of its being so far from the coast. The navigators of past centuries always began their exploration of the isle there. "Even the name Arethusa", Bérard writes, "must have been brought up from the coast in ancient times,

having been imported by foreigners. The name, which has no meaning in Greek, was kept by the Hellenes for three or four watering-places used by sailors."

Ulysses visits Eumaeus in disguise. Next day Telemachus arrives and sends Eumaeus to town, who takes a whole day to go there and back. Later, Ulysses borrows a stick to help himself "on the awkward path". As we have said, Ithaca is composed of two bluffs, the Neriton block and the Neion, which are separated by a high and narrow rocky isthmus. The time taken by Eumaeus to cover the distance suggests that the pigsties were on the Neion and Ulysses' town on the Neriton.

Bérard places the town near Stavros, above Port Polis, a small roadstead in the south-west of modern Ithaca (Thiaki). Excavations were undertaken there in 1930 and 1931 by archaeologist W. A. Heurtley and Miss Benton, but with no result.

Three other places have been identified with near certainty. One is the isle of Asteris, now the isle of Dascalion to the west of Port Polis, where Penelope's suitors lay in wait to kill Telemachus (Plate 27). Another is the domain of Laertes on the bay of Aphalais (Plate 114) in the fertile northern part of the island. The third is the harbour where Athene advised Telemachus to land, to escape being ambushed by the suitors. This is Port Saint Andrew, on the southern tip of Ithaca (Plate 103).

The city itself is still an enigma which defies all efforts of the archaeologists. But perhaps it was badly indicated in the Phoenician periplus which was concerned, above all, with cataloguing harbours, capes, watering-places, and reliefs. If Homer actually went to Ithaca, which is hardly likely (granting, with Simodorus of Amorgos and Pindar, that he lived on the hellenized fringe of Asia Minor, on Chios, or at Smyrna), it is conceivable that he did not find even a trace of Ulysses' manor. It must have been destroyed by fire five centuries earlier, as was the palace of Nestor (see below).

NESTOR AND THE VOYAGES OF TELEMACHUS

Nestor's palace is a most important archaeological site and one of the few to produce clear proof that the Odyssey is not pure legend.

At Eumaeus' house, where he holds a council of war before going to slay the pretenders, Ulysses once more meets his son Telemachus who has also just returned from a long voyage. He had gone off at the beginning of the Odyssey to try to find news of his father. Starting from Ithaca, Telemachus took little more than a night to reach sandy Pylos, the country of Nestor, lord of oxen.

Just the right distance away there is a beach on the Peleponnese where one can land as Telemachus did by sailing straight in. Two archaeologists, Professor Carl Blegen and his wife, went prospecting there in 1939. All they had to start with were the lines of the Odyssey and an item from the geographer Pausanias, writing a century and a half before Christ: "Nestor's Pylos is situated on a spur of Mount Coryphasion."

Professor Blegen is not a man to be discouraged easily. He is perhaps the greatest living archaeologist; it is he who brought to light the city of Troy, following the precise indications of that archaeological genius, Schliemann, but in a shallower stratum, known to archaeologists as Troy 7a.

Blegen searched for a long time on the hills overlooking the beach of Pylos, and behind the two rocky gateways which stand as landmarks for sailors (Plate 10). "If I were a king," he asked himself, "where would I build my palace? Not too near the coast. That would be too dangerous. Somewhere as beautiful as possible, from where I could survey the sea and the land without leaving my fortress." Going from hill to hill — there were hundreds of them and the vegetation was almost impenetrable — Blegen examined the terrain meticulously. One day, a stone sticking out of the ground aroused his curiosity.

He decided to dig there. The results of that excavation have been incredible. Professor Blegen had discovered the very spot which Homer names as Nestor's palace, a palace which had been burnt in 1200 B.C., four and a half centuries before Homer, in a fire probably started by the explosion of a huge jar of oil.

Besides the throne-room, the ante-chambers, the queen's apartments, a hall with a great fireplace and many other rooms, Blegen and his wife found something quite extraordinary: the bath used by the King, a masterpiece of harmonious lines, a basin with rounded rims (Plate 20).

We can be almost certain that Telemachus washed in this bath, and that it was in this room that the lovely Polycaste, Nestor's daughter, rubbed him with fine oil and clad him in a robe "so that he came forth from the bath with the body of an immortal". Drinking-bowls have been found in the room, a sign that the kings drank wine while they bathed themselves.

The bath is not the only souvenir of Telemachus' passage through this area. The Odyssey dwells on the sumptuous luxury of the feast which Nestor gave to the son of his companion-in-arms. Blegen discovered the signs of all this magnificence, which could boast of two thousand eight hundred and fifty-three wine-goblets and seven thousand bowls and jugs. And why should the "embossed cup" which Nestor offered Telemachus on his arrival not be one of those which Blegen now has on exhibit under a corrugated iron roof, in the deserted city where he has been camping for twenty years, and which he is unearthing, bit by bit?

Here we are far from any unsubstantial speculation about the Sirens. Here we have truly come upon the Odyssey once more. Homer did not lie to us about Nestor and his palace, why should he have lied to us about the other heroes and other sites of the Odyssey? Once we have found Nestor's Palace, we are now very sure of the route which Telemachus followed to reach Lacedaemonia from Mycenae. On this level road, where one expects Telemachus to appear at any moment, his chariot drawn by Nestor's oxen, Erich Lessing discovered a stone which once marked the frontier between the kingdom of Nestor and that of Menelaus (Plate 21).

THE ODYSSEY, AN UNFINISHED WORK

In Book XI Ulysses narrates how Teiresias told him: "Go forth under your shapely oar till you come to a people who know not the sea and eat their victuals unsavoured with its salt . . . I give you this token of them, a sign so plain that you cannot miss it: you have arrived when another traveller shall cross you and say that on your shoulder you bear the scatterer of haulms, a winnowing-fan." The Odyssey does not describe this last voyage. Why? Obviously for poetic reasons: another book would have made the dramatic structure of the poem too heavy. But didn't Homer want to write only about a voyage which had a definite tie with reality: his Phoenician periplus would have been of no use to him in describing the landscape in this new voyage. He wanted everything hidden behind his poetic creation to be exact and true. Let me say, by way of conclusion that the Odyssey is a "Baedeker" rewritten by the greatest poet of all time.

So it is not impossible that one day I will find out whether the Galli are, or are not, the isle of the Sirens; and why. I was unable to answer all my children's questions about the Odyssey, but perhaps I shall have those answers for my grand-children.

WITH SCHLIEMANN IN ITHACA

Selections from his book

ITHAKA, DER PELOPONNES UND TROJA

HEINRICH SCHLIEMANN was born on January 6, 1822 in Mecklenburg, the son of a poor Protestant pastor. Even as a child he was fascinated by the stories of the ancient world of Greece and Rome and throughout his life he regarded the accounts of Homer and Vergil as literal records of historical facts. Schliemann owed his success as an archaeologist and his fame as the discoverer of Troy and Mycenae to this unshakeable belief in the veracity of the poets' stories. His discovery of the early Mediterranean cultures in the Aegean area confirmed the historical basis of the Homeric epics and opened up a fresh phase in archaeological research, which shows no sign of diminishing although many of Schliemann's ideas have been substantiated by scientific archaeology.

Schliemann began his career as a village grocer's apprentice. He wanted to go to sea but stayed in Amsterdam after being saved from a sinking ship. Using his own method of study, he learnt English, French, Italian, Spanish, Portuguese, and Dutch while in Amsterdam and in 1846, after learning Russian, he went to Russia for his Dutch employer. A year later he started his own firm, from which he retired as a millionaire 15 years later in order to devote himself to his life-long ambition — exploration of the world of Homer.

In 1868 he wrote his book on Ithaca, and in the following year he married a Greek wife. He began to excavate Troy in 1870 and found Priam's treasure in 1873. In 1876 he began to excavate in Mycenae, 1884 in Tiryns. These are the high points of his career as a archaeologist — a career equal in brilliance to his time as a merchant. Schliemann died on December 26, 1890 in Naples. His corpse was taken to Athens — the capital of that land whose early history had been his life's work.

Publications:
Ithaka, der Peloponnes und Troja (1869); *Troyanische Altertümer* (1874); *Troy and its Remains* (1875); *Mykenä* (1878); *Ilios* (1881); *Troja* (1884); *Tiryns* (1886); all published in Leipzig.
Autobiography, completed by A. Brückner and published by Sophie Schliemann (1892).

ITHACA – THE ISLAND OF ULYSSES

I hired a boat for eleven francs to take me across to Ithaca, and after a rough passage lasting six hours, instead of the one hour it would take under favourable conditions, we reached at eleven in the evening the little harbour of St Spiridon. There, at the foot of the southern slope of Mt Aëtos, I set foot on the ancient kingdom of Ulysses. Tired and hungry though I was, I must confess to a feeling of overpowering joy, as I found myself at last in the homeland of the hero whose adventures I have read and re-read so many times with such passionate interest.

The island is called today Thiaki (Θεάκη), which undoubtedly echoes the name of the island's mythical hero Ithacus, of whom Homer speaks in the Odyssey (XVII, 207). It is composed of a chain of rugged limestone hills and is divided into two almost equal parts by the Gulf of Molo. A narrow isthmus, half a mile wide, joins the two parts, and on the isthmus lies an extensive group of ruins which today is called Palaeokastro, "Oldcastle", the ancient palace of Ulysses according to local tradition (Plate 7). Rocky hills rise everywhere. The highest of them is Mount Anoge in the northern part of the island, Homer's Mount Neriton (Od. XIII, 351; IX, 21) whose "tree-clad flanks" were once "a-quiver with wind-blown leaves", but now is stony and bare, like its companion Mount Neion in the south. Indeed, the whole island is completely denuded of its woods, so that the rain and the dew which were once so abundant (Od. XIII, 245) now come much more seldom to Ithaca.

It has justly been said that nowhere in the world has the memory of ancient Greece been preserved with such vividness and purity as in Ithaca. Immediately after the days of its great hero Ulysses, the island vanishes from the pages of history, and the writers who come after Homer mention Ithaca only to recall its importance in the heroic age. No later happenings mark it out, such as may draw our attention to other places once famous in their day. By A.D. 1504 Ithaca had been almost entirely depopulated by the inroads of pirates, and by the savagery of the wars waged between Turks and Christians. Colonists from the neighbouring islands and the Greek mainland then peopled it once more, retaining to this day the privileges which the Venetian government bestowed on them in the days of its wars with the Turks. Thus all our memories of the place are linked directly to the heroic age. Every hill and rock, every spring and olive grove, remind us of Homer and the Odyssey, and we are carried back in an instant, across the intervening centuries, to the most brilliant age of Grecian chivalry and poetic art.

As soon as I was settled down in my lodging, I hired a guide and a horse and had myself escorted to the little harbour of Dexia which like St Spiridon also lies under Mt Neion and forms part of the great bay of Molo. It is the Φόρκυνος λιμήν, the harbour of Phorkys (Plate 96), where the Phaeacians disembarked Ulysses, still sleeping soundly, and set him down with his treasures first on the shore and then under an olive-tree off the road (Od. XIII, 96–104):

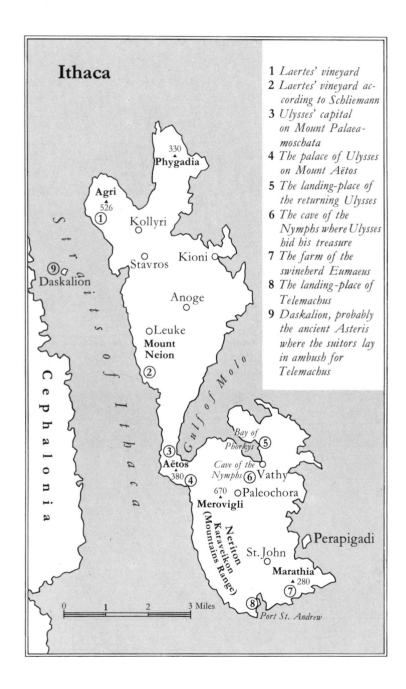

Ithaca

1 Laertes' vineyard
2 Laertes' vineyard according to Schliemann
3 Ulysses' capital on Mount Palaea-moschata
4 The palace of Ulysses on Mount Aëtos
5 The landing-place of the returning Ulysses
6 The cave of the Nymphs where Ulysses hid his treasure
7 The farm of the swineherd Eumaeus
8 The landing-place of Telemachus
9 Daskalion, probably the ancient Asteris where the suitors lay in ambush for Telemachus

"The ship in her rapid seafaring drew toward the island,
toward Ithaca. On its coast is an inlet
sacred to Phorkys, the ancient of the sea,
where two detached headlands of sheer cliff stand forth
and screen a harbour between their steeps
against the great breakers which rage without
whenever the harsh winds blow.
Once they are berthed inside this port
even decked ships can lie unmoored.
By the creek's head is a long-leaved olive tree
and very near it a cave set apart
for those nymphs they call Naiads."

The text which we have quoted describes the locality so exactly that it is impossible to mistake it. We can see two small sharp rocks leaning inward at the mouth of the bay, and close at hand we see the cave of the nymphs on the slope of Mt Neion, one hundred and sixty-four feet above sea-level. And we actually find on the north-west side of the cave a sort of natural door-way, six feet high and a foot and a half wide, which gives easy access to the cave. On the south side there is a circular opening, almost three feet in diameter, which must be the entrance for the gods. Since the cave is over fifty feet deep at this point, it offers no practicable entry for human beings (Plate 99).

Total darkness reigns within. But my guide brought brushwood and kindled a great fire, so that I was able to inspect the cave in all its particulars. It is almost circular in shape and about fifty feet in diameter. From the entrance, one must climb down some ten feet to reach the floor, and one finds the remains of steps which were cut in the rock. On the opposite side one sees the remains of a very badly damaged altar. Masses of stalactites, bizarre in shape, hang from the roof. This is the cave where Ulysses, guided and helped by the goddess Athene, concealed the treasures which he had received from the Phaeacians.

Leaving the cave, we climbed down once more to the harbour of Phorkys and continued on our way to the foot of Mt Aëtos. This hill, five hundred feet high, lies to the south of Mt Neion, from which it is separated by a very fertile valley about a hundred yards wide, which cuts across the little isthmus. To the east, the hill descends sharply at first, and then at a hundred and sixty feet becomes a gentle slope which is watered by excellent springs and covered with flourishing crops. It is bordered by the Gulf of Aëtos. I shall try to show later that this is the harbour of the ancient capital of Ithaca.

THE RUINS OF ULYSSES' PALACE

We climbed Mt Aëtos from the west, the slope being gentler than on the other side. We could see numerous traces of an ancient road, which led at any rate from the palace of Ulysses to the little harbour now called St Spiridon, which also lies on the west of the island, between Mt Aëtos and Mt Neion.

It took me half an hour to reach the southern summit of Aëtos. Here there are the ruins of a tower of rough-hewn stones. The blocks are from three to five feet long and from three to four feet high, laid on top of each other without cement. The tower is square, the sides about twenty-one feet long. In the middle there is an underground receptacle, perhaps a cistern, because all the stones of the structure incline towards the centre, to form a sort of vaulting.

Thirty feet lower down the hill there is a massive encircling wall of similar masonry, while two other walls of cyclopean masonry, provided with defensive towers, run southwest and south-east, scattering their great ruins down the slope to a distance of sixty yards. The top of Aëtos runs northwards from the tower for about eighty yards: it is from eight to ten yards wide and rises gradually about forty feet. The whole space is covered by huge stones, untouched by the hands of man, and excluding the possibility that there ever was a building in this place.

After these stones we come upon the ruins of another square tower, of cyclopean masonry, its sides twenty-five feet long. Then there is a round cistern hewn in the rock, sixteen and a half feet deep, thirteen feet across at the top and nineteen at the bottom. Then the summit broadens out to a perfectly level plateau, extending for forty yards to its northern rim and almost thirty yards broad.

The palace of Ulysses was situated on this plateau. Unfortunately all that can be seen is the ruins of two containing walls, and a little round cistern hewn in the rock for domestic purposes. It is four feet four inches across at the top, almost the same in depth and nearly six feet wide at the bottom. On the northern rim of the plateau, we see the ruins of two great walls which run down to the north-east and the north-west. On the eastern side of the hill, eighteen yards below the summit, there is a large round cistern, also hewn in the rock, thirty-three feet deep, twenty-six feet across at the top and thirty-eight at the bottom. The royal palace was large, some storeys high, and possessed a court-yard, as we know from Eumaeus' words to Ulysses (Od. XVII, 264–8):

Εὔμαι', ἦ μάλα δὴ τάδε δώματα κάλ' Ὀδυσῆος,
'Ρεία δ' ἀρίγνωτ' ἐστὶ καὶ ἐν πολλοῖσιν ἰδέσθαι.
Ἐξ ἑτέρων ἕτερ' ἐστίν · ἐπήσκηται δέ οἱ αὐλή
Τοίχῳ καὶ θριγκοῖσι, θύραι δ' εὐερκέες εἰσίν
Δικλίδες · οὐκ ἄν τίς μιν ἀνὴρ ὑπεροπλίσσαιτο.

"Eumaeus, of a truth this dwelling of Odysseus is noble
easily picked and recognizable amongst many.
See how it rises stage beyond stage with its courts
all properly walled and coped,
and its double doors so securely hung.
No man could reckon it cheap."

The summit of Mt Aëtos is strewn with large horizontal stones, but here and there, for a few yards at a time, it is covered by bushes and weeds, which showed me that there was some soil there as well. I decided at once to undertake excavations at every point where the nature of the ground allowed. But as I had no implements with me, I had to postpone my explorations to the following day.

The next morning, 10 July, I was up early, had a bathe in the sea and drank a cup of black coffee, and by five o'clock was on my way to Mt Aëtos with my workmen. We reached the top at seven, dripping with sweat. I began by setting the four workmen to clear away the scrub, roots and all, and then had them dig up the north-east corner, where, according to my calculations, the noble olive-tree must have stood, from which Ulysses prepared his bridal bed, and round which he constructed his bedroom (Od. XXIII, 183–204):

"Within our court had sprung a stem of olive,
bushy, long in the leaf, vigourous;
the bole of it columnthick.
Round it I plotted my bed-chamber,
walled entire with fine-jointed ashlar and soundly roofed.
After adding joinery doors, fitting very close,
I then polled the olive's spreading top
and trimmed its stump from the root up,
dressing it so smooth with my tools
and so knowingly that I got it plumb,
to serve for bed-post just as it stood.
With this for main member
(boring it with my auger wherever required)
I went on to frame up the bed, complete;
inlaying it with gold, silver and ivory
and lacing it across with ox-hide thongs,
dyed bloodpurple."

44

However, we found nothing but fragments of tiles and potsherds, and at a depth of two feet we reached bedrock. There were indeed many crevices in this rock in which the roots of the olive could have lodged, but I had lost all hope of finding objects of interest to archaeology here.

The next day, 11 July, I was up at four in the morning and climbed Mt Aëtos once more with my four workmen. When we reached the top, we resumed our excavations, and we did not leave a square foot of the ground unexplored at the site where Ulysses' palace had once stood. We also dug between the containing walls and all around the whole top of the hill. But our labour was in vain, for we found nothing more. The only interesting discovery which I made that day was the trace of an ancient road, which descended the north side of the hill from the palace.

ON THE ROYAL ROAD

The next day, 12 July, I set out with my guide, as usual, at five in the morning, first to explore the old road, the traces of which I had discovered the day before, and then to visit the north of the island. The traces of the road are to be found on the steep western slope of Mount Sella, which is really only a continuation of Mt Aëtos, about two and a half miles to the north. It was impossible for me to go there on horseback. But I was told that the road ran on by the village of St John to reach some vineyards by the sea-shore which were traditionally called the Field of Laertes, so I sent my guide ahead there with my horse, and asked another islander to bring me to the domain of Ulysses' father by the old road.

I climbed Mt Sella with great difficulty. It must be a good three hundred feet high, and it rises at an angle of fifty degrees on its eastern side, while the side towards the sea is still steeper. When we gained the top, we still had some thirty-five yards to cover on the other side before we reached the road, which is undoubtedly of very great age, and even in its ruined state still seems something of a marvel. It is completely cut from the rock, some twelve feet wide, and is bordered at intervals of twenty yards by a series of small protective towers built of large, roughly-hewn stones. Huge masses of stone must have been evacuated when this road was being carved in the rock. Its gradient is never less than fifty-five degrees. Three thousand years of winter rains have ravaged it, but enough survives to give us an ample idea of what it was in the great days of King Ulysses. It was along this way, as Homer says, that Ulysses and Telemachus betook themselves to the domain of Laertes (Od. XXIV, 205–7):

Οἱ δ᾽ ἐπεὶ ἐκ πόλιος κατέβαν, τάχα δ᾽ ἀγρὸν ἵκοντο
Καλὸν Λαέρταο τετυγμένον, ὅν ῥά ποτ᾽ αὐτὸς
Λαέρτης κτεάτισσεν, ἐπεὶ μάλα πόλλ᾽ ἐμόγησεν.

"Meanwhile Odysseus and his men had passed the town. Soon they reached the flourishing estate of Laertes acquired by him years before, after great effort."

I climbed down in the same direction, and about half-way along the road I came upon a square stone, eleven feet high, with the (triangular) Greek letter delta carved upon it, measuring twelve inches from apex to base. The islanders call it "Ulysses' letter" and it does in fact appear to be very ancient, so that it may well come from the time of Ulysses. I soon reached the Field of Laertes, where I sat down to rest myself and to read Book XXIV of the Odyssey. The arrival of a stranger is somewhat of an event even in the capital of Ithaca, and much more so in the countryside. I had hardly seated myself when the villagers crowded round me and plied me with questions. I thought my wisest course was to read out for them verses 205 to 412 of Book XXIV, which I proceeded to do, translating it word for word into their dialect. Their enthusiasm knew no bounds as they heard the melodious words ring out in the language of their forefathers of three thousand years ago. They grieved at the terrible sufferings that King Laertes had endured on the very spot where we were gathered, and shared his exultant joy as he found again, in that very place, the beloved son whom he had not seen for twenty years and whom he had mourned as dead. Their eyes filled with tears, and when I had finished my reading, they all came up to me, men, women, and children, and embraced me, saying: "You have made us very happy, we are very, very grateful" (Μεγάλην χαρὰν μᾶς ἔκαμες· κατὰ πολλά σέ εὐχαριστοῦμεν·).

JOURNEY TO THE FARM OF THE SWINEHERD EUMAEUS

After two hours' walk, we reached the famous spring of Arethusa, at the foot of a sheer rock, one hundred and ten feet high, which is called Corax (the raven). The spring must have flowed very powerfully and copiously in ancient times, for in front of it there is a dry river-bed, a hundred feet deep and seventy seven yards broad, which runs down to the sea, five furlongs away. The impetuous waters of the spring must have hollowed themselves this channel in the rock. Now however the spring flows so scantily that less than fifty gallons can be drawn from it each day. Homer speaks of the Arethusa and Raven's Crag in the beautiful lines (Od. XIII, 407–10):

Δήεις τόνγε σύεσσι παρήμενον · αἱ δὲ νέμονται
Πὰρ Κόρακος πέτρῃ, ἐπί τε κρήνῃ Ἀρεθούσῃ,
Ἔσθουσαι βάλανον μενοεικέα, καὶ μέλαν ὕδωρ
Πίνουσαι, τάθ' ὕεσσι τρέφει τεθαλυῖαν ἀλοιφήν.

"You will find him watching his beasts
grubbing round the Raven's Crag and Arthusa's fountain.
Thereby they grow into fat and healthy pigs,
by virtue of the acorns they love
and the still waters of the spring they drink."

The position of the source, which is bounded on the north by the sheer face of the Raven's Crag, and on the south by a slope which falls away to the neighbouring sea at an angle of from fifty-five to sixty degrees, makes it impossible to suppose that herds of pigs could have approached the fountain itself or have been tended on the side of the fountain looking towards the sea. But immediately beyond the Raven's Crag, at a height of two hundred and sixty feet above sea-level, there is a level plateau, very fertile, which is bounded on the north by a ridge of rock some ten feet high. There are some ruins at the foot of the ridge, on the south side, where I discovered the remains of ten structures, each composed of only one room of about eleven feet square. These buildings are side by side in a row, and are made of roughly hewn stones, from three to six feet long and from two to three feet thick and high. Three of the buildings are partly constructed in the rock itself. Ten yards south of these ruins we can see the debris of a building about fifty feet long and wide.

We can identify this plateau without any difficulty. It is the field where the noble swineherd Eumaeus had erected his house and farm-yard, and twelve sties for his pigs. Apart from the fact that there is no other level field in the whole neighbourhood, it accords perfectly with the words of Homer (Od. XIV, 6): "it stood by itself" (περισκέπτῳ ἐνὶ χώρῳ), literally, "in a place visible from all sides", that is, on a plateau (Plate 100). Further, the field is just above the Raven's Crag, and Homer is clearly alluding to this when Ulysses bids his host to cast him down from the lofty rock, if he is not telling the truth (Od. XIV, 398–400):

Εἰ δέ κε μὴ ἔλθησιν ἄναξ τεός, ὡς ἀγορεύω,
Δμῶας ἐπισσεύας, βαλέειν μεγάλης κατὰ πέτρης,
Ὄφρα καὶ ἄλλος πτωχὸς ἀλεύεται ἠπεροπεύειν.

"And if he does not return as I say,
then bid your bondmen hurl me from that great crag
to teach the next beggar not to invent."

We can also recognize in the ruins of the cyclopean masonry ten of the twelve pig-sties which Homer mentions (Od. XIV, 13–16):

Ἔντοσθεν δ' αὐλῆς συφεοὺς δυοκαίδεκα ποίει
Πλησίον ἀλλήλων, εὐνὰς συσίν ἐν δὲ ἑκάστῳ
Πεντήκοντα σύες χαμαιευνάδες ἐρχατόωντο,
Θήλειαι τοκάδες τοὶ δ' ἄρσενες ἐκτὸς ἴαυον.

"All in a row inside the pound he had contrived twelve sties
to lodge his beasts. Fifty each sty held,
of the brood sows, be it understood,
supine on beds of litter in their pens:
as for the boars, they were kept in the yard outside."

A slope leads down from this plateau to the point where the deep river-bed debouches into the sea. The pigs must have been herded down this slope every morning and evening to drink from the water of the Arethusa, because there is no other source in the neighbourhood. It is true that the slope, which is gentle at first, becomes sharper and sharper over the last thirty yards, where it falls away at an angle of thirty-six degrees, and it appears almost impossible that fat pigs, especially sows in farrow, could have climbed up and down it twice a day. But in ancient times there must have been a broad and easy path, going zig-zag down the slope. I spared no pains to try to find traces of it, but as I had no digging implements with me, all my searching was in vain.

Eumaeus' pigs were fed on acorns (Od. XIII, 409). Oak-trees must have been plentiful then on Ithaca. They have completely disappeared from the island today.

THE SAVAGE DOGS

On Tuesday, 14 July, I set out with my guide at five in the morning, on horseback, to explore the south and south-east portion of the island, which lies to the left of the spring of Arethusa. But the terrain proved so difficult that we soon had to leave the horse in a field and make the rest of our excursion on foot. Every farm-house on the island seems to reproduce before our eyes the life of ancient Greece, and we are reminded at once of the description which Homer gives of the farm of the swine-herd Eumaeus (Od. XIV, 5–12):

Τὸν δ' ἄρ' ἐνὶ προδόμῳ εὖρ' ἥμενον, ἔνθα οἱ αὐλή
Ὑψηλὴ δέδμητο, περισκέπτῳ ἐνὶ χώρῳ,
Καλή τε μεγάλη τε, περίδρομος · ἥν ῥα συβώτης,
Αὐτὸς δείμαθ' ὕεσσιν, ἀποιχομένοιο ἄνακτος,

Νόσφιν δεσποίνης καὶ Λαέρταο γέροντος,
Ῥυτοῖσιν λάεσσι, καὶ ἐθρίγκωσεν ἀχέρδῳ,
Σταυροὺς δ' ἐκτὸς ἔλασσε διαμπερὲς ἔνθα καὶ ἔνθα,
Πυκνοὺς καὶ θαμέας, τό μέλαν δρυὸς, ἀμφικεάσσας.

"He found him sitting
in the lodge of his high-walled steading,
which was a landmark because it stood by itself
and was well-built and large.
Without telling his lady or grandfather Laertes,
the swineherd had made it himself
for his absent master's pigs
by lining up boulders from round about
and topping them with a dense hedge of prickly pear.
For outer fence he had run round it a very close-set paling
of heart-oak, the tree's dark core."

The homesteads are always built on a flat piece of high ground. They always stand in the middle of a cattle-yard, and are surrounded by a wall built of small stones untidily laid. The upper portion of this wall is always provided with a hedge of dry thorn and a palisade of pointed stakes. Every farm-house stands solitary in the middle of its fields, and whenever I made for one to buy a bunch of grapes or ask for a drink of water, I was attacked by dogs. I usually succeeded in keeping them at a respectful distance by throwing stones or pretending to do so, but this day, as I was starting to enter a farm-yard on the south of the island, four dogs hurled themselves upon me savagely, and refused to be intimidated by stones or

48

threats. I cried out for help, but my guide had fallen behind and there seemed to be nobody at home. In this somewhat terrifying situation, an expedient luckily occurred to me, which Ulysses had made use of on a similar occasion (Od. XIV, 29–31):

Ἐξαπίνης δ' Ὀδυσῆα ἴδον κύνες ὑλακόμωροι ·
Οἱ μὲν κεκλήγοντες ἐπέδραμον · αὐτὰρ Ὀδυσσεὺς
Ἕζετο κερδοσύνῃ, σκῆπτρον δὲ οἱ ἔκπεσε χειρός.

"When the noisy dogs saw Ulysses
they plunged suddenly towards him, baying:
but he cunningly let fall his staff
and sank to the ground."

Following the example of this prudent king, I sat down calmly on the ground and kept quite still. The four dogs, which a moment before had seemed intent on devouring me, now circled round me and continued to bark, but they did not touch me. They would have bitten me if I had made the least move. But the fact that I behaved so humbly in their presence was enough to soothe the savage beasts.

ULYSSES' CAPITAL

At five in the morning I set out again with my guide to view once more the little plateau above the spring of Arethusa where the ruins of Eumaeus' farmhouse lay, and then to go by the old road to visit the northern part of the island. The road, or rather path, for it is only two or three feet wide, winds around Mount Neion, now called Mount St Stephen, at a height of about two hundred and fifty feet above sea-level. It is almost entirely hewn from the rock, and one can tell at the first glance that it is very ancient. The old inhabitants relate that this was once the only path connecting the two parts of the island, the new road having been built by the English only thirty years ago.

This is no doubt the very path which Homer calls τρηχεῖαν ἄταρπον "the hill-path" (Od. XIV, 1) and ὁδὸν παιπα-λόεσσαν "the awkward path" (Od. XVII, 204), along which Ulysses marched when he set out from his landing-place at Phorkys' harbour, to find his loyal herdsman Eumaeus. It was the way which Ulysses and Eumaeus took when they went together to the royal palace on Mt Aëtos. It certainly lives up to the name of awkward and difficult which the poet gave it, because it is so steep and rugged and slippery in many parts that a man on horseback cannot move along it.

After three hours' march we reached the foot of Mt Aëtos, at a point where the old road formerly forked into one branch leading along the eastern side of the hill to the palace of Ulysses, the other to the northern part of the island. Every trace of the northern road has been hidden by a modern road going in the same direction, but I discovered numerous vestiges of the other as I descended Mt Aëtos.

At the point where the road forked in ancient times, there is a spring with an abundant flow of water. Its interior masonry testifies to its great age, and it fits perfectly the description given by Homer (Od. XVII, 204–11):

᾿Αλλ᾽ ὅτε δὴ στείχοντες ὁδὸν κάτα παιπαλόεσσαν
῎Αστεος ἐγγὺς ἔσαν, καὶ ἐπὶ κρήνην ἀφίκοντο
Τυκτὴν, καλλίροον, ὅθεν ὑδρεύοντο πολῖται,
Τὴν ποίησ᾽ ῎Ιθακος καὶ Νήριτος ἠδὲ Πολύκτωρ ·
᾿Αμφὶ δ᾽ ἄρ᾽ αἰγείρων ὑδατοτρεφέων ἦν ἄλσος,
Πάντοσε κυκλοτερές, κατὰ δὲ ψυχρὸν ῥέεν ὕδωρ
῾Υψόθεν ἐκ πέτρης · βωμὸς δ᾽ ἐφύπερθε τέτυκτο
Νυμφάων, ὅθι πάντες ἐπιρρέζεσκον ὁδῖται.

"They threaded the awkward path till hard by the town,
when they found the running spring, steyned round,
which Ithacus, Neritus, and Polyctor had built.
From this fountain the citizens drew their water.
A grove of black poplars completely encircled it
and the water, ever so cold,
ran down thither from a crag
crowned by an altar to the Nymphs.
Every wayfarer paid reverence there."

This then is the spring where Ulysses and Eumaeus met the goatherd Melanthius, the son of Dolius (Od. XVII, 212–16).

From here we climbed Mount Paleamoschata, which is the immediate northward continuation of Mt Aëtos. We had hired two picks from a farmer in the valley for a few cents, and we made diggings at various points on the summit of the hill and all down the slope till we reached the sea-shore. At a depth of from eight to sixteen inches we came upon fragments of tiles and potsherds at every point, a clear proof that there must have been a city in this place. I think I can affirm with certainty that it is the capital of Ithaca, which Homer speaks of several times (Od. XVI, 471; XVII, 205; XXIII, 137; XXIV, 205).

There was also a city in the valley of Polis (which itself means "city"), which the ancient geographer Ptolemy no doubt had in mind when he spoke of "Ithaca, with its city of the same name" (3:14). The geographer Scylax also refers to it when writing of the Acarnanians of the near-by mainland and has occasion to mention "the island of Ithaca with its city and harbour". But they cannot mean the Homeric capital, because the valley of Polis lies near the sea-shore and is enclosed by mountains. Consequently, no matter what direction one took, one had to "go up" ἀναβαίνειν, from Polis and not "go down", καταβαίνειν. But Ulysses, Telemachus, and their two slaves, "went down" from the city, according to Homer (Od. XXIV, 205–6): κατέβαν.

Further, the vineyard designated by tradition as the Field of Laertes lies nearly eight miles from Polis, but only a little over a mile from Mt Paleamoschata, which I have indicated as the site of the Homeric capital. But since according to Od. XXIV, 205f, Ulysses and his companions reached the Field of Laertes *soon* after leaving the city, they cannot have been coming from Polis. Finally, we know beyond all doubt from Od. XXIII, 135–48 and 370–93, that Ulysses' palace was either in the city itself or very close to it. So when tradition, the allusion to the height of the city in Od. II, 140–60, Cicero's statement that it "nestled among high crags" (de Oratore 1: 44), and the majestic ruins which have defied three thousand years, all proclaim that Ulysses' palace was on Mt Aëtos, we can be sure that the Homeric capital can only have been on the summit and the slope of Mt Paleamoschata.

THE ISLE OF ASTERIS AND THE SUITORS' AMBUSH

When I reached the foot of Mt Paleamoschata, I could not resist the desire to climb it once more, to look for "Hermes' ridge", Ἑρμαῖος λόφος. I identified it without any difficulty as the small rocky hill, eighteen yards high, which is now called Chordakia. This is the only place from which Eumaeus, after leaving the city, could have seen the ship with the suitors in it entering the harbour, full of warriors equipped with shields and double-edged spears (Od. XVI, 472–4). He must have been watching from here when he saw the boat entering the Gulf of Aëtos, which is on the eastern side of the island at the foot of Mt Aëtos and Mt Paleamoschata, and must have been the main harbour of the Homeric capital, and when

he saw it arriving in the little bay of St Spiridon, which is on the western coast of the island where the other side of Mt Aëtos reaches down to the sea, opposite the ancient city of Samos on the island of Cephalonia.

Probably the bay of St Spiridon was always used as a harbour by the occupants of Ulysses' palace, because the western slope of Mt Aëtos is less steep than the eastern, as I have already said, and there was a road which made the ascent in easy stages, winding to and fro like a serpent up the hill. Traces of the road are still visible. The suitors who lay in wait for Telemachus also took it for granted that when he returned from Pylos and Lacedaemonia, he would land at this harbour opposite Cephalonia. Otherwise they would not have set their ambush on this side of the island, meaning to kill him when he landed (Od. IV, 669–71):

Ἀλλ' ἄγε μοι δότε νῆα θοὴν καὶ εἴκοσ' ἑταίρους,
Ὄφρα μιν αὐτὸν ἰόντα λοχήσομαι ἠδὲ φυλάξω
Ἐν πορθμῷ Ἰθάκης τε Σάμοιό τε παιπαλοέσσης.

"I ask you to supply me a fast ship and a crew of twenty men, with which to watch and waylay him
as he comes through the narrow gut
between Ithaca and steep Samos."

Homer also says (Od. IV, 842–47):

Μνηστῆρες δ' ἀναβάντες ἐπέπλεον ὑγρὰ κέλευθα,
Τηλεμάχῳ φόνον αἰπὺν ἐνὶ φρεσὶν ὁρμαίνοντες.
Ἔστι δέ τις νῆσος μέσσῃ ἁλὶ πετρήεσσα,
Μεσσηγὺς Ἰθάκης τε Σάμοιό τε παιπαλοέσσης,
Ἀστερίς, οὐ μεγάλη · λιμένες δ' ἔνι ναύλοχοι αὐτῇ,
Ἀμφίδυμοι · τῇ τόνγε μένον λοχόωντες Ἀχαιοί.

"The suitors set forth,
harbouring sudden death for Telemachus in their hearts,
and sailed the water-quays as far as a stony island in
                                                    mid-sea,
equidistant from Ithaca and craggy Samos,
even the islet Asteris, no large place:
which has a harbour with two approaches
and in it a berth for ships.
There they drew up to lie in wait for him."

I find it difficult to indicate the position of the island of
Asteris. It is often identified with the island of Dascalion,
because this is the only island in the whole strait between
Ithaca and Cephalonia. And the conclusion is then drawn
that the Homeric capital must necessarily have been
situated in the valley of Polis. But I think that I have
given adequate proof that this is impossible, and that the
capital must have been on the slope of Mt Paleamoschata.
I have only to show now that Asteris cannot possibly
have been the island of Dascalion.

Dascalion is twelve miles north-northwest of Aëtos and
it is so small that it cannot be seen from this hill. Thus
the suitors could not have kept watch for Telemachus
from Dascalion, since he was coming from the south and
sailing towards the bay of St Spiridon. Nor could they
have lain in wait there to attack the ship of the young
prince, even if he had sailed as far as Polis, because
Dascalion is six miles west-northwest of this harbour and
only two miles from Cephalonia. If Telemachus was
coming from Pylos, the present-day Navarino, he could
have sailed up the straits between Ithaca and Cephalonia
only if the wind was southerly for sea-faring was then in
its infancy and the art of tacking was unknown.

Now the winds which would have helped Telemachus to
reach Polis would have been unfavourable for the suitors,
for they would have needed a northerly wind to sail in
his direction. Homer says further that Asteris is in the
"middle", μεσσηγύς, of the strait between Ithaca and Cephalonia, which contradicts the distance given for Dascalion
above. Hoping to find further proofs against the identity
of Asteris and Dascalion, I determined to visit the island.

I sailed off, therefore, without delay to the island of
Leucas, where I had been welcomed earlier with such
lively enthusiasm, and found everyone eager to offer me
hospitality. Though I had intended to sail off at once to
Dascalion, they would not let me go till I had recounted all
my travels and read and translated for them a portion of
the Odyssey.

It was glorious weather. By the light of the full moon, I
was able to recognize in the distance all the hills of Ithaca
and Cephalonia and explore the little island of Dascalion
in comfort. It is only a hundred yards long, and at its
widest is only thirty-three yards across, a flat piece of rock

which rises only six feet above the water. According to Homer (Od. IV, 844–5) the island of Asteris had a double harbour. Dascalion nowhere offers an inlet even a yard in length, and in view of the great depth of the surrounding sea, it is impossible to suppose that the local features of the island have changed so much.

It is, however, the only island between Ithaca and Cephalonia, as I have already said. It was therefore supposed to be Homer's Asteris even in ancient times and it was consequently given the name of Asteria. All the geographical indications given by Homer are so exact that I do not cherish the least doubt of the existence of a little island called Asteris in Homer's day, with a double harbour. But the weighty reasons which I have adduced force me to transpose it into the middle of the strait, opposite the southern end of Ithaca. The island must have disappeared in consequence of an earthquake or the inroads of the sea, like so many other little islands.

It was now time for me to take leave of my friends on the islands, and all of us were deeply moved as we said goodbye. One by one they pressed my hand, kissed me and murmured softly, Χαῖρε, φίλε, εἰς καλὴν ἀντάμωσιν: "Farewell, my friend, till our next happy meeting!" I saluted them all very heartily and then went aboard the steamer Athenae, which departed a few minutes later.

It was with profound emotion that I left Ithaca. Long after the island was lost to sight, I was still gazing in its direction. Never in all my life shall I forget the nine happy days which I spent among these upright, virtuous, and lovable people.

A PHOTOGRAPHIC JOURNEY
IN THE PATH OF ULYSSES
by
ERICH LESSING

ERICH LESSING was born in Vienna on July 13, 1923, but in 1939 he emigrated to Palestine. After his studies at the *Technion* in Haifa he worked for two years breeding carp in a Kibbuz located in the Jordan Valley. He spent a subsequent interlude alternately as soldier and taxi chauffeur. But photography was always his first love and from this point on he dedicated himself more and more entirely to it. Near the end of the war he accompanied the English sixth airborne division, reporting the action on film.

In 1947 he returned to Vienna and began a two-year affiliation with the Associated Press. Since 1951 he has been a member of the international photographic group "Magnum Photos" in Paris and New York. At first he specialized in political photographic reports, but for several years now he has gradually been intensifying his interest in series of a particularly cultural nature. His work has appeared in such important international magazines as *Life, Paris Match, Epoca, Picture Post,* and *Asahi,* as well as in many other illustrated journals.

THE GODS ON OLYMPUS DISCUSS THE RETURN OF ULYSSES

O divine poesy, goddess-daughter of Zeus,
sustain for me this song of the various-minded man,
who after he had plundered the innermost citadel of hallowed Troy
was made to stray grievously about the coasts of men,
the sport of their customs good or bad, while his heart
through all the sea-faring ached in agony to redeem himself
and bring his company safe home.

Book 1, lines 1–5

By now the other warriors, those that had escaped
headlong ruin by sea or in battle, were safely home.
Only Ulysses tarried, shut up by Lady Calypso,
a nymph and very goddess, in her hewn-out caves.
She craved him for her bed-mate: while he
was longing for his house and his wife.
Of a truth the rolling seasons had at last brought up the year
marked by the Gods for his return to Ithaca;
but not even there among his loved things
would he escape further conflict.
Yet had all the gods with lapse of time
grown compassionate towards Ulysses — all but Poseidon,
whose enmity flamed ever against him till he reached his home,
Poseidon, however, was for the moment far away
among the Aethiopians, that last race of men,
whose dispersion across the world's end is so broad
that some of them can see the Sun-God rise while others see him set.
Thither had Poseidon gone in the hope of burnt offerings,
bulls and rams, by hundreds: and there he sat feasting merrily
while the other Gods came together in the halls of Olympian Zeus.

Book 1, lines 11–27

Overleaf (1) The Goddess Athene, daughter of Zeus, who helps Ulysses
(2) Wily Ulysses, whose return home from the Trojan War has been delayed for ten years
by Poseidon, Lord of the Sea

In the palace of Olympian Zeus where the gods are gathered, the goddess Athene persuades the Father of the Immortals to allow wandering Ulysses at last to reach his home. Hermes, the messenger of the gods, is to be sent at Athene's request to Calypso's isle, and is there to tell the beautiful nymph of the irrevocable decision of Zeus, that long-suffering Ulysses shall be permitted to return to his native land.

"Ulysses is so sick with longing to see
if it were but the smoke of his home spiring up,
that he prays for death.
I marvel, my Lord of Olympus, how your heart makes no odds of it.
Can you lightly forget the burnt offerings Ulysses lavished upon you,
by the Argive ships in the plain of Troy?"
"My child," protested Zeus, the cloud-compeller,
"what sharp judgements you let slip through your teeth!
As if I could overpass the merit of Ulysses,
who stands out above the ruck of men
as much for worldly wisdom as for his generous offerings
to the Gods that eternally possess the open sky.
It is Poseidon the world-girdler who is so headily bitter against him,
for the sake of that Cyclops whom Ulysses blinded,
even the god-like Polyphemus, their chief figure
and Poseidon's very son: — for his mother Thoosa
(daughter to Phorkys, an overlord of the ungarnered sea)
conceived him after she had lain with the God by the beetling cliffs.
Because of this, Poseidon the land-shaker,
though he dare not quite kill Ulysses, at least implacably frustrates
his every effort to get back to the land of his fathers.
But come, let us put all our heads together and contrive
the man's return; then will Poseidon have to swallow his bile.
Against the concert of the Immortals he cannot stand alone."

Book 1, lines 57–79

Previous page (3) Mount Olympus, home of the Gods
Left (4) Zeus, Father of the Gods, whom Athene begs to allow Ulysses to return home
Right (5) Poseidon, whose anger has delayed the homecoming of Ulysses

TELEMACHUS AND THE SUITORS IN ITHACA

Athene the clear-eyed, the Goddess, answered
and said: "Father and Lord of all, Kronides,
if indeed the ineffable Gods now judge it fit
that prudent Ulysses should return,
then let us call Hermes, our usher, the killer of Argus,
and despatch him straight to Ogygia,
the island of that nymph with the lovely hair:
to warn her how it is become our fixed act that the dauntless one
be allowed to set out homeward forthwith.
For my part I shall go to Ithaca and rouse his son Telemachus,
instilling some tardy purpose into his spirit,
so that he may call his Greek exquisites to council
and give check to the mob of wooers besetting his mother Penelope,
the while they butcher his wealth of juicy sheep
and rolling-gaited, screw-horned oxen.
I will send the youth to Sparta — yes, and to sandy Pylos —
to ask those he meets for news of his dear father's return:
not that he will hear anything, but his zeal
will earn him repute among men."
She ceased, and drew upon her feet
those golden sandals (whose fairness no use could dim)
that carried their mistress as surely and wind-swiftly over the waves
as over the boundless earth. She laid hold of her guardian spear,
great, heavy, and close-grained, tipped with cutting bronze.
When wrath moved the goddess to act, this spear was her weapon:
with it, and stayed by her pride of birth,
she would daunt serried ranks of the very bravest warriors.
Downward she now glided from the summit of Olympus,
to alight on Ithaca before Ulysses' house, by the sill of the main gate.

Book 1, lines 80–103

In the palace on the island of Ithaca Athene encourages young Telemachus to disperse his mother's ninety-eight suitors. However she advises him to voyage first to Pylos, to King Nestor, to seek news about the fate of his father Ulysses. Then swift as a bird, the goddess vanishes.

Left (6) Athene leaves the assembly of the Gods in haste for Ithaca

The minstrel Phemius is singing at the suitors' feast a song which tells of the return of the Achaeans from Troy. Penelope comes grieving into the hall when she hears him and half in tears complains that the minstrel troubles her deeply with his song, reminding her of her lost husband Ulysses.

Left (7) Ithaca, the island home of Ulysses
Below (8) The minstrel singing of Troy and the return of the Achaeans in front of the suitors of Penelope

Telemachus decently cut her short.
"My Mother, why take it amiss
that our trusty singer should entertain us as the spirit moves him?
I think it is not poets who bring things to pass,
but rather Zeus who pays out to men, the Makers,
their fates at his whim: we have no cause against Phemius
for drawing music out of the hard fate of the Danaans.
A crowd ever extols the song which sounds freshest in its ears.
Harden your heart and mind to hear this tale.
Remember that Ulysses was not singular
in utterly losing at Troy the day of his return.
There many others who in the Troad lost their very selves.
Wherefore I bid you get back to your part of the house.
Speech shall be the men's care: and principally my care:
for mine is the mastery in this house."

Book 1, lines 345–355, 358–359

Below (9) Penelope, the wife of Ulysses, and his son Telemachus who have waited loyally for twenty years for Ulysses to return

On the next morning Telemachus, in front of the assembled people, accuses the suitors of continual feasting and revelling, and so of squandering the property of Ulysses. The suitors ungallantly reply that they have stayed so long not through their own fault but through Penelope's. His mother, they say, has promised to choose one of them as soon as she completes the shroud she is weaving for Laertes, Ulysses' father. But what she weaves during the day, she secretly unravels in the night, and for three years now she has thus deceived the suitors.

Unimpressed, Telemachus once more commands the suitors to be gone; then he announces his decision to sail to Pylos, the home of King Nestor, to find news of the fate of Ulysses. The horde of suitors make fun of him. But then Pallas Athene appears to the despondent boy in the form of Mentor, a friend of Ulysses, and the Goddess strengthens his will for the journey. She herself, now disguised as Telemachus, sees to the finding of a ship and twenty oarsmen and to fitting it out for a voyage. With provisions on board and the suitors — thanks to Athene — sunk in a drunken sleep, Telemachus sets out through the night toward Pylos. Once again disguised as the aged Mentor, Athene accompanies him.

TELEMACHUS VISITS KING NESTOR IN PYLOS

Forth from the lovely waters sprang the sun
into its firmament of brass, thence to shine upon the Immortals,
as also upon mortal men walking amid the corn-fields of earth;
while the ship drew into Pylos, the stately citadel of Neleus.
There upon the fore-shore were gathered the inhabitants,
doing sacrifice to the Earth-shaker, Poseidon, the dark-tressed God.

Book 3, lines 1–6

They encountered the throng of the men of Pylos.
There sat Nestor amongst his sons,
with his followers busied about him, arranging the feast
or roasting joints of beef or skewering choice morsels on the spits.
Yet no sooner did they spy strangers than one and all
crowded forward with welcoming hands,
to have them take place in the gathering.

Book 3, lines 31–35

Telemachus makes himself known to King Nestor, explaining that he needs
news of his father Ulysses, not yet returned from Troy.

Then answered him Nestor, knight of Gerenia.
"Dear lad, since you recall to my mind those dreary memories,
hear the tale of what we endured in that fatal land . . .
Manifestly in stratagems of any sort
the palm was borne off by Ulysses, your regal father —
if really you are his son.
A strange wonder takes me as I gaze on you."
Book 3, lines 102–104, 121–123

*Left (10) The entrance to the harbour of Pylos in the western Peloponnese,
where the aged Nestor is king
Below (11) Telemachus presents himself before King Nestor
Overleaf (12) Achaean warriors at Troy*

"Even so we destroyed the tall city of Priam.
It was afterwards, when the god had dispersed the Achaeans
and we had all gone down to our ships,
that Zeus contrived in his heart a sorry return
for the Argives, because they had not, all of them,
been either upright or circumspect.
As for the grisly doom which swallowed so many of them up,
it arose from the fatal anger of the grey-eyed
Daughter of the Great One, who set dissension
between the two sons of Atreus."

Book 3, lines 130–136

*Nestor tells of the feuds in the Achaean army. One half under Menelaus
sailed home as soon as Troy was captured. The rest of the Achaeans under
Agamemnon remained offering sacrifices to appease the anger of the Gods.
Ulysses stayed with Agamemnon while Nestor himself went home early
to Pylos.*

"Thus easily, dear lad, did I return home by myself,
without learning the fate of the other Achaeans.
What news I have gathered since, sitting quietly in my great hall,
that shall you now learn from me without exception, as is your due.
The Myrmidons, they say, those spearmen, got back in good order
under the renowned son of great-hearted Achilles.
It was well, also, with Philoctetes, gallant son of Poias:
and Idomeneus brought back all his company to Crete: —
all, that is, who escaped the war. The sea wrested none from him.
Of the fate of Agamemnon, son of Atreus, word must have come,
even to those remote fastnesses which are your home,
relating the calamity of his return to the woeful fate
Aegisthus had schemed for him. Yet Aegisthus
paid a reckoning even more terrible.
How good it was that a son of the victim survived,
and that he should avenge his great father's cruel death
upon Aegisthus, the sly murderer!"

Book 3, lines 184–198

*Telemachus hears from Nestor of the fate of Agamemnon, who was killed
on his return from Troy by the adulterer Aegisthus. Orestes, the son of
Agamemnon, waited for seven years to avenge his father's death and then
at last slew Aegisthus and Clytaemnestra, the unfaithful wife, his own
mother.*

Above (13) King Priam of Troy on the walls of his city
Below (14) Achaeans try to take Troy by storm
Right (15) The throne-room in the palace of Cnossos in Crete, the home of King Idomeneus
*Overleaf (16) Wall of the citadel at Mycenae where Agamemnon, chief of all the Achaean
war-lords, ruled as king*
(17) Gold death-mask of the King of Mycenae

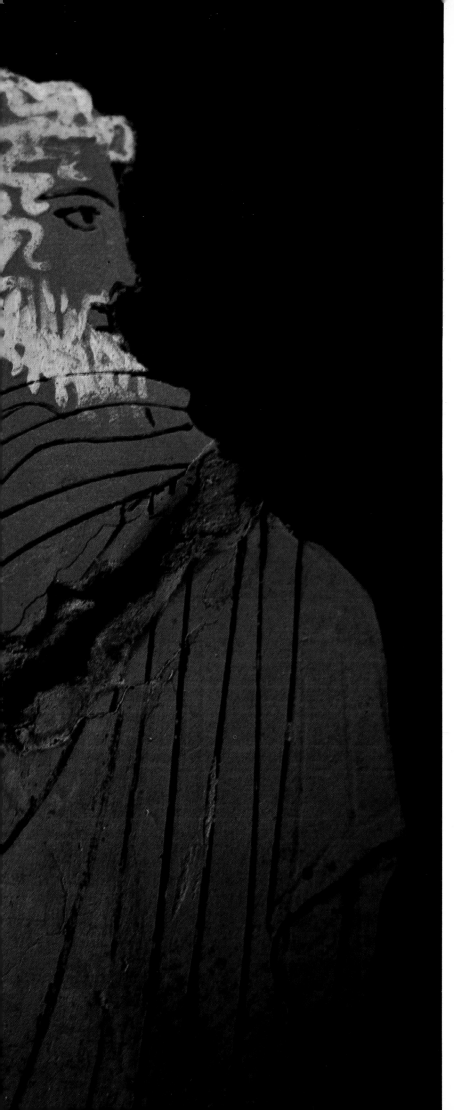

At the end of his story Nestor advises Telemachus to look sharply to his own inheritance in Ithaca and to drive the suitors out. But first he should go to Menelaus in Sparta and learn more of Ulysses' fate, for Menelaus was among the last of the Achaeans to leave Troy.

Athene approves of Nestor's counsel. She vanishes like a sea-eagle from their astounded gaze. Nestor now realizes who it was, disguised as Mentor, who accompanied young Telemachus. Piously he has a bull with gilded horns sacrificed to the Goddess, and a farewell feast for Telemachus is prepared.

Nestor began to address them:
"Quickly, quickly, dear sons, do my bidding,
that I may single out from all the gods for reverence,
divine Athene, who visited me in the flesh yesterday
at the God's solemn feast.
Let one of you, therefore, run to the pastures for a heifer
to be brought as quickly as the neat-herd can drive her here.
Let another hasten to the black ship of large-hearted Telemachus
and bring up all his company save two.
Let some one else bid Laerkes the gilder come,
to lap in gold the horns of the victim.
The rest of you stay in the house
to see that its women busy themselves,
laying the table in our famous hall and arranging seats
and a proper provision of fire-wood and sparkling water."

Book 3, lines 417–429

Left (18) King Nestor, ruler in Pylos, welcomes Telemachus to his kingdom

During this sacrifice beautiful Polycaste,
the youngest grown daughter of Nestor son of Neleus,
had given Telemachus his bath, anointing him with rich olive oil
before she draped him in a seemly tunic and cloak:
so that he came forth with the body of an immortal.

Book 3, lines 464–468

Left (19) Head of a bull with horns gilded for sacrifice to the Gods
Below (20) The bath of King Nestor in the palace at Pylos

TELEMACHUS AT THE HOME OF MENELAUS IN SPARTA

And at the first red pointers of dawn in the sky
they were yoking their horses to the gay chariot
for their next stage. Forth they drove
through the court-yard gate past the echoing porch.
Presently they entered the wheat-lands,
sign that their journey drew towards its close;
Again the sun grew low and the roads were darkened.

Book 3, lines 491–493, 495–497

They came to the country of Lacedaemon,
where it nestled among the hollowed hills;
and they drove up to the home of famous Menelaus.

Book 4, lines 1–2

*Telemachus and Nestor's son, Peisistratus, are welcomed in the palace at
Sparta by Menelaus and his beautiful wife Helen of Troy — especially
when they learn that their guest is the son of Ulysses. They have many
memories of the deeds of Ulysses. Helen, the lovely daughter of Zeus, speaks:*

"Beyond all my listing or telling were the exploits of that hardy one.
Marvellous was this adventure which the iron-nerved man conceived
and dared to execute in the Troad
of unhappy memory to all Achaeans.
He punished himself with humiliating stripes
and threw a coarse wrap about his shoulders as if he were a bondman:
and so went down into the broad streets of the hostile city
amongst his enemies, hiding himself in his foreign shape
and making believe he was a mendicant,
a figure very unlike that he cut in the Achaean fleet.
Yet in this disguise he went through the city of the Trojans —
and not a soul of them accosted him.
But I knew who this man was and challenged him again and again
while he cunningly eluded my questions.
After the washing and anointing with oil
when I was clothing him in new garments I swore to him
that I would not declare to the Trojans that it was Ulysses
before he had got back to the swift ships and the bivouacs.
Then he told me all the intention of the Achaeans."

Book 4, lines 240–256

*Right (21) A view towards Sparta, where King Menelaus has his palace
Overleaf (22) King Menelaus and his beautiful wife Helen, whose elopement with Paris
was the cause of the Trojan War
(23) Ulysses creeps away from Troy after talking secretly with Helen*

Fair Menelaus took up the tale:
"Of all these things, my lady wife, you have said what is needful.
In my time I learnt the counsel and thought of many brave men,
and traversed many countries,
but never set eyes on another man as high-hearted as Ulysses.
The sort of deed his bold heart would imagine and dare to do
was such an adventure as that carved horse
within which all we flower of the Argives lay hidden,
with death and destruction our guerdon for Troy."

Book 4, lines 265–273

Then Menelaus tells Telemachus about his own wanderings on the way home.
Before his return he had heard of the deaths of Aias and Agamemnon from
the sea-god Proteus whom he had beaten by his cunning. He forced the
sea-god to tell him as well the fate of yet a third companion:

"And I found winged words to answer him:
'These men I have now heard of: but name me
that third man who yet lives but lingers somewhere in the broad sea:
or dead? I wish to know it, even though my grief be deepened.'
So I said, and he replied again: 'The son of Laertes,
the lord of Ithaca. I saw him in an island, letting fall great tears
throughout the domain of the nymph Calypso
who there holds him in constraint:
and he may not get thence to his own land,
for he has by him no oared ships or company
to bear him across the sea's great swell.'"

Book 4, lines 550–560

After hearing this Telemachus determines to go home to Ithaca, taking with
him rich gifts from Menelaus.

Right (24) The wooden horse of Troy. Achaeans hid themselves in the horse at Ulysses'
suggestion; when the Trojans pulled the strange beast inside their city the Achaeans came out
of the horse at night, opened the city gates to the rest of their army, and plundered Troy

THE SUITORS PREPARE TO AMBUSH TELEMACHUS

The suitors, carousing in Ithaca, learn that Telemachus has actually sailed off to find news of his father. They are surprised and angry. Antinous, the wildest of them, shouts:

"I ask you to supply me a fast ship and a crew of twenty men,
with which to watch and waylay him as he comes
through the narrow gut between Ithaca and steep Samos:
that this gadding about after his father may cost him dear at last."
He spoke: they cried applause and urged him to execution.
Then they rose up and returned to Ulysses' house.
Not for very long did Penelope remain unaware
of these plots which the suitors were hatching
in the evil depths of their minds:
for the poursuivant Medon told her
what he had overheard of their council,
he being just beyond the court-wall
while they were thrashing out their schemes within.
Medon hasted through the building to bring his news to Penelope.

Book 4, lines 669–679

Upon her came down a heart-corroding agony:
so that she could not even guide herself
to one of the many stools which stood about the house.
Instead she sank to the door-sill of her richly-appointed room
and wailed aloud in piteous fashion:
while round her came crooning
all the woman-servants of the house,
the young ones with the old ones.

Book 4, lines 716–720

While the suitors wait beside the little island of Asteris, between Ithaca and Samos, hoping to ambush and kill Telemachus on his way home, Athene tries to comfort Penelope, who is now mourning both her husband and her son.

Left (25) Storage jars in the time of Ulysses
Right (26) The grief of Penelope. For ten years the suitors have tried to persuade her to forget Ulysses and to choose a new husband to be king in Ithaca
Overleaf (27) Scene of the suitors' ambush by the island of Asteris near Samos, where they plan to fall upon Telemachus and kill him as he sails home

THE GODS DETERMINE
THE RETURN OF ULYSSE.

Dawn rose from her marriage-bed beside high-born Tithonus
to bring her daylight to both gods and men.
The immortals, with Zeus the high-thundering,
their mightiest one, sat down in council:
and to them Athene spoke thus, designing to remind them
of the many misfortunes of Ulysses,
whose long sojourn in the nymph's house lay heavy on her heart: —
"Father Zeus, and you happy ever-living Gods:
henceforth let no sceptred king study to be kindly or gentle,
or to ensure justice and equity. It profits more to be harsh
and unseemly in act. Divine Ulysses was a clement and fatherly king;
but no one of the men, his subjects, remembers it of him:
nor has he power to regain the land of his fathers.
Moreover, there is now a plot afoot to murder his son as he returns
from sacred Pylos or noble Lacedaemon, whither he went
in hope to hear somewhat of his father."
Zeus the cloud-marshal answered her and said, "My child,
too fierce are the judgements of your mouth.
Besides, I think this last move was of your scheming,
for Ulysses to avenge himself on those men when he comes.
You have the knowledge, the power and the skill
to convey Telemachus again to his own place wholly unscathed.
See that it is so: and that the suitors come back too
in their ship, as they went."
He turned to Hermes, the son he loved, and said,
"Hermes, inform this nymph of the love-locks of my fixed decision
that long-suffering Ulysses shall return home as best he can,
without furtherance from gods or mortal men."

Book 5, lines 1–12, 15, 18–32

When at last Hermes attained that remote island,
he quitted the purple sea and went inland as far as the great cave
in which lived the nymph of the well-braided hair.
He chanced to find her within.
In the cavern he did not find great-hearted Ulysses,
who sat weeping on the shore as was his wont,
letting flow his tears while he eyed the fruitless sea.

Book 5, lines 55–58, 81–82, 84

Left (28) The morning sky
Right (29) Hermes, the messenger of the Gods, who brings the fair nymph Calypso the
decision of the Gods about the return of Ulysses
Overleaf (30) Ulysses grieving for his home
(31) The sea around Calypso's isle

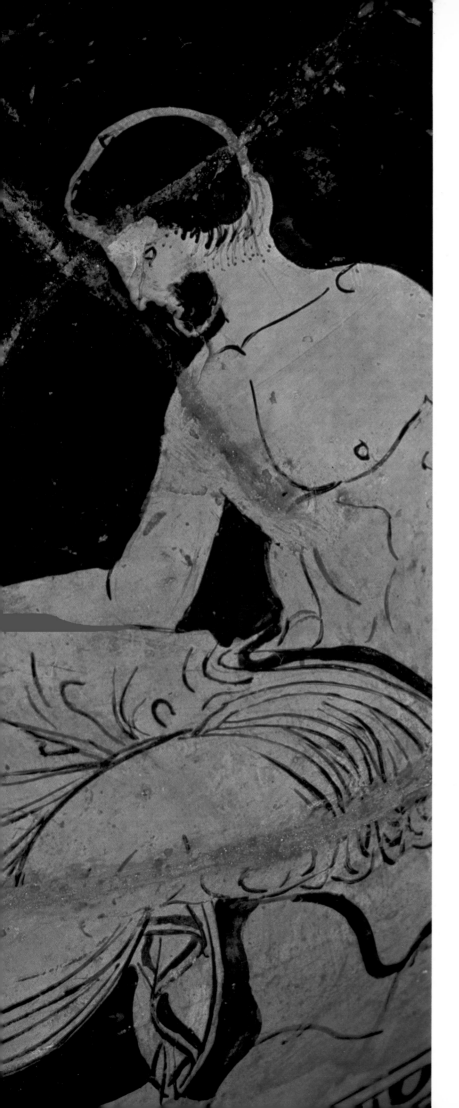

ULYSSES SETS SAIL

The beautiful nymph Calypso tells Ulysses the news which Hermes has brought about the decision of the gods. She helps Ulysses build a raft and on the fifth day sets him out to sea with instructions for the voyage.

The delighted Ulysses spread wide his sail to this fair breeze
and sat down by the stern oar, most skilfully steering.
Nor did sleep once take possession of his eyelids,
so continually he kept gazing on the Pleiades,
or on Arcturus that goes down so late,
or on the Great Bear (they call it also Wain)
which revolves in constant narrow watch upon Orion
and alone of stars will never enter the bath of ocean.

Book 5, lines 269–275

Yet then the God, the Earth-Shaker, spied him
from far off by the mountains of the Solymi,
by which way he was returning from Aethiopia. The mind of Poseidon
was mightily enraged when he saw who was sailing his sea.
With a wagging of the head he began to mutter to himself,
"There now, while I have been away amongst the Aethiopians
these gods have changed their mind about Ulysses . . .
However I think I can give him yet
a long excursion into sorrow."
With this he drove the clouds into a heap
and, trident in hand, tossed together the desolate waters.
He summoned all the violent gusts that were in all the winds
and let them loose, blind-folding sea and land with storm-clouds.
Night leaped into heaven. Mightily the surge rolled up,
for east wind clashed upon south wind, the ill-blowing west
with the north wind from the upper sky.
Therefore the knees and warm heart of Ulysses shook.

Book 5, lines 282–287, 290–297

Left (32) Ulysses and the nymph Calypso, who wants the hero to remain with her for ever
Overleaf (33) Ulysses on the raft on which he leaves Calypso's isle

ΟΛΥΣΕΥΣ

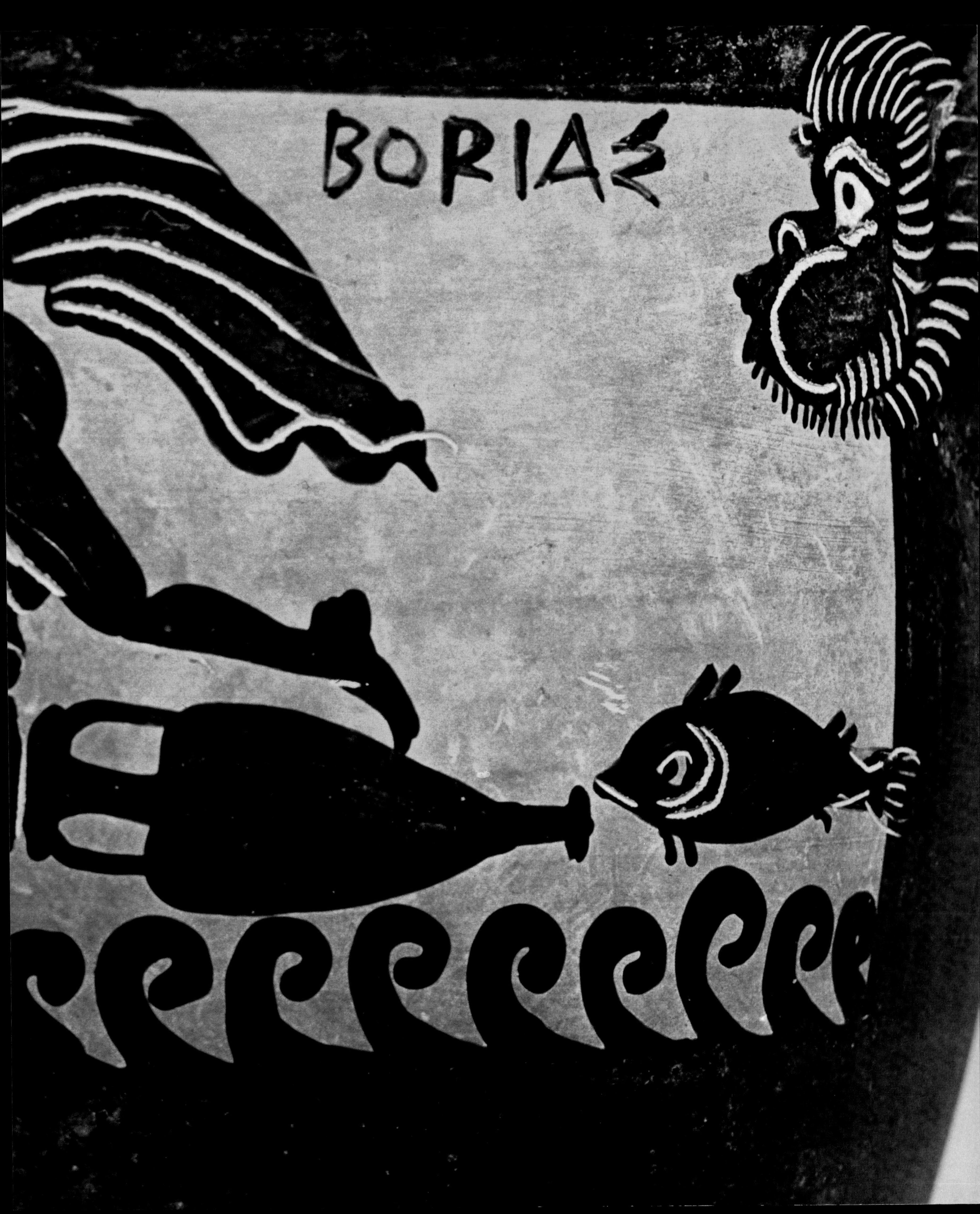
BORIAS

AMONG
THE PHAEACIANS

After Poseidon's storm has wrecked his raft Ulysses has to swim for
three days and two nights. Finally he reaches the island of the Phaeacians,
where the breaking waves almost drown him before he can make the shore.

And there of a surety had woe-begone Ulysses died,
contrary to fate's decree, had not grey-eyed Athene
now given him a deeper wisdom,
by light of which when he once more came to the surface
he swam out beyond the breaking surf and along,
closely eyeing the shore to see if he might achieve
a sheltered landing by help of some spit or creek:
and so swimming he encountered the mouth of a fair-running river
which seemed to him the best spot,
forasmuch as it was clear of reeds and sheltered from the wind.
He felt then the outward-setting current of the river's flow
and prayed to its god in his heart: —
"Hear me, whatever lord you be!
I come to your worshipful presence, a fugitive
from the threats of Poseidon — from the sea."
Thus his petition;
and the god forthwith allayed the current,
smoothed out the eddies and made his way calm,
safe-guiding him within the river's mouths.
Ulysses knees gave way together, and his sinewy arms:
for his reserve of manhood had been used up
in the long fight with the salt sea.

Book 5, lines 436–446, 451–454

Previous page (34) Poseidon

(35) Storm at sea

Right (36) Where Ulysses swims ashore: a beach on the island of the Phaeacians,
modern Corfu

Then Ulysses struggled up from the river . . .
He got under a double bush, two trees with a single root:
one wild olive, the other a graft of true olive.
So closely did they grow together and supplement each other
that through them no force of moist winds could pierce:
nor could the shining of the sun cast in any ray:
nor would any downpour of rain soak through.
Beneath them did Ulysses creep, and set to scraping together
with his own hands a broad bed for himself:
for inside there had drifted such a pile of dry leaves
as would have covered two or three men
well enough for a winter-time, however hard the weather.
When bold Ulysses saw the leaves he rejoiced
and laid himself down in the midst of them
and fell to pouring the litter over his body, till he was covered.

Book 5, lines 462, 476–487

So at last long-suffering Ulysses yielded to his weariness
and slept there; while Athene
proceeded to the district and chief town of the Phaeacian people.

Book 6, lines 1–3

Athene comes to Nausicaa, the king's daughter, as she lies asleep and puts
it into her head to go to the river with her maids to wash the royal linen.
The next day Nausicaa asks her father Alcinous for mules and a cart
to haul the linen down to the river.

At journey's end they came
to the flowing stream of the lovely river
and found the washing-places, within which from beneath
there bubbled up such abundance of clear water
that its force was sufficient to clean the very dirtiest things.
There they loosed the mules from the cart
and drove them down to the rippling water,
where was honey-sweet herbage for their cropping.
Then they took the garments from the waggon in armfuls
and laid them in the shadowed water of the washing pools:
where they danced on them in emulation, each striving
to out-knead the rest.

Book 6, lines 85–92

Left (37) The olive roots where Ulysses lies down to sleep
Right (38) The Goddess Athene, who appears to the king's daughter Nausicaa in her sleep
and persuades her to go washing the next day
Overleaf (39) Maiden washing
(40) The river where Nausicaa washes the linen

ULYSSES
AND NAUSICAA

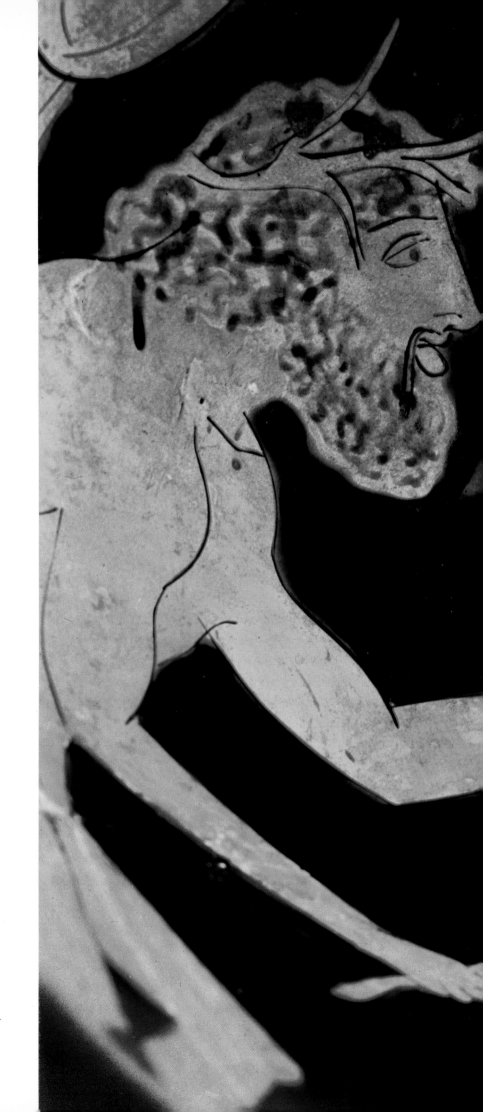

After the washing, the princess Nausicaa and her maids bathe in the sea and play ball beside the river. Their shouts wake Ulysses.

"In what land of men do I find myself?
By the voices I do think them human.
Let me go forward, and if I can see . . ."
Thus muttering Ulysses crept out from his bushes
snapping off in his powerful hands one very leafy shoot
with which to shield from sight the maleness of his body.
So he sallied forth,
like the mountain-bred lion exulting in his strength,
who goes through rain and wind with burning eyes.
After great or small cattle he prowls, or the wild deer.
If his belly constrain him he will even attempt the sheep
penned in solid manors. So boldly did Ulysses
stark naked as he was, make to join the band of maidens:
for necessity compelled him.
None the less he seemed loathsome in their sight
because of his defilement with the sea-wrack;
and in panic they ran abroad over all the spits of the salt beaches.
Only the daughter of Alcinous remained;
for Athene had put courage into her heart
and taken terror from her limbs
so that she stood still, facing him.

Book 6, lines 119, 125–141

Right (41) Ulysses, covering himself with an olive branch approaches Nausicaa: she stands her ground, inspired by Athene

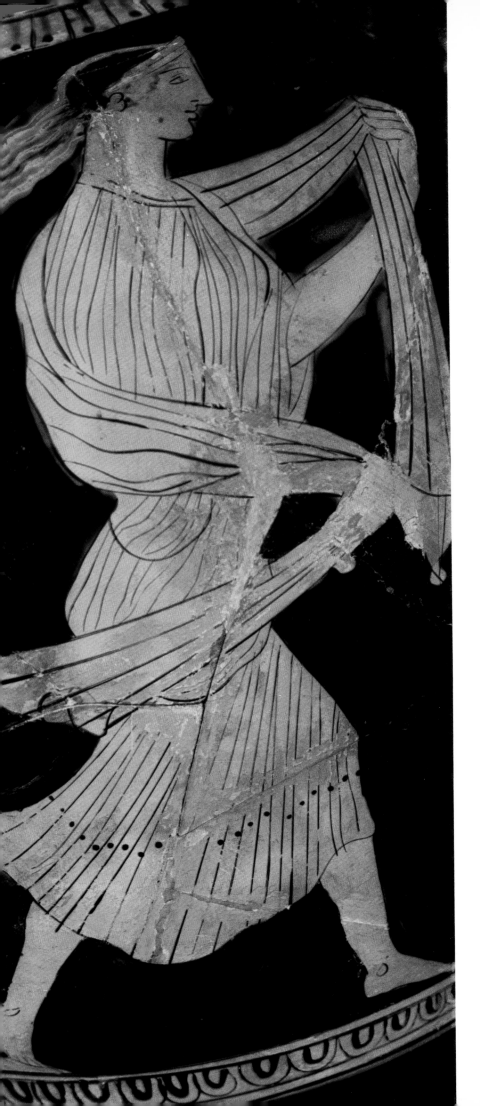

*Nausicaa calls back her maids who have run away and tells them to
bathe, clothe, and feed ship-wrecked Ulysses who has asked
for her help. Then the girls prepare to go home.*
*Nausicaa asks the stranger — Ulysses has not yet given his name —
to wait in the poplar grove of Athene till darkness before entering
the town of the Phaeacians. There he is to look for the palace of
Alcinous, and ask first Queen Arete and then the king himself for
hospitality and help on his journey home.*

The sun sank and they were at the famous grove dedicated to Athene,
where Ulysses tarried and at once prayed a prayer
to the daughter of great Zeus.
"Hear me, Unwearied One, child of Zeus who holds the Aegis.
Especially I pray you now to hear me,
forasmuch as you did not lately when I was broken —
when there broke me the famous Earth-shaker.
Give me to find love and pity among the Phaeacians."
So he prayed. Pallas Athene heard him.

Book 6, lines 321–328

Left (42) One of Nausicaa's companions flees at the sight of Ulysses
*Right (43) The poplar grove of Athene where Ulysses waits till it is dark enough for him
to enter the town of the Phaeacians*

AT THE COURT
OF ALCINOUS

At length Ulysses bestirred himself and moved towards the city:
whereupon Athene for the love she bore him
muffled his shape in a wreath of mist
to prevent any swaggering Phaeacian from standing in his road
and trying by jeers and questions to find out who he was.
For further care there met him in the entrance of the gracious town
Athene herself, grey-eyed and goddess but now subdued
to the likeness of a quite young girl.

Book 7, lines 14–20

Ulysses is shown the way to the palace and the royal family by Athene,
disguised as a young girl. Alcinous welcomes the stranger and entertains
him to a rich supper. Still not revealing his name, Ulysses tells how he
stayed with the nymph Calypso and later was shipwrecked and then saved by
reaching the shore of Phaeacia. Alcinous promises to help him on his way home.

"I shall here and now
fix the actual day of your going. To-morrow, let it be.
To-morrow you shall lie down and slumber soundly,
while the oars of your crew smite the smooth sea,
bringing you all the way to your land and house,
those things you love."

Book 7, lines 317–320

Right (44) Achaeans at a feast like that which King Alcinous held in honour of Ulysses

Next morning Alcinous commands a ship to be fitted out to take Ulysses
home. Then he invites the stranger and various local princes to a
feast in the palace. After the feast the young Phaeacians try their skill
at athletics. They challenge the foreigner to join in as well. When he refuses,
Euryalus, one of the princes, becomes insulting . . .

Deep Ulysses glared at him and thundered:
"Your reviling made the heart beat faster in my breast.
I am no ninny at sports, as you would have it.
Indeed I think I was among the best, in my time,
while I yet heard the prompting of my youth and hands."
He spoke and sprang to his feet.
All cloaked as he was he seized a throwing weight,
a huge heavy stone
far bigger than those with which the Phaeacians had been competing.

Book 8, lines 165, 178–181, 186–188

He whirled it up and flung it from his mighty hand,
and the stone sang through the air.
Down they quailed to the earth, those Phaeacians of the long oars,
those master mariners, beneath the hurtling of the stone
which soared so freely from the hero's hand
that it overpassed the marks of every other.
Wherefore gaily he challenged the Phaeacians: —
"In none of the sports which men use do I disgrace myself.
I can well handle the polished bow. In the thick of each fight
I would be ever the first to loose arrow and bring down my man,
no matter how many followers of mine were there,
shooting at the enemy.
I will send my spear further than any man his arrow."

Book 8, lines 189–193, 201, 214–218, 229

Below (45) Athletic contests among the young men

ULYSSES MAKES HIMSELF KNOWN AND TELLS OF HIS WANDERINGS

*After the games King Alcinous calls the minstrel Demodocus and
orders the young dancers show their skill at dancing to the music of the
harp. The minstrel sings how Hephaestus, the lame blacksmith of the gods,
surprised Ares, the God of war, making adulterous love to Aphrodite, the
Goddess of beauty, how he caught them in a cunning net of steel, and
displayed them to be laughed at by all the Gods in Olympus.
The king offers rich gifts to the stranger so that he shall not return home
empty-handed. Euryalus, who has insulted the stranger at the games, now
makes it up to him by giving him a finely-wrought sword. Then the whole
assembly goes in together for a feast in the royal palace.*

And when they were filled with drink and food
then Ulysses addressed Demodocus.
"Demodocus, I laud you above all mortal men:
I know not if it was the Muse, daughter of Zeus, that taught you,
or Apollo himself. Anyhow you have sung the real history
of the mishaps of the Achaeans, their deeds, sufferings, and griefs,
as if you had been there or had heard it from eye witnesses.
But now change your theme and sing
of how Epeius with the help of Athene carpentered together
that great timber horse, the crafty device,
which wise Ulysses got taken into the citadel
after packing it with the men who were to lay Troy waste."

Book 8, lines 485–495

So he said: and the minstrel, fired by the God,
gave proof of his mastery. He sang
how the sons of the Argives quitted their hollow den,
and poured out from the horse, and made an end of Troy.
He sang the share of each warrior in the wasting
of the stately town, and how Ulysses, Ares-like,
attacked the house of Deiphobus with great Menelaus.
There, he said, Ulysses braved terrible odds
but conquered in the end, by help of resolute Athene.
Thus ran the famous singer's song: but Ulysses melted
and tears from his eyelids bedewed his cheeks.

Book 8, lines 499, 514–522

*Left (46) Ulysses with a throwing-spear
Overleaf (47) The Minstrel whose singing brings Ulysses to tears, thus revealing who he is
to the amazed Phaeacians
(48) The wooden horse of Troy*

When Alcinous notices the grief of his guest he bids the minstrel be silent
and asks the stranger about his name and story, which assuredly must be
connected with the fate of the Achaeans at Troy.

Many-sided Ulysses then began:
"Lord Alcinous, most eminent, I am Ulysses, son of Laertes:
a name which among men spells every resource and subtlety of mind:
and my fame reaches heaven.
However, let me recall the tale of the calamitous homeward journey
with which Zeus afflicted my return from Troy.
From Ilion the wind served me to near Ismarus of the Cicones.
I sacked the city and slew them."

Book 9, lines 1–2, 19–20, 37–40

Below (49) Ulysses driving a chariot
Right (50) Ulysses in tears
Overleaf (51) The ship of Ulysses leaving Troy
(52) Sunrise at sea

AMONG
THE LOTOS-EATERS

"Thereafter for nine days I was driven
by ravening winds across the sea.
On the tenth day we made the land of the Lotos-eaters,
men who browse on a food of flowers.
And so it was that as each tasted of this honey-sweet plant,
the wish to bring news or return grew faint in him:
rather he preferred to dwell for ever with the Lotos-eating men,
feeding upon Lotos and letting fade from mind all memory of home.
I had to seek them and drag them back on board."

Book 9, lines 82–84, 94–98

Left (53) Palms on the island of Djerba, the land of the lotos-eaters
Below (54) A bowl of fruit, the food of the lotos-eaters

THE LAND
OF THE ONE-EYED
GIANTS

"I constrained the rest of my adherents to hurry abroad,
lest perhaps more of them might eat Lotos
and lose their longing for home.
They embarked promptly and sat to the rowing benches:
then in their proper ranks, all together, they swung their oars
and beat the sea hoary-white.
We left in low spirits
and later came to the land of the arrogant iniquitous Cyclopes
who so leave all things to the Gods
that they neither plant nor till."
Book 9, lines 100–108

*Ulysses and his companions land first on a small island, within sight of
a larger one where the Cyclopes dwell; they feast all day on wild goats which
they have killed, and twelve of them set out the next day to explore the island.*

"As we came to the nearest point of land
we could see a cave at its seaward extremity
— a lofty cave, embowered in laurels.
Actually it was the lair of a giant,
a monstrous creature who pastured his flocks widely
from that centre and avoided traffic with any man.
He was a solitary infidel thing, this ogre, and fearfully made.
I ordered my faithful crew to stand by the ship
and guard the ship, while I picked the twelve men I judged best
and set off with them. I took,
as an afterthought, a goat-skin of potent wine, very mellow."
Book 9, lines 181–183, 187–190, 193–197

"Soon we were within the cave, to find its owner absent,
grazing his goodly flocks in their pastures.
So we explored the cave, staring round-eyed.
We built up a fire, made a burnt offering,
helped ourselves to cheese and ate as we sat there inside the cavern
waiting for our man to come home from the pastures.
He brought with him an immense burden of dried wood,
kindling for his supper fire, and flung it upon the cave's floor with a
crash that sent us scurrying in terror to its far corners."
Book 9, lines 216–218, 231–236

Left (55) The harbour of the island of the Cyclopes on the west coast of Italy
Overleaf (56) Volcanic spring in the land of the one-eyed giants
(57) The Cyclops Polyphemus, son of the sea-god Poseidon

"So far he had been wholly engaged in work,
but now he rebuilt the fire and looked around
and saw us. 'Why, strangers,' said he, 'who are you
and where have you come from across the water?'
So he asked, and our confidence cracked at the giant's booming voice
and his hugeness. Yet I made shift to speak out firmly,
saying, 'We are waifs of the Achaeans from Troy.'"

Book 9, lines 250–252, 256–259

*The Cyclopes' chief, Polyphemus, rejecting Ulysses' request for a friendly
reception, slyly asks where the Achaeans' ship is. Ulysses, just as clever, replies
that he and his twelve companions are the only survivors of a shipwreck.*

"So I said. His savagery disdained me one word in reply.
He leapt to his feet, lunged with his hands among my fellows,
snatched up two of them like whelps and rapped their heads
against the ground. The brains burst out from their skulls
and were spattered over the cave's floor, while he broke them up,
limb from limb, and supped off them to the last shred."

Book 9, lines 287–291

*Next morning the monstrous Polyphemus drives his flock from the cavern
and closes up the doorway with a great slab of stone. Ulysses works out a plan to
get Polyphemus drunk with wine and then stab out his one eye with a burning pike.*

"So we held the burning pointed stake in his eye and spun it,
till the boiling blood bubbled about its pillar of fire.
He let out a wild howl which rang round the cavern and drove us
hither and thither in terror. He wrenched the spike from his eye
and it came out clotted and thick with blood.
The maddening pain made him fling it from his hands,
and then he began to bellow to the other Cyclopes living about him
in their dens among the windy hills."

Book 9, lines 387–388, 395–400

*The wily Ulysses has told Polyphemus that his name is "Nobody". So that
when the other Cyclopes come rushing in reply to his howls for help and ask
what is the matter, they turn away again as Polyphemus shouts from the
cave that "Nobody" has hurt him. During the night Ulysses makes ready
for their escape from the cavern. He binds the rams together in threes,
one companion under every middle ram.*

"That meant three rams for each shipmate: while for myself
there remained the prize ram of all the flock. I took hold of him,
tucked myself under his shaggy belly
and hung there so, with steadfast courage: clinging face upwards
with my hands twisted into his enormous fleece.
Thus we waited in great trepidation for the dawn."

Book 9, lines 431–436

Above left (58) Polyphemus about to eat one of Ulysses' companions
Below left (59) Ulysses offers Polyphemus the wine through which he falls into a drunken sleep
Right (60) Ulysses and his companions put out the eye of the drunken Polyphemus

The trick works — though Polyphemus strokes each ram as it leaves the cave. Soon Ulysses and his companions reach the open air in safety and get back unharmed to their ship. When the Achaeans have rowed away to a safe shouting distance from the island, Ulysses cries out to Polyphemus and insults the giant's father, Poseidon, the Lord of the Sea.

"'Cyclops, if any human being asks of you
how your eye was so hideously put out,
say that Ulysses, despoiler of cities, did it;
even the son of Laertes whose home is in Ithaca.'"

Book 9, lines 502–505

Left (61) Ulysses escapes from the cave of Polyphemus under the belly of a ram
Below (62) Leaving the land of the Cyclopes

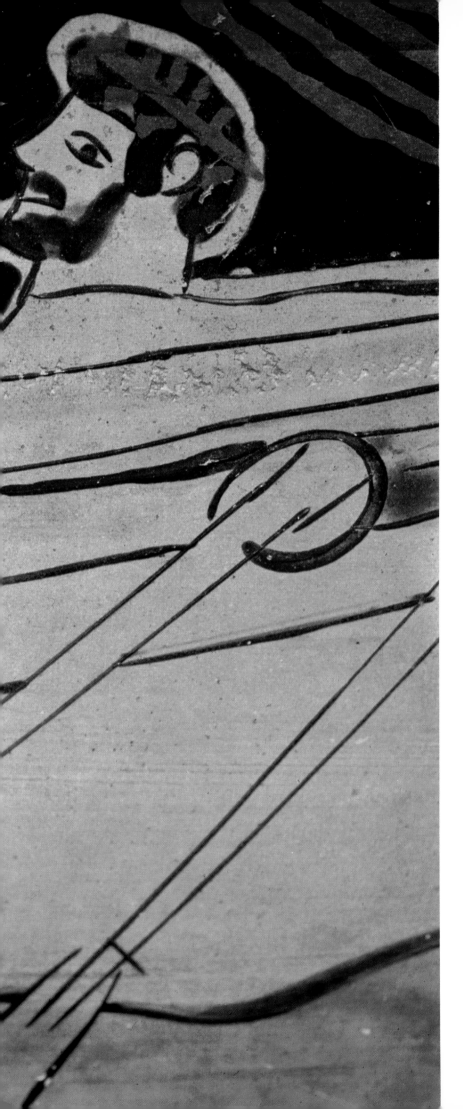

AEOLUS, LORD OF THE WINDS

The furious Cyclops tries twice to smash Ulysses' ship with huge stones which he hurls with giant force into the sea. Then he calls upon Poseidon:

"'Hear me, dark-haired Girdler of the earth,
if indeed I am yours and you my sire.
Grant that there be no homecoming for this Ulysses,
son of Laertes of Ithaca.'"

Book 9, lines 528–531

Zeus is angry at Ulysses' behaviour and he rejects the thank-offering of the Achaeans. It seems that the gods have heard Polyphemus' curse.

"We lay down by the water's brink till dawn's rosy showing:
when I roused the force and bade them embark and cast off.
Soon they were aboard and ready on their thwarts,
sitting to the oars and frothing the sea with their well-timed strokes:
our voyage being sad, as we had lost a part of our fellowship
and glad, that we had delivered our own souls from death."

Book 9, lines 560–566

"So we came to the Aeolian island. In that sea-cradled fastness,
within a bulwark of invincible bronze from which the cliff falls sheer,
lived Aeolus son of Hippotas, a friend of the eternal Gods."

Book 10, lines 1–4

Aeolus, who has been put in command of the winds by Zeus, plays host to the Achaean wanderers for a month. When they finally leave he gives Ulysses a carefully tied bag with the storm winds bottled up inside.

So they sail safely for nine days and nights. But when the fires on Ithaca are already visible Ulysses falls asleep. His companions, imagining it to contain secret treasure, foolishly open the bag. A terrible storm blows up and the ships are eventually driven back to the island of Aeolus.

Ulysses, in his despair, asks the ruler of the winds for help a second time, in vain! Aeolus shouts angrily:

"'Get off the island instantly, you vilest thing alive!
Am I to make a habit of maintaining and fitting out
one whom the Gods hate?'"

Book 10, lines 72–74

*Left (63) Achaean oarsmen
Overleaf (64) Stromboli, the island of Aeolus whom the Gods have appointed as keeper of the winds
(65) The wall of bronze on the island of Aeolus*

THE ADVENTURE
AMONG
THE LAESTRYGONS

"On the seventh day we made the fortress of Lamos,
which is nicknamed Tall-tower by its people, the Laestrygons.
Upon our arrival my other shipmasters
steered straight into the cove and there moored their ships,
each tightly to the next, together: not that it mattered,
for inside the haven there was never any swell, small or big,
but a white calm constantly prevailed.
I however kept my own ship outside, yet near:
making fast our lines to a rock at the extreme end of the point.
I told my fellows they must discover
what the bread-eaters of this part were like
and chose two of them to go, with a third for messenger."
They went ashore asking after the king of the island and his subjects ...
But when they came to that great house they found his wife inside,
a mountainous woman whose ill-aspect struck them with horror.
She summoned Antiphates, her powerful husband, from the assembly.
His notion was to murder my men in cold blood.
He seized hold of the first
and proceeded to eat him for his dinner out of hand.
The other two sprang away in headlong flight
and regained the ships, while the master of the house
was sounding an alarm throughout the city.
This brought the stout Laestrygons in their thousands
pell-mell together — not human-looking creatures, these, but giants.
They gathered missile stones each a man's weight and cast them
down on us from off the cliffs. There went up from the fleet
the ghastly sounds of splintering hulls and dying men,
while the natives were busy spearing my people like fish
and collecting them to make their loathsome meal.
As they were so engaged in killing all within the close harbour
I drew the sharp hanger from my side and cut the hawsers of my ship,
shouting orders the while to her honest crew
how they must be urgent upon their oars
if we were to escape a terrible fate.
Like one man they spumed up the water in dread of death,
and my ship darted out from the cliffs into the welcome main.
All other vessels which had gone inside went down together:
so it was in very disheartened mood that we rowed on,
having lost every one of our dear comrades."

Book 10, lines 81–82, 91–96, 100–103, 109–110, 112–134

*Right (66) The rocky coast of the Laestrygons on Corsica where the fleet of Ulysses is
reduced to a single ship*

THE ENCHANTRESS CIRCE

"We came to the island of Aeaea, where lived a formidable Goddess,
Circe of the luxuriant tresses."

Book 10, lines 135–136

*Ulysses first scouts out their position and sees far away a wisp of smoke
showing that the island is inhabited. On his way back through the thick
forest he brings down a mighty buck, which makes a fine meal for the
Achaeans. Next morning he divides his men into two platoons, himself in
command of one, Eurylochus of the other.*

"So tall Eurylochus marched off his two and twenty men,
all of them weeping aloud.
The twenty and two who stayed with me cried in sympathy."

Book 10, lines 208–209

Left (67) The island of the enchantress Circe in the Gulf of Gaeta
Below (68) The wood at the foot of Monte Circeo, where Ulysses slays the great stag

"The party threaded the woodland glades
till they found the hewn walls of Circe's house
on a site which overlooked the country-side.
Wolves from the hills and lions,
victims of her witch's potions, roamed about it.
She came at once, opening her doors to bid them in.
In their simplicity all went in to her: except Eurylochus
who thought it was some trick and stayed behind.
She showed them all to thrones and seats and confected for them
a mess of cheese with barley-meal and clear honey,
mulched in Pramnian wine.
With this she mixed drugs so sadly powerful
as to steal from them all memory of their native land.
After they had drunk from the cup
she struck them with her wand; and straightway
hustled them into her sties,
for they grew the heads and shapes and bristles of a swine,
with swine-voices too.
Only their reason remained steadfastly as before."
Book 10, lines 210–213, 230–240

Eurylochus alone comes back to the ship and he tells Ulysses the story of
his men's misfortune. Hearing it Ulysses sets off alone to the house
of the enchantress Circe.

"I left ship and shore and plunged into the solemn wood,
till near the great house of drug-wise Circe;
when there came from it to meet me Hermes of the gold rod,
seeming to be a quite young man, of that age when youth
looks its loveliest with the down just mantling his cheeks.
He called my name and took my hand, saying:
'O unhappy one, do you again hazard the wild-wood alone?
Your followers, no other than hogs to all appearance,
are penned in the deep sties of Circe's house.
Do you come to set them free?
I tell you, yourself shall not get away but will join the others
and be pent with them.
But listen: I can save you and deliver you from this evil
by a potent drug in whose virtue you can enter Circe's house
and yet remain immune. Hear the manner of Circe's deadly arts.
She will prepare you refreshment, and hide a poison in it:
but against you her spells will not avail,
forbidden by this saving charm I give you.
Let me explain your course of action.
When Circe strikes you with her long thin wand
draw the sharp sword that is on your hip and make for her
as if you had a mind to run her through.'"
Book 10, lines 274–295

Left (69) Circe with the magic potion which changes the companions of Ulysses into swine
Right (70) (71) The companions of Ulysses turned to swine
Overleaf (72) The grove of Circe
(73) The magic plant which Hermes shows Ulysses for an antidote against the drugs of Circe

"I halted at her gate and called. The Goddess heard, opened and bade me in."

Book 10, lines 310–313

Following Hermes' advice, Ulysses frees his companions but then remains a whole year with Circe. When he pleads with the goddess for their return to Ithaca, Circe tells him that he must first travel to the kingdom of Hades, the God of the Underworld, to question the seer Teiresias about his return home. Then the goddess tells Ulysses how to reach the Underworld and what he must take with him as offerings to appease the souls of the dead that thirst for the blood of sacrifice.

Below (74) Ulysses compels the enchantress Circe to turn his companions back into men again
Right (75) Ulysses and Circe

AT THE EDGE
OF THE UNDERWORLD

"We could sit and watch the wind and the helmsman
lead us forward, daylong going steadily
across the deep, our sails cracking full,
till sundown and its darkness covered the sea's illimitable ways.
We had attained Earth's verge and its girdling river of Ocean,
where are the cloud-wrapped and misty
confines of the Cimmerian men.
We beached the ship on that shore
and put off our sheep. With them we made our way
up the strand of Ocean till we came to the spot
which Circe had described.
There Perimedes and Eurylochus held the victims
while I drew the keen blade from my hip, to hollow that trench
of a cubit square and a cubit deep.
About it I poured the drink-offerings
to the congregation of the dead,
a honey-and-milk draught first, sweet wine next, with water last of all;
and I made a heave-offering of our glistening barley."

Book 11, lines 10–15, 20–28

Right (76) The Lake of Avernus, one of the gates of the Underworld
Overleaf (77) The sacrificial ram with whose blood Ulysses attracts the souls of the dead

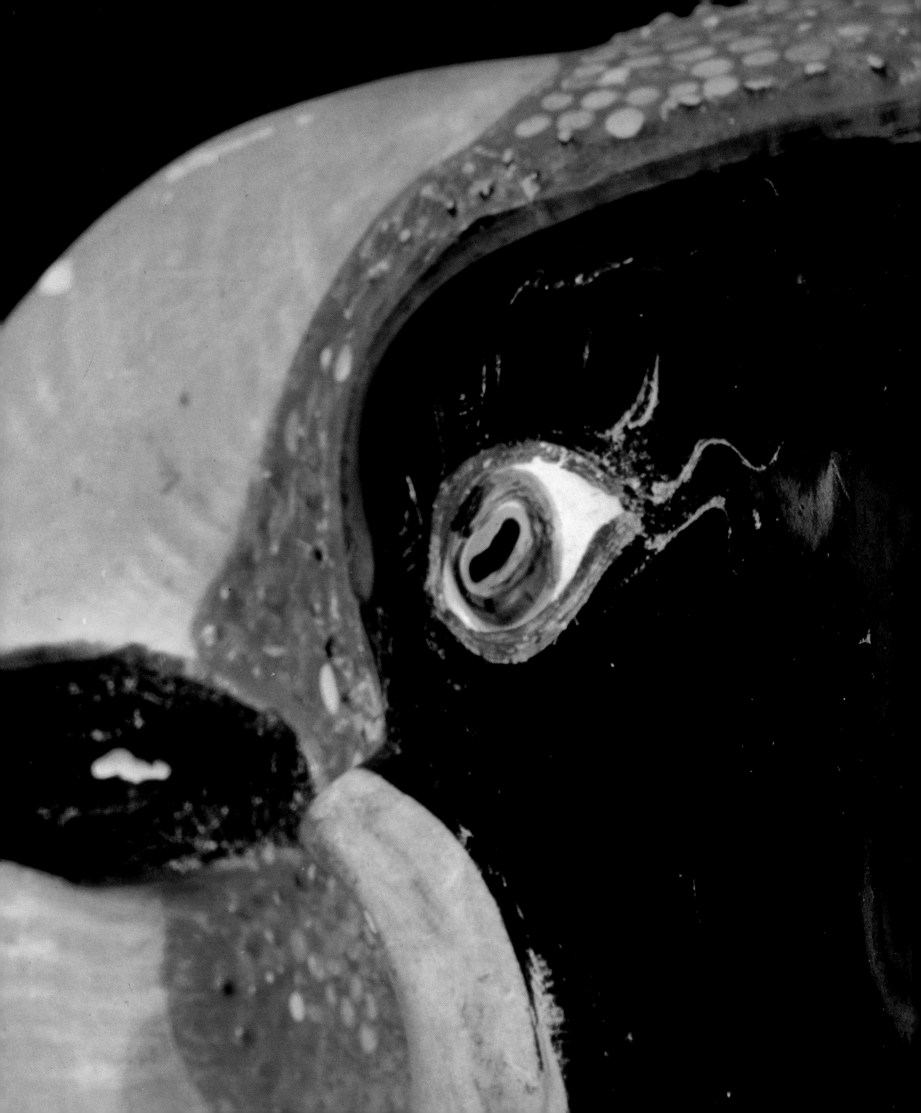

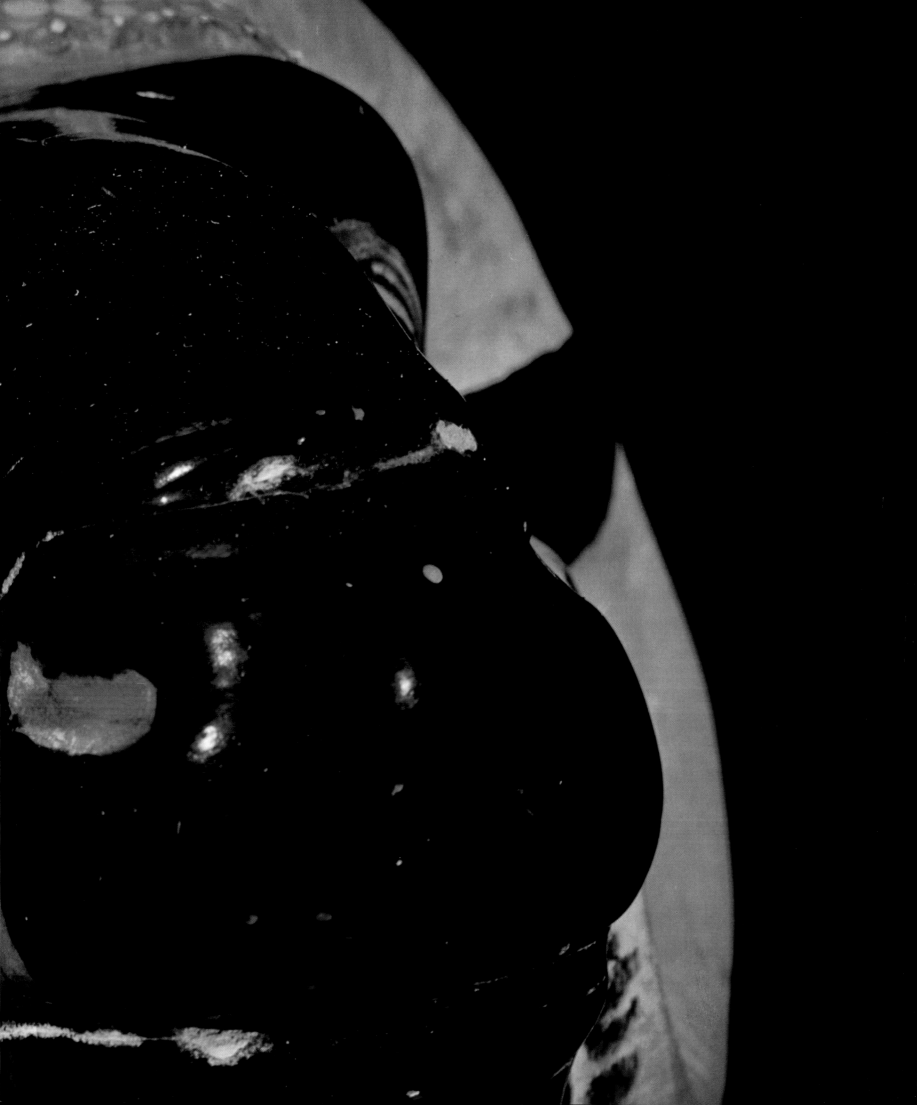

Left (78) The sacrifice of Ulysses
Below (79) Ulysses and the soul of Elpenor, who complains
that his body lies unburied on the island of Circe

"After I had been thus instant in prayer to the populations of the grave
I took the two sheep and beheaded them across my pit
in such manner that the livid blood drained into it.
Then from out of Erebus they flocked to me,
the dead spirits of those who had died,
The first I knew was the spirit of my fellow, Elpenor,
whose body was not yet interred under the ample ground."

Book 11, lines 34–37, 51–52

At last the spirit of Theban Teiresias appears and recognizes Ulysses:

"'You come here,
renowned Ulysses, in quest of a comfortable way home.
I tell you the God will make your way most hard.
I tell you that your movements will not remain a secret
from the Earth-shaker, whose heart is bitter against you
for the hurt you did him in blinding the Cyclops, his loved son.'"
Book 11, 100–103

*Ulysses is promised a delayed but happy homecoming, provided he and his
men keep their hands off the herds of the sun-god. Thereupon, a long train
of souls of the dead appear, first his mother and then a great number of
noble ladies, then the heroes who fell at Troy, chief among them Achilles.
Ulysses speaks with them all, then leaves the Underworld filled with horror.*

*Below (80) Achaean warriors at Troy
Right (81) Ulysses questions the prophet Teiresias
about the chances of his reaching home*

PASSING THE SIRENS

Ulysses returns once again to Circe to bury poor Elpenor. Circe welcomes the Achaeans with a cry:

"'A hardy adventure, men, this going down to Hades alive.
Now you will twice encounter death,
whereas others do die but once.'"

Book 12, lines 21–22

Then Circe informs Ulysses of the dangers and adventures which await him on his voyage and how he can surmount them.

"Back into the island went the Goddess, while I rejoined the ship.
After a while to my crowd I spoke gravely: 'Friends,
I do not mean to keep to myself, or among just one or two,
the disclosures now made me by Circe, but I will publish them freely
in order that we may die — if we die — informed;
or else trick death and fate to get clean away.
Her first warnings concern the Sirens and their flowery meadow.
Our prime duty will be to turn a deaf ear to their singing.
Only myself may listen, after you have so fastened me
with tight-drawn cords that I stand immovably secured to the mast,
and if I beg you or bid you let me loose,
then must you redoubly firm me into place with yet more bonds.'
I repeated this till all had heard it well,
while our trim ship was borne towards the island of these Siren-sisters
by the breath of our fair breeze."

Book 12, lines 143, 153–161, 163–167

Ulysses seals the ears of his companions with wax lest they hear the song of the Sirens. He alone, bound fast, listens to the seductive singing.

"Such words they sang in lovely cadences. My heart ached
to hear them out. To make the fellows loose me
I frowned upon them with my brows.
They bent to it ever the more stoutly while Perimedes and Eurylochus
rose to tighten my former bonds till we were wholly past
and could hear no more the Sirens' words nor their tune:
then the faithful fellows took out the wax
with which I had filled their ears, and delivered me from bondage."

Book 12, lines 192–200

Left (82) The morning sun upon the sea
Right (83) One of the Sirens, whose singing bewitches passing sailors
Overleaf (84) The ship of the Achaeans passing the Sirens: Ulysses bound to the mast

THE ADVENTURE
WITH SCYLLA

"We had left that island behind when I began
to see smoke and broken water:
the thundering of breakers came to my ears.
My crew took fright: the oars slipped from their grasp."

Book 12, lines 201–203

*Now Ulysses orders his companions row hard and he tells the steersman to
guide the ship clear of the spume and the breaking seas lest it be swallowed
up by the whirlpool. Ulysses, however, does not mention to his companions
the terrible Scylla about whom Circe has warned him. Instead he takes up
arms himself to ward off the man-eating monster.*

"We went on up the narrow strait, thus anxiously.
On this side lay Scylla, while on that Charybdis
in her terrible whirlpool was sucking down the sea:
My crew turned sallow with fright, staring into this abyss
from which we expected our immediate death.
Scylla chose the moment to rape from the midst of the ship
six of our party — the six stoutest and best.
I happened to cast my eye back along the thwarts, over the crew,
and thus marked their dangling hands and feet as they
were wrenched aloft, screeching my name for the last time
in voices made thin and high by agony."

Book 12, lines 234–236, 243–250

*Previous page (85) Isole li Galli in the Gulf of Sorrento, known as the
Islands of the Sirens
Left (86) Scylla
Right (87) Scylla's rock
Overleaf (88) The steersman of Ulysses' ship
(89) Scylla*

THE KILLING OF THE CATTLE OF HELIOS

"Now we were through the danger
of the Skurries and of Scylla and Charybdis.
We neared the God's good island where Helios Hyperion
kept his broad-browed splendid cattle and many flocks of fat sheep.
So I spoke earnestly to my followers:
'Hear me, long-tried and suffering ones, while I tell you a thing.
In their warnings Teiresias and Circe were very stringent with me
to beware this island of Helios, Delighter of Mankind.
She foretold that here might be our last and deadliest peril.
Wherefore let us drive right past the place and avoid it.'"

Book 12, lines 260–263, 270–276

*But his companions will not listen to Ulysses' warning. They slaughter the
sacred cattle and stay on the island seven days.*

*Meanwhile Zeus, told of the outrage, decides to wreck the ship. Hardly
are the Achaeans at sea once more when a terrible storm comes up. The
helmsman is crushed by the crashing mast and Zeus splinters the ship and
shatters the crew with a bolt of lightning. Only Ulysses is able to save himself.
Straddling the overturned ship's keel, he is driven back by the storm to the
rocks of Scylla and Charybdis. The whirlpool Charybdis sucks the timber
down into the depths while at the last moment Ulysses is flung into a fig-tree
which overhangs it. Here he waits, hanging above the awful depths, till the
whirlpool spouts forth the ship's keel and mast again.*

"I let go and dropped with sprawling hands and feet,
to splash heavily into the water
on the lee side of these great beams.
Across them I sat and paddled hard with my hands.
The Father of Gods and men spared me further sight of Scylla,
else should I inevitably have died."

Book 12, lines 442–446

Previous page (90) Scylla's tail smashing the ship
(91) Scylla's hand
Left (92) Scylla grabbing the ship's crew
Overleaf (93) The cattle of Helios
(94) One of Ulysses' companions in despair over the slaughter of the sacred cattle of Helios

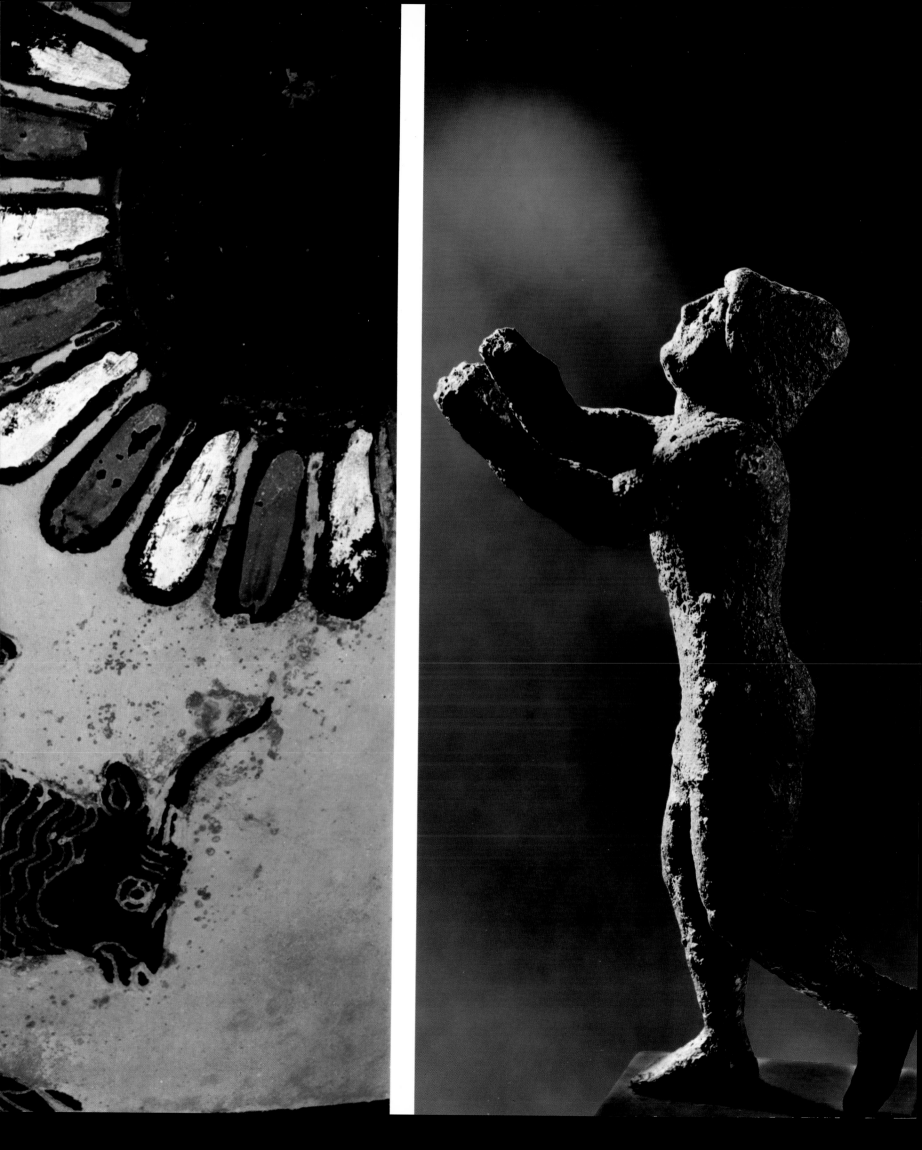

"So I drifted for nine days.
In the tenth darkness the Gods cast me ashore on Ogygia,
Where lives Calypso, the high but humane-spoken Goddess
who greeted me kindly and tended me.
Yet why rehearse all that? Only yesterday I told it within
to you, O King, and to your famous wife.
It goes against my grain to repeat a tale already plainly told."

Book 12, lines 447–453

THE RETURN
OF ULYSSES TO ITHACA

King Alcinous repeats his agreement to bring Ulysses home to Ithaca in one of the fast Phaeacian ships. After a feast in honour of his departure Ulysses goes on board with many presents from the Phaeacians and is borne swiftly towards Ithaca through the night.

So she went, cleaving the ocean surges and bearing within her
a man deep-witted as the Gods,
one who had in the past suffered heart-break
as the sport of men's wars and the troublous waves,
but who now slept in tranquil forgetfulness of all he had endured.
Upon the rising of that most brilliant star
which is the especial harbinger of early dawn,
the ship in her rapid seafaring drew toward the island,
toward Ithaca. On its coast is an inlet
sacred to Phorkys, the ancient of the sea
where two detached headlands of sheer cliff stand forth
and screen a harbour between their steeps.
The mariners knew this bay of old:
they drove in with their ship.
They filed down off her benches,
raised Ulysses from the hollow hull and bore him to land
just as he was, on his sheet and gay carpet.
He was yet lost in sleep as they bedded him gently on the sand.
Then they passed ashore his belongings, the treasures
with which by Athene's contriving
the Phaeacian nobles had speeded his parting.

Book 13, lines 88–98, 113, 116–121

So Ulysses has at last reached his home. But Poseidon is still angry, and so after asking the permission of Zeus he takes his revenge on the Phaeacians who brought Ulysses home: within sight of their own people ship and crew are turned to stone.

Left (95) The rock above Charybdis
Overleaf (96) The bay of Phorkys in Ithaca

In the land of his fathers
Ulysses stirred and woke from sleep.
Not that he knew his whereabouts . . .
So to its King Ithaca showed an unaccustomed face,
the pathways stretching far into the distance,
the quiet bays, the crags and precipices, the leafy trees.
He rose to his feet and stood staring at what was his own land,
then sighed and clapped his two palms downward upon his thighs,
crying mournfully, "Alas! and now where on earth am I?
I fear that both right instinct and honesty of judgment
must have been absent among the Phaeacian chiefs and councillors,
for them to abandon me in this strange country.
They swore to land me on prominent Ithaca, and are forsworn.
May Zeus the surveyor of mankind and scourge of sinners
visit it upon them in his quality as champion of suppliants:
and now, to make a start, let me check my belongings and see
if the crew took off anything in their boat when they vanished."
Whereupon he totted up his tripods and their splendid cauldrons,
the gold and goodly woven robes.
Not a thing was gone.
So his lament must be entirely for his native land
as he paced back and forth in bitter grieving
beside the tumultuous deep-voiced waves,
till Athene in male disguise manifested herself and drew nigh,
seeming a young man, some shepherd lad, but dainty and gentle
like the sons of kings when they tend sheep.

Book 13, lines 187–188, 194–200, 209–223

Athene tells Ulysses that he is now in Ithaca. At first he tries to conceal
from her who he really is and invents a false story. But Athene smiles and
tells him who she is. Then she works out a plan with Ulysses for the
destruction of his wife Penelope's suitors. When they have hid the gifts from
the Phaeacians in a cavern Athene changes Ulysses into a beggar and
advises him to go first to the swineherd Eumaeus. There he is to wait till
the Goddess has led his son Telemachus home from Sparta.

"You will begin by joining company
with the swineherd who keeps your swine:
a man of steadfast feelings toward yourself
and devoted both to your son and judicious Penelope.
You will find him watching his beasts
grubbing round the Raven's Crag and Arethusa's fountain."

Book 13, lines 404–408

Left (97) The wanderer Ulysses
Right (98) The Goddess Athene
Overleaf (99) The treasure cave where Ulysses hides the gifts which the Phaeacians have
given him
(100) The farm of the swineherd Eumaeus

ULYSSES VISITS EUMAEUS

Meanwhile Ulysses strode up the hill-path
that climbed straight from the timbered plains
into the highlands, the way Athene had pointed him
to that devoted swineherd who cared more for his lord's substance
than any other of the serfs Ulysses owned.
He found him sitting in the lodge of his high-walled steading
which was a landmark because it stood by itself
and was well built and large.

Book 14, lines 1–7

*The swineherd Eumaeus welcomes the stranger who announces himself as a
man from Crete and tells amazing tales of all his voyages. Meanwhile
Athene has led Telemachus safely around the suitors' ambush home to Ithaca
from Sparta. On landing Telemachus orders his companions to make straight
for town. He himself goes first to the swineherd Eumaeus. The faithful
swineherd welcomes the homecomer Telemachus like a son and introduces the
stranger to him. Telemachus too greets the disguised Ulysses warmly and offers
him food and new clothes. Next Athene advises Ulysses to let his son know
who he his. She gives him back his noble appearance. Telemachus, astounded
at the beggar's divine transformation, takes the handsome man for a god:*

But Ulysses said, "I am no God:
liken me not with the Immortals.
In very deed I am your father, the Ulysses
for whose sake you have grieved and endured adversity
and suffered indignities from men."
He spoke and kissed the lad, yielding
to the tears he had hitherto held back.

Book 16, lines 186–191

*Together Telemachus and Ulysses plan the destruction of the suitors.
Ulysses is to make his way, still disguised as a beggar, into the suitors'
feast while Telemachus makes ready for the final struggle.*

Left (101) The loyal swineherd Eumaeus
Right (102) Ulysses beside the fire of the swineherd
*Overleaf (103) The bay where Telemachus lands secretly after being warned by Athene
of the suitors' ambush*

Disguised as a beggar Ulysses approaches the suitors' feast and begs them
in turn for food. Antinous insults him and throws a stool at his back.
Penelope, waiting still for her long-absent husband and sitting full of grief
in her upper room, hears the row and asks that the beggar be brought to
her so she can question him for any news of Ulysses.

Left (104) Ulysses disguised as a beggar at the suitors' feast
Above (105) The grief of Penelope

That night Ulysses talks with Penelope without revealing who he is, although he sees that she has remained faithful to him. At Penelope's bidding the old nurse Eurycleia washes the stranger's feet.

While he spoke the hoary woman had taken the burnished foot-bath
and poured in much cold water before stirring in the hot.
Ulysses had been sitting towards the hearth,
but now sharply turned himself to face the shadow, as his heart
suddenly chilled with fear that in handling him
she might notice his scar, and the truth come to light.
Yet so it was, when she bent near in her washing.

Book 19, lines 386–392

But Ulysses stops the old woman from announcing her discovery. He begs her to wait till the next day when he hopes to cut down the annoying suitors.

Left (106) The feet of Ulysses are washed
Below (107) Eurycleia recognizes the beggar as Ulysses by the scar on his leg

ULYSSES TAKES REVENGE

At the feast on the following day, while the suitors again insult Ulysses disguised as a beggar, Penelope brings out the great longbow that belonged to Ulysses and says:

"Now my suitors, see your test plain. Here I set the huge bow
of god-like Ulysses. Whoso easiest strings the bow
with bare hands and shoots an arrow through the twelve axes —
after him will I follow, forsaking this house, my husband's home."

Book 21, lines 73–77

But none of the suitors is able even to string it. Then Ulysses begs to be allowed also try the test of the bow. Ridiculed by the suitors but encouraged by Telemachus Ulysses takes the bow:

Ulysses the master of craft had by now handled
and surveyed the great bow up and down. Calmly he stretched it out
with the effortless ease of a skilled musician
who makes fast both ends of a piece of twined cat-gut
and strains it to a new peg in his lyre.
Changing the bow to his right hand he proved the string,
which sang to his pluck, sharp like a swallow's cry.
Distress overwhelmed the suitors and they changed colour.
Zeus declared himself in a loud thunder-peal;
and long-suffering royal Ulysses rejoiced
that the son of devious-counselled Cronos should make him a sign.
He snatched up the keen arrow which lay naked there upon his table —
all the others which the Achaeans were so soon to feel
being yet stored in their quiver —
and set it firmly upon the grip of the bow.
He notched it to the string and drew;
and from his place upon his settle, just as he sat,
sent the arrow with so straight an aim
that he did not foul one single axe.
The bronze-headed shaft threaded them clean,
from the leading helve onward till the last ones.
Then he cried to Telemachus, "Telemachus,
the guest sitting in your hall does you no disgrace.
My aim went true and my drawing the bow was no long struggle. See,
my strength stands unimpaired to disprove the suitors' slandering."

Book 21, lines 404–427

Left (108) Ulysses with the bow

Meanwhile the cowherd Philoetius, who has always remained loyal to Ulysses,
has closed the gates of the courtyard so that none shall escape the end they deserve.

Therewith the wily Ulysses shed his rags,
grasped the bow with its filled quiver
and made one leap to the door-sill,
where he tumbled out the swift shafts at his feet
before calling in a great voice to the suitors.
"At last, at last the ending of this fearful strain!
Before me stands a virgin target never yet hit."

Book 22, lines 1–6

He levelled the bitter arrow at Antinous,
shot, and took him with the shaft full in the throat.
Right through his graceful neck and out again went the point.
He rolled over sideways, letting the cup fall from his stricken grasp
and thrusting back the table with a jerk of the foot.
The life-blood spurted thickly from his nostrils.
One outcry broke from the suitors when they saw the man fall.
They sprang in terror from their thrones.

Book 22, lines 8, 15–19, 21–23

Below (109) Having passed the test of the bow Ulysses slays the suitors with deadly accuracy

Ulysses kills one suitor after another with his arrows. After using the last he arms himself with sword and spear and continues the slaughter. Telemachus joins in too, so do Eumaeus and a cowherd, while Athene supports them in the guise of Mentor. The traitorous and adulterous maids too, who made love to the suitors, now meet a grim and grotesque end: they have to clean the bloody mess from the hall and then all twelve of them are hung by the neck on high. Eurycleia goes to summon Penelope and her handmaidens.

But it was with a cackle of laughter
that the old dame climbed towards the upper room,
to warn her mistress of the beloved husband's return.
Her knees moved nimbly
and her feet tripped along to the lady's bed-head
where she stood and spoke her part.
"Awake dear child, Penelope,
open your eyes upon the sight you have yearned for all these days.
Ulysses has appeared, at this end of time.
He has reached his home and in it slaughtered
the recalcitrant suitors who for so long vexed the house,
ate his stored wealth and outfaced his son."

Book 23, lines 1–9

But Penelope cannot believe Eurycleia or Telemachus. Endowed by Athene with divine beauty, Ulysses himself comes before Penelope and says:

"Proud lady, the heart that the lords of Olympus gave you
is harder than any true woman's. None but you
would pitilessly repulse the husband who had won his way home
after twenty years of toil."

Book 23, lines 166–170

But only when he has shown Penelope by a sure sign which only he could know that he is really Ulysses does she throw her arms around his neck and cry:

"My Ulysses, forgive me this time too,
you who were of old more comprehending
than any man of men.
The Gods gave us sorrow for our portion.
Be not angry with me, therefore, nor resentful,
because at first sight I failed to fondle you thus.
The heart within me ever shook
for terror of being cheated by some man's lie,
so innumerable are those who plot to serve their greedy ends."

Book 23, lines 209–210, 213–217

Above left (110) Ulysses slaying a suitor
Below left (111) The last suitor hides behind a table
Right (112) Ulysses comes before Penelope

Ulysses' first journey is to his old father's farm.

Meanwhile Ulysses and his men had passed the town.
Soon they reached the flourishing estate of Laertes.
Now Ulysses had a word for his son and the serfs.
"In with you smartly to the well-built house," he said,
"meanwhile, in view of my long absence abroad
I shall go to test if my father knows me again by sight, or not."
He handed his arms to the two thralls
who went straight in, as Ulysses proceeded
through the rich fruit-farm, on his quest.

Book 24, lines 205–206, 213–214, 216–221

Above (113) Laertes, the aged father of Ulysses
Right (114) The rich farm of Laertes

Ulysses makes himself known to his father and tells him that he has killed the
suitors who have courted Penelope for so many years and squandered his property.
In the town trouble is brewing as the noble Achaeans learn of the suitors'
death. Angrily some make a foray to avenge the death of their sons on
Ulysses. A fight flares up, but Athene spreads peace on both parties.

Athene, the daughter of aegis-bearing Zeus, shouted
with such force as to halt the array.
"Let be your deadly battle, men of Ithaca," she cried.
"Without bloodshed is the affair best arranged."
The voice of the Goddess blenched them all with fear.
In their panic the weapons slipped from their grasp
and fell together to the ground, as the Goddess called.
They turned their faces toward the town for dear life,
while with a roar the great long-suffering Ulysses
gathered himself for the spring
and launched after them, like an eagle in free air.
But instantly the son of Cronos flung his lurid levin
which fell before the grey-eyed Goddess,
the dread Father's own child; then did Athene cry to Ulysses,
"Back with you, heaven-nourished son of Laertes,
Ulysses of the many wiles. Hold back.
Cease this arbitrament of civil war.
Move not far-sighted Zeus to wrath."
So Athene said, she the daughter of aegis-bearing Zeus.
Ulysses obeyed, inwardly glad:
and Pallas, still with Mentor's form and voice,
set a pact between them
for ever and ever.

Book 24, lines 529–548

Left (115) Zeus the Thunderer, who helps Athene make peace among the men of Ithaca

THE ODYSSEY IN ANCIENT ART
by
HELLMUT SICHTERMANN

HELLMUT SICHTERMANN was born on November 21, 1915 near Posen — like Schliemann the son of a Protestant pastor. He attended high school in Bromberg and in 1938 began studies at Berlin university in Classical archaeology, the history of art, and philosophy. After six and a half years interruption by military service and imprisonment he proceeded to the doctor's degree in 1948 in Berlin. Since then, he has acted as technical expert in the German Archaeological Institute first in Berlin, then Madrid, and since 1955 in Rome.

The special areas of research with which Sichtermann has been concerned are: the relation of ancient art to Greek Mythology; the effects of ancient art in post-antiquity, in particular in the time since the Classical period; and the connexion between archaeological scholarship and other branches of learning.

Publications:

Apart from numerous articles in scholarly journals he has published: *Ganymed. Mythos und Gestalt in der antiken Kunst* (Berlin 1953); *Sophokles* (Bremen 1959); *Die griechische Vase. Sinn, Gestalt und Kunstwerk* (Berlin 1963); *Laokoon* (Stuttgart 1964).

ULYSSES AND HIS TIMES

We all know that Ulysses and his companions belong to the world of "myth" and that their adventures are legends. But there is no such thing as absolute timelessness. Even what appears to be purely mythical is not entirely without reference to time and place. When a story is told, for instance, it deals with the past and that fact in itself is enough to fix the story in some conception of the past as it is remembered by the people who hear the story now — even though the story itself is fiction. How much more real, then, must stories be about the past which, however mythological they may be, are also based on some remote events in history, or upon epic actions which were accepted as history?

This is the case with Homer's Odyssey. Much scientific and literary study, of course, has been expended on it. Nowadays, no one takes it so literally as to undertake excavations to find the traces of the "real" Ulysses, as was being done not so very long ago by romantic-minded archaeologists and classicists alike. But modern scholarship definitely recognizes that not everything in Homer is sheer poetic imagination. There are secret links which bind this myth to some reality of history. The songs of Homer must be an echo of great events in which important figures of the Mycenaean age played a part. His poems stir the imagination of readers and direct them to epic, heroic, and sometimes comic and human events which for Homer took place in the past, in history, but in a period and a culture (that of Crete and Mycenae) to which he was closer than we are today.

In some sense we can recreate that distant time by listening to the poem. But there are other ways. If we wish to picture the age which Homer conjures up in more specific detail, we must go and see the palaces of Cnossos and Pylos and the tombs of Mycenae where we can study, in fact actually be in the presence of stones and structures among which the kings and heroes of the Odyssey lived and fought and suffered, and where they found their last resting-place. It is precisely this, to make a more physical contact with Homer's world (and with the blind singer's poetry as well), that photographer Erich Lessing for months studied ancient art and archaeological documents and hunted down the stones and scenes of the Odyssey throughout the Mediterranean world, finally incorporating many of them into this book.

The throne-hall of an Homeric king cannot have been very different from the hall of the palace of Cnossos in Crete, which has been one of the happy discoveries of modern archaeology. This throne (see Plate 15) is simple and monumental, with tutelary griffons on either side, and the installations of King Nestor's palace must have been very much like those which recent excavations have brought to light in Pylos (Plate 20). Looking today on the mighty walls and the impressive Lion Gate of Mycenae (Plate 16) we get a sharp idea of what a fortified town was like in ancient times. We can recognize the majestic simplicity of life as it is painted in the Odyssey when we see the great provision jars of the Cretan palaces (Plate 25) and the splendid vessels in the shape of oxen found in the tombs. These vessels reveal a practical relation, an intermingling of "art" and "real life" which has largely escaped our confused society today (Plate 19).

Of course one must be careful. It is a difficult and often misleading thing to trace too exact links between epic and history. But this need not put us off if we remember that a highly imaginative unity exists between art and epic, between poem and history. It is toward this unity that the poetry of Homer leads us, as surely as the treasures of art and archaeology. It is impossible to prove that the magnificent gold mask (Plate 17) of the sixteenth century B.C., which covered the face of a chieftain in a tomb at Mycenae, was fashioned actually and precisely to reveal the real visage of Agamemnon. But it shows us a great prince and hero of that age — and that is precisely what Agamemnon was.

THE GODS AND DEMONS OF HOMER

Homer, of course, was not a chronicler of historical events as we understand the terms. Whatever its historical basis was, he gave his epic the grandeur of a divine and mythical setting. It teems with gods as well as men. Athene guides, helps, and advises her friends and favourites among the mortals on earth. Poseidon tries to destroy Ulysses because he is enraged by the blinding of his earthly son Poly-phemus. The oxen which Ulysses' companions kill, bringing ruin upon them, are in the final incident of the poem not the property of an ordinary countryman but belong to Helios the Sun-God. And Zeus is enthroned above all, not always wise but nevertheless a powerful ruler. These gods have no bodies, and when they take on visible form factual history falls silent and great art alone can speak.

In the age in which Ulysses was supposed to live, there were not pictures of the gods which corresponded to the grandiose visions of Homer, and even, when the Odyssey was being composed (probably in the eighth century B.C.) the canvas was equally bare. Giving Homer's visions a bodily form was a long, slow process. Artists, sculptors, and writers laboured for many centuries to penetrate the mystery behind them. Every effort made by the Greeks and all antiquity to portray the gods was fired by the original vision of Homer, and we can sense his influence on every representation of the gods which has come down to us. In the majestic beauty of the classical statues of Athene, preserved for us in careful Roman copies (Plates 1 and 28), we see the guardian goddess of Telemachus exactly as in the naive bronze statuettes (Plate 38) from the frontier regions of Greek culture. Even in the smallest Greek pictures of Zeus the power of the "ruler of gods and men", can be sensed the presence of a deity who can sit enthroned in calm dignity, or hurl down destruction from Olympus in a bolt of lightning (Plates 4 and 115). When we see him depicted sending Athene on a mission, in the presence of his Goddess-wife, Hera, and Hermes (Plate 6), we think at once of an episode in Homer. And when we find Hermes setting out in travelling-cloak and hat and winged shoes (Plate 29) we suspect that he is hurrying to meet Calypso or Ulysses, as related in the Odyssey. The impressive trident of Poseidon gives us a vivid sense of the divinity of its holder, even in tiny bronze statuettes (Plate 34): the way the god holds it is enough. And could the ruler of the waves appear more majestic than he does in the noble bronze statue (Plate 5), which itself came out of the ocean in 1926 off Euboea? Ulysses saw him thus when he brought disaster on the ship. Homeric gods are Greek, and the Greek gods are Homeric: they show themselves equal and united in the manifestation of their divine power. In this sense, much of ancient Greek art can be viewed as illustrations for the Odyssey and the Iliad.

Besides the gods, there were also demons. The Sirens, Polyphemus, and Scylla are not just extras in the great action of the Odyssey. They are powers that exist in their own right with their own proper significance. In Greek art the Sirens (Plate 101) appear again and again in bronze and clay, in painting and sculpture. The gruesome head of the Cyclops Polyphemus with his one eye in his forehead (Plate 57) was represented many, many times. Ever the monster Scylla embellishes bronze utensils and earthenware vessels (Plates 86, 89, and 92). We can mark the creative influence of Homer in these pictures — although many of them were created by artists who postdated Homer by two, three, and four hundred years.

LIFE AMONG THE GREEKS

The poet who sang of these gods and demons, of these heroes and their feats, did not live in the days which he conjured up by his songs. He could only become the singer of these tales when the long process of time had begun to turn the heroic past into myth. But what an impressive figure he must have become in the eyes of his contemporaries, when he set out to turn the myth into poetical form! At first unable themselves to transform the poet's mighty visions into pictures, artists began by portraying the man himself, naively enough, but with a powerful artistic sense: he is shown seated, holding his lyre (Plates 8 and 47), concentrated and reduced to the essentials of his being. He appears as the prototype of the poet as such, a witness to the early Greek way of life, distant in time from the Homeric epic, but linked to it inwardly by a thousand threads.

The same unity pervades all our examples of Greek art and culture, no matter what century they come from. And so we have little difficulty in understanding pictures which belong to a Greek world far removed in time from the age of the Odyssey. They still evoke vividly that ancient world which had not entirely disappeared in the Greece of the pre-classical and classical age. Homer's Phaeacians drank like the Attic drinkers who appear on a vase from pre-classical Athens (Plate 44). The young Greeks of Homer's Ithaca played and raced like the youths we see on an impressively beautiful relief from archaic times (Plate 45). And we may picture the warriors in combat at

Troy just as the vase-painters of Athens showed them (Plate 80); it does not matter whether or not their dress and weapons correspond to the historical reality. When a Greek potter many centuries after Homer makes a drinking-horn in the form of a ram (Plate 77), we still sense something of the sacrificial rams of Homer in this tiny but incredibly powerful work, just as we recognize the Oxen of the Sun (Plate 93) on an Ionic vase from the Italy of the sixth century B.C. The luxuriant beauty of the fruits of the earth, of which Homer sang, can likewise be sensed in the clay imitations (Plate 54) done by the artists of Rhodes. The same Greek spirit lives in all of them, the reflection of a way of life, dimly perceived, which lends the passing centuries a kind of unity in our eyes.

THE FIGURE OF ULYSSES

The Greeks who came after Homer soon began to look for pictures of the Odyssey itself. They wanted to see what they had hitherto only heard about, above all they wanted pictures of the hero himself, the great sufferer, the prudent, wily — and very human — Ulysses.

He soon became a timeless figure like Homer's gods, and he appears in the early efforts of the most archaic Greek art just as in the productions of late Roman times. Bronze statuettes from Greece have captured something of his essence, as did the works of Roman artists who leaned heavily on their older models (Plates 2, 23, and 102). His noble, patient suffering is still depicted on gems of later times, where he often appears in an attitude of mourning and in utter loneliness (Plate 30).

But the picture of Ulysses is not complete without his adventures and achievements. Any reader of the Odyssey wants to see him as something more than a lonely symbol, and more even than a single figure detached from the wider context of his story — like the picture of Ulysses as charioteer or spearsman (Plates 46 and 49). He must be seen along with his companions, or confronting Circe, Polyphemus, Scylla, and the Sirens. He must be followed on all his journeys till he returns home to the wife who has waited for him so loyally (Plate 112).

But when we turn from the lonely, symbolic figure of Ulysses to Ulysses as a man of action with a particular destiny, the Homeric and Grecian timelessness of the pictures is not so apparent. Antiquity needed to express itself in pictures, and the process of self-expression lasted for centuries. The pictures which have survived are therefore witnesses to the various historical settings in which they were painted. They are stamped with the external traits, which we today can sum up as "style", and they are penetrated with the spirit of whatever age they happen to have been produced in, both in the choice of themes and in the way these themes are developed. This historical process cannot be disregarded. It did not leave the subject-matter of the pictures unchanged but affected it intrinsically, so that the contents, the chants of the Odyssey, were given a new life and meaning in the course of this development. While therefore the subject-matter remains to a certain extent timeless, the form given to the picture was conditioned by their times, and both these elements have an equal claim on our consideration. How, then, are we to approach these pictures — as illustrations to a famous text, or as works of art in themselves?

THE PICTURE AND THE SONG

These are some of the questions which the reader of the Odyssey will ask on seeing Erich Lessing's pictures, but they are not the only ones. Before we try to contemplate the pictures, we must ask ourselves in general what is the relation between the word and the picture, between the picture and the word.

What then is the Odyssey to us really? Is it pure poetry, the sheer art of words, the spoken or written language which needs no visual aid? A blind singer wrote it. Should we not try to match his inward gaze? Do not all these concrete images contradict or at least limit the spirit of the poem? Do they perhaps control and direct our imagination too much?

We might easily think so, if we just could yield totally to the spell of Homer's verse. If we were fortunate enough to understand the poet's original language, all the images we need might form in our mind's eye as we read the poet's harmonious lines; and pictures which others offer us would only hobble us.

But the masterly language which makes us relive the story of the great and sorely-tried Ulysses, and feel and suffer with him in his adventures, is only one way to the heart of the story. For all its power, the language, while remaining the loveliest and easiest way, does not exclude aids to an appreciation of Homer. His poetry itself, because it is a great and authentic work of art, points beyond itself and beyond the limits of its own artistic forms. It is not merely "poetry", and anyone who reads it just for its poetry will miss its substance. The outward form is enough to tell us that it is only a selection from sources which preceded it, and continued to flow on around and after it. But in its essence, the Odyssey shows how a poet mastered and interpreted a universal human experience, which can be embodied not only in the hexameters of the song but in the manifold creations of the graphic arts.

The purely academic (and literary) scholar will confine himself perhaps to the poetry, but those who are interested in mythic action will turn at once to the pictures, where they can learn much that is novel and unexpected. And if they can glimpse the major outlines of a comprehensive symbolism behind the work of Homer, they will look for the symbols in the works of art where the word falls silent and only the picture speaks.

The differences (and difficulties) are of course great, even in the most superficial comparison of poetry and picture. We have the whole of Homer's poem, a living, breathing thing from first to last. It grips us, bears us along and lets us drop — and all the time we feel a single creative imagination at work. But the visual arts have left us only a jumble of ruins, the debris of centuries, swept together from many lands and across many seas. The pictures were made by many different artists, to suit many different occasions. They were painted, chiselled or engraved on many kinds of material. They survive as a random collection which sheer chance has left us from what was once a brilliant and comprehensive profusion.

The expert in art and archaeology can tell a tale of woe about the labours which this ruined heritage has caused him, and, confronted by such material, the layman may well be dismayed at finding himself faced by a mass of lore which has more questions to ask than it has answers to give.

But as soon as we start to put all these objects into perspective, the lines of the pictures, the light and shade of statues and reliefs begin at once to come to life. They seem to react as we approach, they respond to the questions which we put, and a real dialogue is set up between pictures and viewer.

We have already contributed a kind of order by the very fact that we have decided to include these works and no others in the circle of "illustrations of the Odyssey". The act of selection always brings a particular attitude and certain principles into play. When we start to put the works selected into some sort of order, this attitude is brought into the open.

Anyone who starts with Homer's poetry will naturally wish to use the Odyssey and its sequence as the guiding line for the arrangement of his pictures. But if he is looking for the adventure of the hero behind the poetry, he will take the development of the action as his guide, and not the poetic narrative which so often doubles back upon itself. If he wishes to learn how various peoples and ages have reacted to the poem, he will arrange the surviving pictures in their chronological order or distribute them over the map of the Mediterranean. He who is not quite happy with any one of these approaches will perhaps try to combine them all.

All· these various methods (and more) have in fact been used. The first collection of ancient pictures followed the action of the epic closely. Efforts were later made to take various guiding-lines from the history of art. Sometimes individual works were presented as a series of isolated, but provocative examples.

Today we have given up the notion of imposing of an all too mechanical order. We try instead to reach the unifying factors which underly the variety of the approaches. It is of course the Odyssey itself which forms the link. It was the Odyssey which impelled scholars of earlier times to make their collections of pictures, and it is the Odyssey which has created this book, which presents a selection and an arrangement which will perhaps appear old-fashioned to future generations. The pictures follow the order of the books of the Odyssey itself and so provide what may be called "illustrations" of the text.

Used in this way, and in this context the word "illustrations" is worth examining carefully. We all know it well, and it naturally suggests so strongly a definite connexion between word and picture, between text and image, that we unhesitatingly judge an epic picture by its value as an illustration. The criterion is simply this: how well does the picture render the actual words of the text?

But this attitude does not do justice either to the subject-matter or the real meaning of the picture. The pictures are works of art, and there is no such thing as an authentic work of art if it is merely a slavish copy of a literary model. Art must go deeper than the surface meaning of the words of the epic, if it is to make a real assertion in its own right. It may then depart literally from the actual wording but still express the same kind of truth, or the same truth expressed in a different way.

Folklore and saga and epic use the medium of words, so here, too, one must justify that "in the beginning was the word". But words only have the power of provoking the need for a picture and of evoking that picture when they are "mythic" words. And then the picture no longer depends entirely on the word. It derives from the myth. Neither the artist who painted the picture nor the sculptor who chiselled the statue had the least idea that they were being "inspired" by any given text. They felt that they were portraying the very same action which the poet had striven to present. They thought that they were rendering the events "as they really happened", for that was the function of the arts, whether poetic or graphic.

We read in the eighth book of the Odyssey that Ulysses will recognize Demodocus as a divinely-inspired singer, if he can describe accurately and in proper sequence the adventure of the wooden horse, in which Ulysses had taken part: "Tell me all this in order," Ulysses says, "and then I will maintain that the God's good grace has conferred the bounty of inspiration on your singing." A faithful description is demanded as well as a song. And without the singing, the facts were likewise worthless. But people could paint as well as sing, so the artists too tried to render the story "in order", and they too wished it to be proclaimed to all men that the God's good grace had granted them the bounty of inspiration for their art.

This does not mean that it is wrong to view the pictures in the light of the text, and then return to the text after contemplating the pictures. The two processes are complementary, both work hand in hand to create the great work of art which we know simply as the Odyssey.

This holds true — in a remarkable way, I think — for the pictures in this book. The reader who derives full satisfaction from contemplating them, can enjoy them as a series of illustrations for the Odyssey and leave aside the question of when they were painted. But below, to complete the pictures, an historical framework is provided so that they can be seen as elements in a rich development within which they have their definite place. To make the lines of evolution clearer we shall have to mention many examples. Even so, in this space we can offer no more than a limited selection from the great profusion of pictures that has survived.

THE FIRST CENTURIES
AFTER HOMER

When the Odyssey was composed, the rich glories of Mycenaean art belonged to the distant past, and the classical age was still far away. The art contemporaneous with the writing of the Odyssey was of a simple "geometric" type, to which Homer's poetry eventually was to add grandiose dimensions. Pictorial art followed *after* Homer; in his time it was largely undeveloped and to keep pace with his vision was beyond its capacity.

Hence there are few examples of geometric art which qualify as scenes from the Odyssey. There is an engraved bronze fibula (brooch) from the second half of the eighth century B.C. (London, British Museum) which shows a horse on wheels with rectangular openings in its side, and this must certainly be the famous wooden horse with which Ulysses duped the Trojans. But two other examples, which are sometimes cited — a vase-painting of a shipwreck (München, Museum antiker Kleinkunst), and another showing a man and a woman who may be Hermes and Circe (Ithaca, Museum) — are really quite uncertain; the most we can say is that they are possibly from the Odyssey.

The really descriptive pictures only occur when all the songs have been sung and written down, and then we have pictures with distinctive features linking them to the epic — to which however they add their own poetic traits. Various sites on the Greek mainland, but also in Italy, the scene of so many of Ulysses' adventures, yielded the first fragments, random samples of the growing urge to see shown in pictures what the singers had sung.

The Odyssey must have been only a century or two old when an artist in Eleusis near Athens decorated the neck of a large amphora (jar), with a picture of the blinding of Polyphemus (Plate 60). He hardly felt bound to keep to the words of his text, probably thinking that he knew the story exactly as Homer did, and he told it in the way his medium allowed. Polyphemus is not lying down but seated, not asleep but still holding the cup of wine in his hand. He does not let his eye be pierced by the stake without a struggle, but grips it with his left hand. He is not clearly depicted as one-eyed, indeed, he is given a normal profile. The stake is held by three men, not four. But the important elements coincide with Homer, and no one would dream of suggesting the scene was not from the Odyssey. It is clearly the blinding of a helpless giant by the combined effort of smaller men, which can only be the blinding of Polyphemus. Would the artist have been more correct and impressive, if he had kept still closer to the text? I do not think so. In spite of the discrepancies, we are shown everything that we need. The cup indicates that the giant is drunk. The painter cannot show a sequence like a writer, and so when he wants to bring out the decisive rôle of Polyphemus' drinking, he has to show the beaker. He is not interested in mathematics, and once the number of attackers is more than one he is content. He was however keen on showing that Ulysses played a leading rôle. He did this by giving Ulysses a clearer and more delicate complexion than his companions.

The amphora was found only in 1954. Two years earlier a fragment of a vase had been found in Argos in the Peloponnese which depicts the same scene. It comes from the neck of a mixing-bowl (krater), and only part of the scene is left, but the most important part. On the left is Polyphemus, lying naked on a bed of round stones, already half sitting up. On the right, two of Ulysses' companions are approaching — only the foot of a third is preserved — lifting the stake high above their heads, ready to plunge it into the eye of the giant. This picture is closer to the text of Homer: the posture of the giant is better suited to a sleeper than being seated. The wine-cup is also missing — a sleeping man would not have one. The artist has heightened the horror of the scene by showing great drops of blood falling from the giant's pierced eye on to his face and neck.

To these two early pictures from the Greek mainland we must add another very similar one from Italy, found in the Etruscan city of Caere. The painter has put in some cheese-driers and milk-pails, behind the giant, a detail mentioned by Homer. And over the drawing he has written proudly, "Made by Aristhonotos", which makes this one of the earliest signed works of art in Europe. It is probably as early as the first half of the seventh century B.C. It is certain that the painter, by putting in his signature, meant to affirm that the epic picture owed its existence to *him* (Rome, Palazzo dei Conservatori).

The story of the blinding of Polyphemus is cruel and exciting, but it is at the same time almost a simple comic burlesque. It was the very thing to hold people's attention and it almost begged to be put into picture form. The survival of so many of the pictures of Polyphemus may well be due to chance. But it is clear that Polyphemus received preferential treatment by artists which remained a fashionable subject for works of art. We have other pictures of the Polyphemus episode from the sixth century B.C., perhaps not so stark, powerful or monumental in their impact as the three mentioned above, but even though they have become more diffuse and "ballad-like" they are still centred on the gruesome kernel of the action. Some surviving base-paintings reproduce the story much in the same way as those we have already mentioned. But there are always some additional touches, which give each painter's work its grisly individuality: human limbs in Polyphemus' hands, Ulysses' companions being roasted over a fire. Each succeeding painter obviously felt he would give a clearer description than anyone before him had done.

These vases are the product of schools of art which flourished for only a comparatively short time. In some cases we know little about them but their date. But the city of Athens, with its most brilliant period of development still to come, soon began to contribute to the theme. From some times perhaps before 500 B.C. comes a little beaker, from the hand of an Attic master, who painted it with scenes from the Odyssey, and naturally one of these is the blinding of Polyphemus (Berlin, Staatliche Museen). This time the giant is really asleep, stretched out on the ground. His face is turned outwards, so that we see clearly that the great stake held by Ulysses and his companions is piercing his right eye. The fact that Polyphemus here has two eyes may be due to the inability of the painter to depict a one-eyed face, but on the other hand Polyphemus was not described as one-eyed in all versions of the story. A little later, early in the fifth century, a black-figured wine-jug from Attica, now in the Louvre, Paris, follows Homer once more on this point. The giant is again half sitting up on the ground, but the two attackers are pointing the stake directly against his forehead, where his single eye must be situated. Further, on the left of the main scene, the painter has shown the stake being made red-hot preparatory to the blinding, which is impossible in the time-sequence as the right of the picture shows the same stake already doing its work.

This brings us right into the epic world of Attic vase-painting, which has left us such a living profusion of the most diverse myths. Its pictures, though similar in subject-matter and in composition, are strikingly different from those of earlier times and other parts of Greece. Instead of the monumental impact and the powerful simplicity of the earliest portrayals, we find a more detailed but looser anecdotal style, which strays very easily from the central theme. Can it be accidental that among all the many red-figured vases of Attica, from just before the great classical period, none have been found depicting the blinding of Polyphemus? As Athens was moving towards its divinest hour when gods and men seemed to blend in one harmonious majesty, there was hardly room for what was merely crude and violent. Another day had to dawn before the old stories could be clad in new forms and the bolder themes acquire new life.

But let us continue for the moment with this first period of confrontation, when the Homeric material was being given its earliest visual form. We need not go beyond the theme of Polyphemus. This figure and the ordeal it inflicted on Ulysses stirred the imagination deeply. The adventure which followed the blinding of Polyphemus, the escape from the cave, is preserved on an Etruscan vase of the seventh century and in a bronze relief on a tripod from Delphi which is not much later (Aegina, Museum). The seventh century also supplies the painting on an Attic jug found on the island of Aegina which shows the escape of Ulysses and two of his companions. This theme is also represented in early Attic black-figured vase-painting. A lekythos (small slender jar) now in Munich (Plate 61) shows Ulysses and one of his companions tied to the bellies of the rams. The essentials are so carefully studied that the scene becomes a most impressive piece of animal painting. A tree is shown beside the ram, so Ulysses must have already escaped from the cave.

There are other black-figured vases which depict this scene, but the red-figured painting of the fifth century did not treat the theme very often. There are three pictures early on, but they are still in the line of the older type of painting.

Sixth-century artists showed a special delight in story-telling and had a preference for the unusual and fantastic. Naturally they found other themes to their liking in the fairy-tale parts of the Odyssey. Several paintings on black-figured vases show Ulysses sailing past the Sirens' rock, an adventure sometimes depicted in short and summary fashion, sometimes in fuller and more precise detail. A late Corinthian vase from the middle of the sixth century (Boston, Museum of Fine Art), and a black-figured wine-jug somewhat later (Switzerland, private collection), show three Sirens, which is a departure from Homer. The number three then became the rule. They have the name "Seren" written beside them, while Ulysses has "Olyteus" and the cry, "Let me loose!" This classic comic-strip technique is to indicate the seductive force of the Sirens' song, and shows also that the painter was still ready to use "the word" where it served his purpose.

Other black-figured paintings show either only one Siren in front of Ulysses, or a group of Sirens singing or playing instruments, the thought of Ulysses sailing past being left to the viewer's assumed knowledge of the story. From red-figured vase-paintings we have a detailed representation on a stamnos (jar) in London (Plate 83). It shows the ship with Ulysses, the steersman, and the rowers on board. One of the three Sirens is visible, throwing herself suicidally from the rock into the sea. None of the Sirens has a musical instrument, but one of them has the graphic and seductive name "Himeropa" — "she whose voice awakens desire".

When depicting the Sirens the painters have in general followed Homer closely. But they have also added in a great deal which is not in the Homeric tradition. The Odyssey does not give the Sirens the bodies of birds, but all these early vase-paintings portray them in that form, and exceptions begin to occur only much later. Moreover, Homer says nothing of the suicide of the Sirens after their failure to seduce Ulysses. He may have presumed that such things were generally known, though of course some of these embellishments of the story itself may have been added for the first time after Homer's day.

Along with Polyphemus and the Sirens, it is the enchantress Circe who is most often featured in the early pictures. She usually appears along with Ulysses. He is threatening her with his sword, or she is offering him the magic potion, as on a particularly beautiful black-figured lekythos from Eretria on the island of Euboea. Here one of Ulysses' companions, with the head of a pig, is moving off to the left, while the enchantress is seated in the centre, holding a wand in her right hand and offering a great bowl to Ulysses, who is seated on a rock (Plate 69). Other vase-painters have enriched the scene with more details, crowding in as many of Ulysses' companions as possible and giving each the head of a different animal. This variation is not to be found in Homer, who, moreover, does not speak of partial transformations. He tells only of luckless sailors being changed into swine, complete with bristles. The painters proceeded differently, since they had no other way of indicating that the animals were not really pigs but men transformed.

These animal-headed men occur again and again on vase-paintings of Circe, including the later red-figured vases. There is a lekythos from Eretria on which the painter has gone to great pains to make the transformation particularly vivid. One of the hapless monsters, who has the head of a pig, is moving on all fours — but his hands are still human. Another sailor nearby, also half-beast, half-human, is crouching in the same position (Plate 70).

But the artists did not confine themselves to painting men with heads of animals. When the context was clear enough, they did not hesitate to show complete transformations, nor did they confine themselves to swine. Wild boars or panthers, for instance, were also portrayed.

Polyphemus, the Sirens, Circe — these adventures were narrated by Ulysses himself, not directly by the poet, who appears only in the role of reporter. This confirmed the artists in their conviction that they were portraying events which had reached the poet also in the state of "raw materials", and had not therefore been invented by him. They found this fact a challenge, no doubt, which stimulated them as much as the fascination of the stories themselves, and we can be sure that these adventures also circulated in forms which differed from those given in the Homeric epic. The purely Homeric matter, especially the books ·which narrate the adventures of Telemachus, was necessarily less arresting, less full of associations by contrast. Even to the untutored reader, it must have appeared much more obviously an invention of Homer. The artists must have felt the challenge to their inventiveness most strongly when dealing with an episode which is not narrated either by Ulysses or the poet in person, the story of the Trojans being duped by the wooden horse, told in the Odyssey by the bard Demodocus.

It was of course the astonishing man-made animal itself which had first to be presented to the viewers. We have already met it, though in a fragmentary state, on a brooch of the geometric period. The relief on the neck of a large amphora on the island of Mykonos (Plate 48), gives a complete picture of the scene with all the details necessary for understanding it. The horse's feet are provided with wheels, and, so that there can be no mistake, the flaps in its body are left open to show the heads of the men inside.

In fact, two arms holding swords and a third holding a shield can be seen hanging from the hatches. Nothing could be clearer, though one wonders where there is room for the bodies of the men supposed to be locked inside. Other warriors, also Greek presumably are already surrounding the horse, though according to the epic the soldiers on foot penetrate the city only later. The soldier on the right, with his foot on one of the wheels, must be a Trojan, though he is bearing weapons, which is again a departure from the poem. Clearly the artist had little concern for accuracy of detail. His main interest was to make his picture speak for itself.

This splendid vessel from Mykonos, which also shows other horrors of the Trojan war, must be put as early as perhaps 670 B.C. A good hundred years later, a Corinthian vase provides a picture of the same story, which is further repeated in the red-figured vases of the fifth century.

There are others of course, but their interpretation is doubtful, or they do not fit into any known category. The woman shown on an amphora from the island of Melos about 600 B.C. may be Calypso, with the god Hermes standing before her; but it could easily represent some other woman who also received an important message from the god. Later artists took up the theme of Ulysses' quarrel with Aias (or Ajax) over the weapons of Achilles, some showing the heroes coming to blows, as on a red-figured lekythos from Tarentum in Italy, others eliminating the violence, as on a black-figured pelike (broad-based jar) in Naples. The weapons are not shown in all the paintings, but some add Athene or Agamemnon to the groups.

On the whole, not very much has survived from this early period. In Corinthian vase-painting, where very many other epics are represented, there are only a few scenes from the Odyssey, and the reliefs on the bronze bands of the shields from Olympia in Western Greece, which contain a profusion of themes from the sagas, have not supplied any certain pictures of the Odyssey. Even in the black-figured and early red-figured vase-paintings themes from the Odyssey are relatively scarce. Scenes from the Iliad are quite another matter. From the early period on, they occur in almost bewildering confusion, so much so that the number of pictures of the Odyssey seem almost insignificant beside them. This may well seem remarkable since the Odyssey was no less loved and read than the Iliad. But it contained too little that could be condensed into pictures, it was not stimulating enough for an original imagination, and above all it lacked the favourite artistic themes of those centuries, wars and fights. There were of course plenty of scenes of violence in the Odyssey, but they did not show well-matched warriors in heroic combat but crude force and triumphant treachery. These scenes continued to be depicted, along with the fabulous events, whenever artists painted the Odyssey at all. The time was not yet ripe for a profounder interpretation of the human aspects of the Odyssey. As Friedrich Gottlieb Welcker has so well said, men preferred the "fabulous adventure" to the "simple human relationship", the "fantastic" to the "homely".

THE CLASSICAL AGE

In the fifth century, the period of classical Greek art, choice of subject and manner of presentation begin to undergo a change which can be followed clearly in the scenes from the Odyssey. New themes appear and older ones are treated differently. We have already noted some vase-paintings which are still tributary to the older type of art. Now sculpture intervenes in the development of the pictorial. Here should be mentioned the "Melian Reliefs", small clay tablets mostly from the island of Melos, which were nailed to wooden sarcophagi or to small wooden caskets used as funeral offerings. They are from between 470 and 440 B.C. Here we find themes from Ulysses' home-coming, which had hitherto been neglected by artists. There is the first meeting of Ulysses and Penelope; he in the guise of a beggar, she still bowed down by grief (Plate 112). This presented either as a group of two figures or with Telemachus, Eumaeus, and Laertes included. Or there is the scene of Eurycleia washing Ulysses's feet in front of the columns of the palace while Telemachus looks on. These are tranquil groups with fine spiritual feeling, from which we may deduce that similar representations existed in the great art of the period.

The feeling that a viewer gets of being presented with imitations, or even plain copies, which does not occur when looking at the early epic scenes, recurs again and again with many of the pictures of the fifth and even later centuries. Archaeological research, in fact, has in many cases been able to trace the lost models once existing

213

in "great" art, so that the study of epic scenes in classical and post-classical times now become more and more part of the history of art. But this must not be allowed to distort our view of what actually remains, "pastiche" though much of it is.

When we note that the artistic themes of the Melian Reliefs are repeated elsewhere, and especially that the figure of the pensive, grieving Penelope enjoyed particular favour (Plates 26 and 105) — some important remains of statuary also illustrate this fact —, the conclusion is unavoidable that some great work of the early classical period must lie behind the composition. Possibly it was not immediately called "Penelope", but was linked up soon after its appearance with the name of the wife of Ulysses who so loyally awaited his return. The archaeological difficulties of the question may be judged from the fact that a similar torso of "Penelope" has recently come to light in Persia!

The red-figured vases of the fifth century, also reflect the richer themes of the emotional mood and the meeting of friends. We see for the first time pictures of Nausicaa, the charming Phaeacian maiden. It is true that Pausanias claims to have seen her on the Calypso Casket, a coffer of cedarwood which stood in the temple of Hera at Olympia and which was richly decorated with subjects from the epics. This would put the first picture of Nausicaa about 600 B.C., but it is certain that Pausanias saw nothing of the kind, as there were no scenes from the Odyssey at Olympia. The vase-paintings, however, are unmistakable. An amphora at Munich, with a pictorial frieze running round the body of the jar, shows Ulysses standing naked

and miserable on the left, with two very small twigs in his hand. He is asking for shelter (Plate 41). To the right, two girls are running away (Plate 42), while three others stand their ground calmly. This same set of figures is very beautifully presented, with certain changes, on the lid of a pyxis (round box) in Boston (Plate 39), which even shows the pebbles on which Ulysses is walking.

It is not always possible to identify each personage in these vase-paintings and the artists themselves did not always aim at giving individual traits. Some pictures are, however, clear for us because of the recognizable grouping of the figures or of sufficiently recognizable characteristics, like the vase-painting of the late fifth century which portrays a majestic white-haired man (Plate 18). The artist certainly meant to show King Nestor, and he has succeeded admirably.

The composition is also remarkable on a large red-figured cup from Chiusi in central Italy, which on one side shows Telemachus, with Penelope grieving in front of her great loom (Plate 9), on the other Eurycleia washing Ulysses' feet (Plate 106). The arrangement of the figures is very similar to that of the Melian Reliefs. But there are certain differences, which cannot be explained merely by the fact that the cup is from the Attic, the reliefs from the Ionian school. On the Chiusi cup Ulysses is standing, while in the Melian Reliefs he is sitting down, and his weapons and dress are different. His old nurse has already recognized him by his scar, as her attitude shows. Her name is given as Antiphata, which is contrary to the Odyssey. We cannot but think that a new source underlies the whole composition, and scholarly acumen has in fact identified the source in a tragedy of Sophocles which gave a different version of the home-coming of Ulysses, although we now only have fragments of this play.

A marble relief in the National Museum of Athens, however, follows the text of the Odyssey closely. It shows clearly the terrified Eurycleia letting Ulysses' foot fall back into the basin, while Ulysses, seeing that he has been recognized, seizes her by the throat to enforce silence. Penelope appears behind Ulysses, not seated, however, but standing at her loom, unweaving once more the threads.

These are precisely the pictures which were imitated in popular Roman art. The clay statues of the Roman period are at one with the Melian Reliefs in showing Penelope sitting mournfully at her loom, under which stands the basket of wool that became her emblem (Plate 26). There are also imitations and adaptations of the recognition-scene, where the climax of the event is vividly portrayed. One version (Plate 107) shows the nurse still holding Ulysses' foot, with its revealing scar, while Ulysses in dismay puts his hand over her mouth to prevent her betraying the secret too early. The tenseness of the moment is heightened by the way Ulysses turns to Eumaeus, who is coming from the rear unaware of any thing unusual.

We can hardly assume that these works of popular Roman art depend directly on the Greek art of the type displayed in the Melian Reliefs. Most probably both types have common models in the great works of classical art. These prototypes cannot be identified more particularly, but our literary sources tell us that the painters, which means

above all Polygnotus, the first great classical master, took up themes from the Odyssey with surprising frequency. It is hard to say whether this was due to his personal preference or to one of the tendencies of the age. Speculation is severely limited by the fact that none of his paintings survive.

Another thing that makes tracing the origin difficult is that Polygnotus obviously did not confine himself to the text of Homer. His "Philoctetus" portrays a scene first heard of long after Homer, as does his painting of the theft of the palladium by Ulysses and Diomedes — two themes which then never disappeared from graphic art. Other themes are no doubt more "Homeric" but they are still novel and unusual. Ulysses appears in a painting of the cruel sacrifice of the Trojan king's daughter Polyxena, and he plays an important part in the painting which depicted the discovery of Achilles among the daughters of Lycomedes. The Propylaeum collection in Athens contained all these pictures, along with the "Nausicaa", while the small town of Plataea possessed a "Massacre of the Suitors" by Polygnotus, and Delphi a "Journey of Ulysses to the Underworld". Derivatives of these two paintings may perhaps be seen on Attic red-figured vessels; one, a skyphos showing the massacre of the suitors (Berlin, Staatliche Museen), from the same hand as the "Penelope" cup from Chiusi mentioned above, the other a pelike (small jar) in Boston. The vase-paintings do not entirely agree with the descriptions of Pausanias, our main source for the work of Polygnotus, but some definite links can be discerned. The vases, however, need not be regarded as mere copies. Even as small vase-paintings they are imposing and gripping, especially the Boston pelike (broadbased jar), where the spectre of Elpenor rises up before Ulysses, who has just offered sacrifice in the presence of Hermes (Plate 79). And all the terrors of the slaying of the suitors are well brought out on the skyphos, which displays a power of invention of a greater artist, though the vase-painting retains a character of its own. The scene is divided between the two sides of the cup, but Ulysses remains the central figure. We can sense years of repressed grief and pent-up anger in the way he bends his bow. The arrows are directed at three suitors grouped around a couch. One has already been hit in the back, another has his hands raised to parry the shot, the third holds a table in front of him like a shield. This last motif recurs in other pictures of the massacre of the suitors and so probably goes back to Polygnotus.

A similar composition, also probably influenced by Polygnotus, is found in one of the reliefs decorating a strange building, a heroon or "hero's shrine", in the ancient city of Trysa in Lycia, Asia Minor. Though a relatively modest piece of work, the scene is important because it probably dates from the beginning of the fourth century. Here too we see the stirring scene of the actual shooting (Plate 109): Ulysses is bending his bow and the suitors are already hit or flying terrified to shelter. One of them is again using the flat of a table for a shield (Plate 110). The relief, now in the Kunsthistorisches Museum in Vienna, formed part of a whole series depicting scenes of the Trojan war, including the eventual capture of the city (Plates 12, 13, 14, and 51).

Other painters of classical and post-classical times also painted scenes from the Odyssey. The examples we will mention here are no longer in a state of preservation, nonetheless, their earlier existence is witnessed in the writings of the ancients. Nicias of Athens painted Ulysses before Teiresias in the underworld — and also with Calypso. Parrhasius painted Ulysses' feigned madness and the healing of Telephus in the presence of Ulysses. Pliny narrates that the painter Nicomachus, who lived at the end of the fourth century B.C., was the first to depict Ulysses with the pilos, the pointed sailor's cap. Unhappily this isn't true, because there are many earlier pictures of Ulysses in this sort of cap, which was to become his permanent emblem. Echoes of the work of these classical masters too are faint and rare: a few reliefs, gems, and vase-paintings, on which no final verdict can be passed as to their degree of faithfulness to their early models. A silver drinking-vessel with reliefs, in Copenhagen, is worth mentioning: it perhaps reproduces a "Philoctetus" of Parrhasius, in which Ulysses appeared.

Classical statuary is necessarily less rewarding than painting, because the latter had more psychological possibilities of doing justice to the newly-discovered themes. Outstanding among the few surviving remains is the late classical statue of Ulysses in Venice, a very beautiful piece of work, which probably formed part of a group portraying the theft of the palladium. But in statuary of this period the Odyssey is on the whole overshadowed by the Iliad, not only with regard to mythological themes, but much more in the visual rendering of the Homeric gods, which had by now been brought to an absolute climax. The Odyssey lacked the youthful enthusiastic surge which could soar at times to sublime inspirations in the Iliad. The classical age was unable to respond to the same extent to the profoundly human side of the story of the Odyssey. The interest of the age remained centred for a great deal upon the fabulous and heroic themes.

THE END OF THE CLASSICAL AGE

Antiquity was very far indeed from being over-awed and solemn when dealing with its myths, and it could produce mocking burlesque as well as profound interpretations. It was possibly in the comedies of the Sicilian Epicharmus, who lived at the beginning of the fifth century B.C., that Ulysses was first presented as a comic figure, and a Boeotian cup from the end of the fifth century B.C. (Nauplia, Museum) shows us the unexpected scene — which is in sharp contrast to Homer — of the men turned into swine by Circe making merry at table. The really grotesque vase-paintings which take comedy to the limits of the absurd are also from Boeotia, from the shrine of the Cabiri in Thebes. Two cups portray Ulysses and Circe as ridiculous figures, each time before a great loom, once as the magic drink is being offered (London, British Museum), and again when Ulysses threatens violence if she does not return his men (Oxford, Ashmolean Museum). Here Circe is still actually stirring the drinking-bowl with her wand while Ulysses,

naked and pot-bellied, is rushing at her sword in hand. Another cup makes fun of the adventure on the raft. It shows Ulysses careering over the sea, straddling two amphoras (Plate 33), hunting fish with a trident, while Boreas, the god of the winds, blows him onwards. It would be wrong to see anything like modern scepticism and disrespect in these pictures. The fun was still aimed at the myth as a reality of faith and not as a fiction outside the religious sphere. We should not be alarmed at the direct and "natural" feeling of the Greeks for their gods, nor at their facility for combining their ideas of the human and the divine.

Another example of the transformation and deformation of classical art is the type of painting with which the Greek colonists of southern Italy decorated their vases from the end of the fifth century till well into the fourth. The artists have departed very far from the early high classical art, though charm and gaiety are still present in their work. Their paintings were on vessels which were mostly intended as funeral offerings, so they too do not lack profounder traits; but they nearly always take their origin from theatrical representations when they deal with mythology, which means that as a rule they at least border on the comic. Like many other scenes from the Iliad and the Odyssey, the blinding of Polyphemus becomes exaggerated and farcical.

One of these vase-painters, who also painted a grotesque "Slaying of Dolon", decorated a vase (now in Paris) with the scene of Ulysses consulting the blind prophet Teiresias in the underworld.

In this Ulysses is sitting in the middle on a heap of

stones, with Eurylochus and Perimedes standing beside him. Before him lies the head of the sacrificial ram, behind which another ram is lying on its back. Just in front of the ram's head, almost touching the sole of Ulysses' shoe, the white-haired head of the blind Teiresias is rising up out of the ground, while Ulysses stares at him wide-eyed (Plate 81). Possibly some dramatic work is behind this rather than Homer, for in Homer the whole shade of Teiresias arrives at the pit but does not come up out of it.

In addition to these early pictures, which still belong to the fifth century we have some later ones from south Italy. A water-jug in Naples confronts us with the peculiar obscurity, or indeed vagueness, which is often seen in the treatment of mythological themes on the vases of this region. On the left a woman is standing, holding a mirror, then there is a woman sitting down with a water-jug in her lap. In front of her stands a young man with a lance and either a band of pearls or a leafy twig. Between the seated woman and the youth, there is a gravestone, beside which is written, near the woman, the word "kale", Greek for "beautiful". The word "Telemachus" is written near the youth. The picture on the right shows a bearded man with a sword, sitting on a heap of stones. A woman, standing, offers him a box. The word "Ulysses" is written between them (Plate 32). A precise explanation of the two pictures is impossible. The "second wedding" of Ulysses has been suggested, or Ulysses and Eurycleia, for the first, Penelope and Telemachus at the grave of Ulysses for the second. Some commentators have tried to make Calypso out of the word "kale", but this is most unlikely. Perhaps, however, these are scenes from the theatre which have nothing to do with Homer, or just mythical names and figures which have been confused with well-known types of south Italian vase-paintings.

A mixing-bowl in Berlin is clearer. It presents a subject hitherto unknown in works of art, the visit of Telemachus to Nestor (Plate 11). Telemachus is standing on the left, a youth with long hair, his pointed cap in his hand. The white-haired Nestor is standing in front of him, in royal garments, with his mouth open to speak and his hand raised in a warning gesture. Behind him a girl is approaching with a basket of fruit and cakes. Also represented in the vase-paintings of southern Italy is Ulysses' voyage past the rock of the Sirens, and here again we meet with comic traits which suggest that the paintings were inspired by the theatre rather than the epic.

The Etruscan works also represent the reflected glory of classical art, but for all their debt to the Greeks they develop a structure and a significance of their own. I have already mentioned some early pictures. In the forcible and direct way in which they give expression to the myth, they are on a level with Greek art. Even the later works have an immediate charm of their own, and one finds hard to regard them as mere interpretations of Greek classical motifs.

A pepper-wood sarcophagus in Orvieto, for instance, which strikes one as being typically Etruscan — delighting in bloodthirsty subjects and realistic presentation. The sides show the slaughter of the Trojan captives who were sacrificed by Achilles, and also the slaying of Polyxena, while the ends show Ulysses threatening Circe (Plate 74) and calling up Teiresias from the underworld by sacrificing a ram (Plate 78). The scene with Circe shows the two main characters surrounded by the swine-headed men familiar in Greek art.

The Circe episode also occurs in the engravings on the back of Etruscan bronze mirrors. One of these shows on the right a seated female figure, offering a bowl to a man standing in front of her (Plate 75). He seems rather young to be Ulysses, but the offering of the magic potion is the same as on earlier Greek vase-paintings.

A large number of scenes from the Trojan War and from the Odyssey are found in post-classical times on Etruscan burial-urns, which are richly decorated with reliefs in the style of their Greek models. There are several examples of the Circe episode (Plate 71), as well as of Polyphemus and the Sirens, and the rare Scylla episode (Plates 86 and 92). The scenes which take place after Ulysses' return are particularly impressive. One alabaster urn shows the suitors banqueting, with Ulysses already present — unrecognized. He is seated at the extreme left of the picture, dressed as a wandering beggar and seeming quite insignificant, while the suitors are gazing at Penelope who is entering from the right (Plate 104). The gruesome end is also depicted (Plate 110), when the parasites are slaughtered mercilessly by the arrows of Ulysses and the sword of his son Telemachus. These stories from a distant land (and past) must have held a powerful fascination for Etruscan artists. They returned to them again and again to decorate the urns to which they committed their dead. On such occasions, one does not choose a subject to which one is indifferent!

THE POST-CLASSICAL PERIOD

All the above has taken us very far, in space and time, from classical Greek art, and it looks as though classical art as such has slipped by unnoticed in the process. Where are its pictures of the Odyssey, such as we are entitled to hope for after the promising beginnings in that early period?

We have mentioned great pictures which have disappeared. We have seen new themes being treated in the art that has survived. And we have met a new way of viewing the myths and of interpreting them in civilized, complex ways. But all this must appear feebler, less gripping and imposing, than the early powerful pictures, which, though less civilized and sophisticated, were still closer to primitive human nature. We need only compare the striking wooden horse on the amphora from Mykonos (Plate 48), with the harmless little beast which the red-figured vases fuss over. The pictures of the classical century appear to us to contain too much "art", too little myth, too little real utterance.

But the fact that these later pictures are less exciting should not prevent us from seeing the mighty achievement of classical art. It was a transitional period; but in breaking loose from the old, it opened up the way for later development, which could not have been based on the archaic alone. To develop, art had really to become "artistic", which entails a certain loss of power and simplicity, but the loss often brings the freedom which characterizes all progress.

From the fourth century on, art in the sense of forms and styles never lost its influence in the portrayal of the Homeric myth. In the centuries following the classical period, artists, in fact, turned with new energy to the Homeric themes, among others. These were centuries which acknowledged no non-artistic restrictions. Artists felt little obligation to such things as "noble simplicity and grandeur". Artists went to work with any and all technical means at their disposal, ruthless even with their artistic media. Yet they were centuries which remained purely Greek and "mythic".

Hellenistic baroque of the third and second centuries produced once more "Homeric" groups in bold compositions, including subjects from the Odyssey. In popular art — Roman lamps, clay figures, bronze reliefs on utensils and couches, sarcophagi, mosaics, copies of ancient sculpture — one theme was so often represented that we can reconstruct it at least in its main outlines. Polyphemus is sitting on a rock holding by the arm the lifeless body of one of Ulysses' companions, while Ulysses is creeping up cautiously, a bowl of wine in his hand, poised for instant flight. Part of this group is reproduced in a Roman bronze statuette in Paris, which shows Polyphemus devouring the dead body of his victim (Plate 58), and its counterpart, the cautious Ulysses, is preserved on a fragment of a sarcophagus in Naples (Plate 59). Among the large-size statues, a statue of Ulysses in the Vatican and one of Polyphemus in the Capitoline museum give us the best idea of this group, which is psychologically subtle in spite of all its baroque massiveness. In the productions of popular art it has been added to here and there by further figures, notably in the great mosaic of the late Roman villa in Piazza Armerina in Sicily portraying the same theme.

Polyphemus, as might have been expected, enjoyed a new popularity in this emotionally-charged, "Hellenistic baroque" art which worked in large dimensions. This popularity became marked probably in the second century B.C., the age of the temple of Zeus at Pergamum (Troy). Presumably the crudest scene from the Polyphemus episode, the blinding of the giant, was remodelled at that time. The escape of Ulysses under the ram certainly belonged to this cycle. It is represented by two Roman copies in marble, in an excellent state of preservation, now in the Villa Albani and in the Palazzo Doria in Rome. There is also a ram in the Toledo, Ohio, museum, that shows traces of Ulysses. Even the difficult theme of the adventure with Scylla was attempted. Apart from the remains of large-size copies in marble, there are echoes of Scylla scenes in popular Roman art, as, for instance on the bronze relief in London dating from the first century (Plate 92).

No doubt there was much artistic refinement in all this, but to regard it just as artificial exaggeration would be to mistake the spirit of that age. It was not just the mood of the artists which made them depict graphically the more dramatic aspects of the stories from the Odyssey. The portrayal also touched on new, essential aspects of the original epic, which were in fact adaptable to baroque forms of visual presentation.

But that was not the only artistic achievement of the Hellenistic period (second and third centuries B.C.). It made a very essential discovery, which our age in particular, especially the readers of this book, will be able to appreciate. It saw that beyond the characters and action of the Odyssey the landscape, the setting in which everything took place, was an intrinsic element of the voyages and adventures of Ulysses.

Graphic proof that the Hellenistic age produced great landscape paintings with scenes from the Odyssey depends largely on the existence of an extraordinary and complete unique piece of Roman art: the frescoes with "landscapes from the Odyssey" which were found in a house on the Esquiline in Rome. They are so badly preserved that today no photographic reproduction can give a true idea of their value. But it is worth while trying to form a clear idea of their importance in the history of pictures of the Odyssey. Landscape itself has been taken as the real subject of the painting and is no longer just the backdrop for the action. This striking approach is quite novel, and it displays a wider feeling for one of the essential elements of the Odyssey, the landscape, which did not exist in art before. We must not, of course, look for geographical exactness here — the scenes are all part of the myth. The landscapes are idealized as an imaginative enhancement of the Mediterranean. If we have a similar sense of the myth when we are looking at actual landscapes of the Italian coasts, these may well correspond to much of the scenic art of the ancient past.

The frescoes derive from late Greek art, at least to some extent. Taken as a whole, however, they reflect Roman taste and show us the Roman approach to the epics of Homer.

THE ROMAN PERIOD

This brings us to Roman representations of myth and all the problems in interpretation which they pose. Many paintings are simply more or less faithful reproductions of Greek art, and we have already had occasion to speak of some Roman antiques which preserved at least the themes of lost Greek works. But there are many other Roman works which deal more freely with the traditional material. The clay reliefs used by the Romans to decorate buildings often depicted Greek myths. The washing of Ulysses' feet (Plate 107), has already been mentioned because of its close connexion with Greek art. Another notable Roman relief shows Ulysses' ship sailing by the Sirens' rock. Ulysses is tied to the mast (Plate 84), and his expression of feverish restlessness is brought out as effectively by the artist as the untroubled calm of the oarsmen and the ship gliding over the waves.

Pompeii, too, provides certain scenes from the Odyssey. In a wall painting (Plate 24) a completely fantastic version of the Trojan horse episode is given. On the right we see the horse, standing stiffly on its long legs in front of a tower, while a number of men are making fierce efforts to drag the colossus forward. Others are dancing or jumping excitedly around the straining men. A row of upright figures may be seen in the background, and behind them rises a number of what may be lances or spears. A statue of Pallas Athene stands on the left, before which a number of figures at prayer or sacrifice may be distinguished. A woman bearing a torch is walking across the upper part of the picture. Not much of Homer has been preserved here, but the crucial moment has been caught and rendered competently. The painting is fluid — almost "impressionistic" — but executed with a very sure touch.

ILLUSTRATIONS

Obviously the Romans, too, did not make fidelity to the text of Homer their supreme goal. And yet in Roman art there is much that is just a literal attempt to turn narrative into picture, in a way more evident than was the case in the earlier centuries. But here especially we find links with what is pre-Roman and Hellenistic. The Odyssey landscapes of the Esquiline, independent though their artistry is, are also something like mere illustration, because they are so true to the text and give so many Greek names. By the time their Hellenistic models were painted, a change of attitude had long made itself felt with regard to "picture and song". Art had exhausted its most spontaneous expression, and at the same time, a new type of interest in the actual text of Homer arose, almost like that of modern scholars. The mythic narratives no longer had a popular independent life of their own, but could only be experienced through the text of the epics. They had become "academic". Eventually the "Iliad" and "Odyssey" were taken as "personifications", in material, visible, and tangible form, and mounted their

pedestals as statues. Then pictures of the cruel Cyclops Polyphemus or the Sirens with their seductive song or the grieving Penelope were no longer wanted. People wished so see instead "Odyssey, Book So-and-So", — a representation of some particular Homeric description. Naturally they began to demand that the pictures should conform exactly to the text. Indeed, they wanted the pictures to appear beside the text to be able to check their accuracy. And so finally something was evolved which today we still call "illustration": the complete text with the pictures beside it.

Very little of it has survived, because such manuscripts were written and illustrated on perishable material. But with the help of other witnesses, in clay or stone, we can at least imagine what such illustrated parchment scrolls must have looked like.

As usual, the artistic tradition is less well documented for the Odyssey than for the Iliad. However, from as early as Hellenistic times (the third and second centuries B.C.), we have a series of "Homeric bowls", hemispherical clay vessels with thin walls, which reproduce the relevant text of epic or tragedy beside their small pictorial reliefs. The emperor Nero, who clearly had a magnificent collection, already called these vessels by the name which is used for them today. Here, too, pictures from the Iliad are more numerous, and they also include representations of scenes from other literary epics which are now almost completely lost, as well as from classical Greek tragedy. From the Odyssey, the "Massacre of the Suitors" deserves to be mentioned in particular. All these pictures give the impression of belonging to larger cycles of illustrations, which presented whole episodes. They are probably imitations of models in gold and silver, which suggests that other forms of Homeric illustrations already existed.

There is another set of antiques which points even more clearly to the existence of the cycle of pictures from which they originate, the so-called "Tabulae Iliacae", the Trojan plaques. They are small marble reliefs from early imperial Roman times, depicting scenes from the Homeric epics with (and sometimes without) the relevant texts. Their purpose is unknown, but everything from simple wall decoration to special teaching aids has been suggested. Only two reliefs with scenes from the Odyssey have been found: a fragment showing the adventure with Circe, very detailed in its execution, with emphasis on the reproduction of the palace; and a complete relief, without inscriptions. The latter consists of a central panel showing Poseidon, surrounded by twenty-four more panels, each of which gives a scene from one of the twenty-four books of the Odyssey. Some ancient scholar with a mathematical bent, (or perhaps a mathematician with a scholarly bent) has here turned the various and complex sequences of the epic's action into a kind of geometrical game. The reliefs have been poorly preserved, and the scenes they show are not at all characteristic of the books. They are always the opening scenes, another arbitrary, mechanical trait, which prevented them from being recognized for what they are, when first discovered. But it allows us to deduce that these reliefs were modelled on a fully illustrated Odyssey, from which they took the opening scenes in each case. Such a model must have contained from four to five hundred scenes, and can hardly have been anything but a papyrusroll.

Thus insubstantial paper took the place of stone, bronze, clay, or ivory, and it cannot be accidental that the method of illustration came into use at the same time, giving word and picture together. These purely illustrative pictures of the papyri were not "vase-paintings", nor were they decorations for religious buildings or burial urns or sarcophagi, nor for couches, coffers, tripods, or ornaments. But they did not exist on their own account either, to be contemplated for their own intrinsic value as art objects. They were aids for reading and understanding the text, not "art for art's sake" but art put to the service of the written word. The importance of this fact, which is also a change, can hardly be overestimated. And it calls for a word of explanation, or perhaps an excuse from us, for having spoken so little of the various settings of the pictures which we have been discussing. Why do nearly all the early pictures appear on vases, why others on mirrors, couches, urns, sarcophagi? And why do we not hear of pictures existing in their own right, which were painted only to be looked at, without regard to any particular purpose or setting?

Of course, it has been suggested that purely illustrative art existed in early times, which must have been less pretentious than that which served higher — religious — purposes. But modern sentiment is often strongly at work if we feel that one ancient picture is "more profound", another "more an illustration". Our present critical opinion is too subjective to be sure which was which originally. At any rate, there is no extrinsic evidence or exact criterion by which these two types of art can be exactly distinguished, as for instance by separating them according to the kinds of vessels on which they were placed.

When we do ask what the "more sublime meaning" may have consisted in, we are rapidly plunged into an inextricable tangle of private feeling and conflicting thoughts. The early vase from Eleusis (Plate 60) with the blinding of Polyphemus was found in a child's grave, and there is no satisfactory answer to the question of why this picture was chosen for a child. "They were tales told to children", it has been suggested. But was that the reason for placing precisely this blood-thirsty story beside the dead child? The same story also appears on very different utensils. No doubt, the meaning of the picture depends to some extent on the purpose assigned to it. But have we any way at all of recognizing the difference in intended meaning and purpose between a vase-painting, for example, a temple decoration, an engraving on a mirror, and a relief on an urn? Ulysses giving the bowl of wine to Polyphemus has been reproduced on the decoration of a bed, on a sarcophagus, and in a floor mosaic. Since we have no clear indications in contemporary literature to tell us why, must not every attempt at explanation end in inconclusive speculation?

Matters are not made much simpler by scattered literary references and numerous monuments available from Roman times. And not much help is given by the shorter or longer additions which point to the symbolism behind them. When for instance a late sarcophagus shows a Siren dressed like a philosopher with a book in the form of a scroll in his hand, this undoubtedly refers to the seductive powers of philosophy. But when the garden of the enchantress is depicted in a wall-painting of a Christian catacomb, there is such a complex world of theological speculation behind it that we cannot precisely grasp the meaning of the representation. And since in the last resort *every* speculative application, every effort to find the basis for the comparison presupposes associations of ideas (and facts) which are not at our disposal in general, but can only be determined by a precise knowledge of the whole actual environment, we just have to give up in most cases.

The objection could also be made that by detaching the image from the object which it decorates, we are neglecting its *artistic* character: a vase-painting must be seen along with the vase, an architectural relief along with the whole building.

But a very simple fact does appear in both cases. It is always the same picture which is assigned to different purposes and placed on different objects. Even when thus affected by slight alterations and additions, the kernel itself remains untouched. The voyage past the Sirens' rock is the same on a Corinthian vase and on an early Christian sarcophagus, the blinding of Polyphemus is the blinding of Polyphemus on a vase in a tomb of the seventh century and in an Etruscan painting of the second pre-Christian century. Differences that may occur are accidental, due to contemporary conditions, and so are a matter for scientific research and not for pure contemplation. They may be interesting, "something to know about", but they do not contribute to the one possible interpretation of the actual process of creation. The fact that a Greek mother told her child the story of Polyphemus or that a Christian saw the seductive power of philosophy in the Sirens is of no essential significance for the real content of the story of Polyphemus or the Sirens — just as the original incident and idea behind it are essentially unaltered whether the picture is put on a vase or on a mirror.

But it were these essential ideas that gave rise to the myth and the incidents of epic enabling the songs to be sung and the images to be created: ideas which changed with the constant surrounding changes not in spite of their being the same, but because of their being the same — because they can never be fully known and portrayed but can only be sought after. The history of each theme of the Odyssey is therefore composed of two things: its original idea and man's constant effort to express it, to understand it.

CONCLUSION

In conclusion, let us look at one of the mightiest attempts ever made by man to grasp the idea of the Odyssean themes. It was made at a time when vase-paintings and furniture decorations no longer seemed satisfactory, when men also found that pure art, working independently of time and place, was no longer sufficient, and when they wished somehow to unite the two components of myth: art and reality, art and nature. The painted landscape, as we can still see it in the house on the Esquiline, was in fact just illusion. Now the earth itself was to become "mythic" landscape. It was to remain what it was and at the same time serve as the theatre of a higher reality.

It was in the first century A.D. that a Roman emperor ordered the Odyssean myth to be performed where it had "in reality" taken place. Polyphemus was to be placed in his cave, Scylla by the sea, and not just as some form of dramatic show put on for a day or two, such as had undoubtedly been produced before, but as really enduring myth — that is, in the form of art — colossal statuary representing the themes of the Odyssey. This was certainly the search for the idea of the myth: if the myth had once been reality, and if art was the credible portrayal of the myth, then both could and must be united!

Eight years ago during the tunnelling of a road, the mighty ruins of the Emperor's effort came to light, in a cave by the sea at Sperlonga, in the Italian landscape of the Odyssey. The ruins were in a deplorable state of confusion. But we had not only to mourn losses. Among the enormous piles of broken, colossal statuary (some figures were twenty feet high), an inventory in poetic form was found, listing the contents of the Emperor's vast exposition of mythic sculpture, and for good measure, an inscription giving the names of the artists of at least one group of the statuary.

From explicit accounts by the Roman poet Faustinus, a friend of the poet Martial, the historian may conclude that these groups of Homeric figures were installed in the cave in the time of Faustinus, about A.D. 92–97. The archaeologist has the somewhat more difficult task of piecing them together from the ruins, and then of trying to insert them properly into their place in the history of art.

It is an immense task which may take years. Meanwhile, however, some preliminary conclusions can be arrived at. One is that the present way of showing sculptures in the museums is incorrect. This has been proved at least for the colossus of which not much more than the legs have been preserved. The statue must be Polyphemus, and the figures grouped around him are the companions of Ulysses, who are advancing to blind the sleeping giant. Ulysses too has been preserved, at any rate his head. (A relief in Catania shows a similar grouping, and considering how ancient art preferred to retain a composition once it had been invented, we must take it as a fairly exact repetition of the group in Sperlonga.) Unfortunately, the head of Polyphemus appears to be irretrievably lost, but great efforts are being made to complete a reconstruction. The colossal group, which was to raise the myth from the realm of art to the realm of nature, probably stood in one of the large neighbouring caves; contemplated today, as a project, the whole idea seems a baroque, a mistaken effort at uniting two levels! But what power there is, all the same, precisely in this aesthetic error! And how close it comes to the Odyssey itself! Even the sceptic must concede that in spite of the lack of good taste, the attempt to unite what should not be united — art and nature — can succeed in regard to the Odyssey because art and nature become one at the level of the myth. Did the Romans suspect or know this, or was their success in the Sperlonga caves just the accidental result of an aesthetic error? We shall probably never know.

Meanwhile all sorts of questions about the cave and its groupings come to mind. It is not quite certain that the two other groups, the ship with the falling steersman, and the companions of Ulysses attacked by Scylla, originally belonged together, as the present position of the sculptures suggests. The poet Faustinus speaks of the shattered ship *and* of the Scylla group, and yet no fragment has yet been found which would link the two groups. Yet connexion cannot be excluded: Scylla's powerful hand (Plate 91) is clutching the hair of a man, who could be the steersman (Plate 88). He has fallen head foremost on to the ship, with his head strangely twisted and pressing against the timbers. A bronze relief from Boscoreale near Pompeii proves that such groupings did occur. It shows on the right bow of a ship with the fallen steersman. Scylla is in front of him, crushing the hapless sailors in her monstrous arms (Plate 92) — and with one of her hands she has just grasped the steersman by the head.

Another question is how to establish and classify exactly the style and quality of the sculptures. The three artists whose names appear on the ship are none other than those whom Pliny names as the creators of the famous Laocoon. They were, as he says, from Rhodes. But we do not know when they lived, and expect analysis of the style of the statues (at Sperlonga or in the Laocoon) has reached no clear results. To make things more difficult the Polyphemus group is clearly different in quality from the rest. Is it an original or a copy? Is it also from the three Rhodians? And did they themselves produce this piece of sculpture only for Sperlonga? Or was it produced hundreds of years earlier, at the height of Hellenism? Or, in the last resort, is the whole thing a set of copies from beginning to end? Though these questions may have a decisive effect on modern notions of the development or certain aspects of Mediterranean art, no judgement is yet possible.

But, just on the level of what is tangible and provable, the find is a joyful event. For it proves the setting up of the sculptures in a cave by the sea at Sperlonga in the first century of Roman imperial times. The creative elements in the effort were Roman power and taste, bowing before the Greek myth. The result, however interpreted, is an impressive final chord in the whole concert of ancient representations of the Odyssey. What came after the first century was really no more than an echo.

It is a far cry from the potsherd in Argos to the colossus of Sperlonga. But in all the ruins the idea of what the Odyssey means shines clearly clarity for anyone who knows how to look. In this respect too the giants in the Sperlonga cave may be a symbol: before their miserably fallen majesty, we painfully try to re-create their original outward form. But an inward beauty is still inviolate before our eyes. It is concentrated in the head of Ulysses (Plate 50), which, whatever group it belongs to, from whatever century it was created in, always remains "Ulysses" — just like the tiny figure on the bronze tripod from Olympia, neither baroque nor monumental, which was fashioned many centuries earlier. We must follow attentively the results of archaeological research. But we must always return, unconfused by any artistic theories, to the contemplation of the original pictures and words. This was the way of one of the first commentators on ancient portrayals of the Odyssey, the erudite Christian Gottlob Heyne, writing at the end of the eighteenth century. Heyne in effect laid down a practical law both for research and contemplation: "Anyone can raise doubts and questions about Ulysses and the Odyssey, and anyone can answer them. But if one reads the poet himself or contemplates the work of the artists who have portrayed his poems, one would need to have little sense of art or poetry not to forget at once all this far-fetched subtlety of speculation and scepticism. Then our whole mind is filled with the true Ulysses, one who always retains his presence of mind, acts with prudence and constancy, suffers with steadfastness and never loses sight of the set goal before him."

LITERATURE ON THE ANCIENT ILLUSTRATIONS OF THE ODYSSEY

Attempts to collect ancient pictures inspired by the Odyssey into one volume began in modern times with the book published in 1801 by the German painter Johann Tischbein, *Homer nach Antiken gezeichnet* (Homer in Ancient Illustration), for which the classical scholar Christian Gottlob Heyne wrote the major texts. This quite unsystematic publication was followed in 1836 by the *Galleria Homerica* of Francesco Inghirami of Florence, which simply followed the story sequence of the Odyssey. The same organization was used seventeen years later in Friedrich Overbeck's *Galerie heroischer Bildwerke* (Heroic Selective Gallery) and in the *Bilder-Atlas zum Homer* (Pictorial Atlas to Homer) of Richard Engelmann (1889). An English edition of the latter work was published in 1892. In 1882 J. Harrison had published the *Myths of the Odyssey,* and in the same year Johannes Bolte's doctoral dissertation appeared, *De monumentis ad Odysseam pertinentibus.* This took the history of art as its organizational pattern, presenting the pictures and objects according to what style they showed and what artistic period they dated from. So did Franz Müller's *Die antiken Odyssee-Illustrationen* (The Ancient Illustrations of the Odyssey), which had grown out of his doctoral dissertation of 1908.

These works, which were mostly only collections of drawings, were supplemented by the corresponding entries in W. H. Roscher's *Ausführliches Lexikon der griechischen und römischen Mythologie* (Complete Lexicon of Greek and Roman Mythology) (1884–1937). The *Enciclopedia dell'Arte Antica* (Rome 1958, still in the course of publication) gives the latest material, with pictures and references to the relevant literature, under the various entries dealing with names from the Odyssey (Calipso, Circe, Diomede, Nausicaa, Polifemo, Sirene, Ulisse, etc.), and in the general articles on "Illustrazione" and "Omeriche, Illustrazione". A short survey is given by G. M. A. Hanfmann in the *American Journal of Archaeology* 61 (1957), pp. 71 ff. The earliest pictures have been reproduced and discussed recently by K. Schefold in his *Frühgriechische Sagenbilder* (Munich 1964) (Early Greek Epic Illustrations).

Special Works:

Black-figured vase-paintings of the Odyssey (Circe, Polyphemus, the Escape under the Ram, the Sirens), see: C. H. E. Haspels, *Attic Black-figured Lekythoi* (1936). — The escape under the ram: see also M. Bieber in *American Journal of Archaeology* 47 (1943), pp. 378 ff. — For Polyphemus, see P. Courbin in *Bulletin de Correspondance Hellénique* 79 (1955), pp. 1 ff. — For the reliefs from Melos, see P. Jacobsthal, *Die Melischen Reliefs* (1931). — For Penelope Mourning, see G. Neumann in *Archäologischer Anzeiger* 1962, pp. 852 ff.

Classical statues and paintings, see G. Hafner, *Geschichte der Griechischen Kunst* (Zürich 1961), p. 258 and *passim;* see also the index to this book.

Etruscan Mirrors, see E. Gerhard, *Etruskische Spiegel* (1870–97), text out of date, but with abundant illustrations. — Etruscan Urns, see H. Brunn, *I Rilievi delle Urne Etrusche* (1870–96), text out of date, but with abundant illustrations.

On Hellenistic groups of figures, see M. Renard in *Hommages à Léon Herrmann* (1960), pp. 655 ff.

Landscapes of the Odyssey, see P. H. von Blanckenhagen in *Römische Mitteilungen* 70 (1963), pp. 100 ff. (in English).

Roman sarcophagi, see C. Robert, *Die antiken Sarkophagreliefs,* vol. II (1890).

Tabula Odysseaca, see K. Weitzmann in *American Journal of Archaeology* 45 (1941), pp. 166 ff.

Christian art, see *Comptes Rendus des séances de l'Académie des Inscriptions et Belles Lettres* 1941, pp. 103 ff.; 1945, pp. 26 ff., 54 ff. Also Th. Klauser in *Jahrbuch für Antike und Christentum* 6 (1963), pp. 71 ff.

THE FORMS AND TECHNIQUES OF
GREEK POTTERY-PAINTING

KYLIX
Early form: late 7th century B.C.
Classical form: about 575 B.C.

KANTHAROS
About 600 B.C.

RAM-RHYTON
Late 6th century B.C.

SKYPHOS
Middle 7th century B.C.

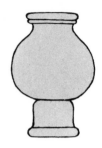

PSYKTER
About 530 B.C.

The beginnings of Greek pottery-painting can be traced back to approximately 1100 B.C. and the then purely ornamental *geometric style,* which was to perdure until the 7th century before Christ. It was Athens that led in the production of such geometrically patterned vases, and it continued to maintain its predominance in the late-period with the adoption of strongly stylized silhouettes of funeral processions. Much later the epoch was christened the "Dipylon-culture" on the basis of the rich pottery finds which were located in a cemetery in the area of the athenian double-gate (dipylon) that straddles the festive highway to the Acropolis.

In the early part of the 6th century, in the wake of the declining archaic period, *Corinthian pottery-painting* managed to work its way to the fore. At the mid-point of the same century, however, once *attic painting* had effected its final break-through in figurative contour and etched drawings, Athens was able to recover its former supremacy; this supremacy remained undisputed until approximately 420 B.C. By then a general paralysis had taken hold of the artistic production of its pottery wares. The short-lived *attic white-ground* lekythoi represent the only exceptions.

Pottery-painting not only flourished on the mainland, but also on the Greek islands as well, where, in fact, the typical characteristics of the *Ionian school* were formed. Under the influence of the Greek colonists the forms and techniques of pottery-art became at home in all of Greece,

NECK-AMPHORA
Early form: early 11th century B.C.
Classical form: early 6th century B.C.

PAUNCH-AMPHORA
About 700 B.C.

PRIZE-AMPHORA
('panathenaic' shape)
Probably 566 B.C.

COLUMN-KRATER
Early 6th century B.C.

VOLUTE-KRATER
Early form: about 575 B.C.
Classical form: about 500 B.C.

230

HYDRIA
Early form: about 700 B.C.
Classical form: about 575 B.C.

OINOCHOE
Early 7th century B.C.

PYXIS
Early form: 8th century B.C.
Classical form: early 5th century B.C.

ALABASTRON
Middle 7th century B.C.

LEKYTHOS
Second half
6th century B.C.

especially in Sicily and lower Italy. Italian pottery-painting bore a reciprocal relationship to *Etruscan art*. But consequent to the advent of *hellenism* in the 2nd century B.C., an oriental and partially relief-like decoration once again occupies the foreground.

Greek pottery is generally decorated with filling-ornament and pictorial representations. On the basis of the various techniques we can distinguish three forms of pottery-painting:

(1) The *black-figure style*. The representation is executed directly onto the bare clay in black ink. In its earliest form the figures were drawn in silhouette, but they were later supplemented with incised or painted "relief linea". The

fully developed style begins in the late 7th century B.C. and ends in the hellenistic period, about mid-second century B.C.

(2) The *red-figure style* coated the pot with a concentrated wash of black pigment, carefully avoiding the outlined figures. The reserved figures consequently took their color from the unpainted red clay background. This style was inaugurated about 530 B.C. and ended about 300 B.C.

(3) The *white-ground lekythoi* exhibit polychrome paintings on a light slip. The development of the style begins in the initial quarter of the 5th century B.C. and ends about 100 years later.

CALYX-KRATER
About 530 B.C.

BELL-KRATER
About 530 B.C.

STAMNOS
About 530 B.C.

PELIKE
About 530 B.C.

ULYSSES
by
C. KERÉNYI

C. Kerényi was born on January 19, 1897 in Temesvár in Hungary. He studied at the University of Budapest, where he took his degree as doctor of philosophy and became in 1927 assistant professor in the history of ancient religion. His own leanings in historical scholarship brought him into the Ulrich von Wilamowitz-Moellendorff school but with a special interest in the phenomenon of religion. This was later to bring him into contact with Walter F. Otto (author of *The Homeric Gods*).

In 1929 he made a prolonged stay in Greece and since then has been continually occupied with research and writing in Italy and Greece, extending his interest from Greek and Roman literature — to which he had mainly devoted his early work — to include what he describes as the "sensual heritage" of antiquity: the archaeological monuments and sites. Thus very early he followed a personal course in Classical scholarship which took him through studies normally the domain of the specialist: literature, art, religion, and mythology.

Taken as a whole his work aims at a comprehensive view of the classical world from the standpoint of the "sensual heritage"; a view which sees the concrete and the abstract as a unity, as they were united in antiquity. Between 1934 and 1943 he was professor for Latin and Greek at the universities of Pécs (Fünfkirchen) and Szeged. He then left Hungary in voluntary exile in Ascona in Switzerland whose citizenship he has taken.

His interest in psychology brought him contact with C. G. Jung, his humanism with Thomas Mann, a connexion evidenced by a well-known correspondence (Mann–Kerényi, *Gespräch in Briefen,* 1960). Kerényi is a member of the Norwegian Academy of Sciences and an honorary doctor of Uppsala University. Apart from his work on ancient religion and mythology he is especially interested in the novel and its early forerunner in Greek literature, the Odyssey.

His most important works are:

Die griechisch-orientalische Romanliteratur, 1927, 2nd ed. 1962;
Apollon, 1937, 3rd ed. 1953;
Die antike Religion, 1941; 4th ed. as *Die Religion der Griechen und Römer,* 1963; published as *The Religion of the Greeks and Romans,* 1962; 2nd Italian ed. 1951; French ed. 1957.
Die Mythologie der Griechen, 1951, 3rd ed. 1965; published as *The Gods of the Greeks,* 1951; 2nd Italian ed. 1962; French ed. 1952; Swedish ed. 1955.
Die Heroen der Griechen, 1958; published as *The Heroes of the Greeks,* 1959; Swedish ed. 1960; Italian ed. 1962.
Die Mysterien von Eleusis, 1962.
Autobiographical:
Unwillkürliche Kunstreisen, 1954; Swedish ed. 1957.
Tessiner Schreibtisch, 1963.

Further English and American Publications:
Asklepios. Archetypal Image of the Physician's Existence (New York 1959; London 1960).
Prometheus. Archetypal Image of Human Existence (New York and London 1963).
C. G. Jung and C. Kerényi, *Essays on a Science of Mythology* (New York 1949 and 1963); *Introduction to a Science of Mythology* (London 1951).
Paul Radin, C. Kerényi, and C. G. Jung, *The Trickster* (London 1956).

THE PRE-ODYSSEAN ULYSSES

"And so we see Homer as the men
of his time saw him, a poet singer
among poet singers."

ALBERT B. LORD[1]

THE 'ULYSSES THEME'

Aristotle praises Homer because he chose a unit of action for the Odyssey (as he also did for the Iliad) and did not try to depict the whole life of Ulysses. The material was there however, as Aristotle implies. He mentions the boar-hunt on Parnassus and the feigned madness of Ulysses. Actually, the first incident is told briefly in the Odyssey, when the scar on the hero's foot, by which the nurse Eurycleia recognized him, has to be explained (Plate 107). Possibly Aristotle was thinking of some fuller version of the story, or it escaped him for the moment that Homer recounted it briefly. He could read the story of the madness in the Cypria, an epic which he refused to ascribe to Homer. Sophocles wrote a tragedy called *The Madness of Ulysses,* and details about him not in the Iliad or Odyssey could be gathered from post-Homeric literature. Aristotle took it for granted that the whole story of Ulysses was pre-Homeric, and it is not unreasonable to follow Aristotle in the main.

In doing so, we are supported by the conclusions drawn by Professor W. B. Stanford of Dublin University, in his fine book, *The Ulysses Theme.* The lasting popularity of the hero, which moved James Joyce and the Greek novelist Niko Kazantzakis in our own days to link themselves — disguised as "Ulysses" or "Dysseas" — to Homer's hero, is clearly based on the fact that his creation was and remained more than his own invention. It has a dynamism and a weight of its own, perhaps best described, as Professor Stanford thinks, as "archetypal" in the sense

of Jungian psychology. It sets up a reciprocal dynamic interaction between the ancient theme of the Greek hero and each new author who takes it up. When Goethe (who planned to write a poem on Nausicaa), Tennyson, and others linked themselves so closely to Ulysses, it was certainly not mere imitativeness or homage. These conclusions, which have been formed by a literary critic with no psychological prejudices, can hardly be gainsaid. There is a difference between the influence of Prometheus and Ulysses on the one hand, and Hamlet and Othello on the other, which cannot be explained by aesthetic reasoning.

In the figures of Greek mythology, potentialities of man and the world were expressed, which, in the act of seeking self-expression, became still more vigorous. Once they had come to light in this way, they were like the "entelechies" in the philosophy of Aristotle, actualizations in the highest degree of their essence, and so became unforgettable. The gods are simpler figures, dwelling in the sphere of pure being, the heroes more complicated, swaying between divinity and humanity. Though there is a fixed kernel which can be recognized in the story of any given hero, the heroes can by no means be reduced to *simple* archetypal forms. Ulysses would then be only the embodiment of wiliness, with all the fascination which comes from wiliness being a human potentiality. But the question is whether a mere outline, nothing more than a personification of wiliness, could really exercise *such* a fascination. The heroes of folk-lore are such simplifications. In force and influence, they cannot compare with the heroes of Greek mythology. We must look closely at the hero to perceive all the elements in his make-up which were disclosed by an ancient power of vision which later become unusual — but then we note them. In the case of Ulysses, a vision was there long before Homer, and evidence pointing towards that earlier stage exists.

THE SOMNOLENT ULYSSES

First there is the name of the hero. Ulysses is its latest form, in Latin. It brings the classical Latin form, Ulixes, closer to the Homeric name, Odysseus. On the Greek mainland the hero was long called Olysseus, a name which can be read on vase-paintings. It must have been pronounced like this in western regions, as the Latin "Ulixes" testifies. On the basis of the non-Homeric pronunciation and the relationship of the hero to countries which he did not touch in his misdirected travels, we can circumscribe a region where the pre-Homeric Ulysses may have been a well-known figure. It was greater than the kingdom of Homer's Ulysses. It embraced the so-called Ionian Isles from Zacynthus (Zante) to the peninsula of Leucas, and two towns, perhaps on Leucas and the adjoining Acarnanian coast. The linguistic region, where the transition to the form Ulixes was possible, extended at this point, where the Adriatic is narrowest, over to Italy. In Epirus, the hero wandered and hunted in the land of the Thesproti, which possessed a famous entry to the underworld, and also visited the region of Parnassus. The whole district of the mountains between the Acarnanian coast and Boeotia seems to have known him otherwise than through Homer.

He became a royal figure when he was transferred to an existing or imaginary palace in Ithaca — like the kings of Mycenae who were the heroes of the epic songs. That was the great change in his mythic existence before Homer. In his previous condition, he could also have been called "god", though not a great god like "the gods who lived in ease" spoken of by Homer, who still, however, cared for men and could suffer wounds on their behalf. A "daimon" would be perhaps the best description of him, if this word in Greek did not contain the element of "being a man's destiny". He does not seem to have been worshipped as a hero at a grave in Ithaca, though a feast of Odysseus, the "Odysseia", was celebrated there. If he had had a shrine, a votive offering would not have been dedicated to him in a cave of the nymphs, where, like the thirteen three-footed kettles from the ninth or eighth century B.C., reported by Homer,[2] a picture of a nymph bearing (strangely enough) the name of Ulysses has been discovered. It dates from the second century B.C. We are very lucky to be able to note the impression which he left, other than by means of Homer's poems, on peoples dwelling on the other side of the Adriatic. It probably also extended to the eastern side, which was not occupied only by Greeks but also by Illyrians and certainly by the remains of an older Mediterranean population.

The Etruscans had preserved memories of an impressive feature. It is probable that some Greek historian writing of the Etruscans recorded the fact. Plutarch took it over from him in his "How should young people learn poetry?", which says as follows: the Etruscans related that Ulysses was a sleepy-head and therefore "hard to approach". Was his somnolence part of his craftiness? At any rate, deep sleep overcame him on board the Phaeacians' ship and we are not told that Athene was the cause of it, as after his arrival in the land of the Phaeacians. Ulysses was deposited on the strand without waking up. Plutarch associated the Etruscan story with this, and it might be thought that it was composed on the basis of the Odyssey. But the detail that Ulysses was unapproachable refutes this idea. It is mentioned nowhere else. Mythic beings sleep in order to be unapproachable. It is part of their craftiness and prevents men from disturbing them. The same sleep is narrated of Telepinus, a son of the Weather-God worshipped by the Hittites in Asia Minor. He goes into hiding, taking with him the corn and depriving the earth of fertility and nourishment. His brother the Sun-God sends out the eagle to search for him. The gods are in despair, wondering if they will survive. The great gods, like the lesser ones, have already hunted in vain for Telepinus and the eagle's search, too, is fruitless. Then the bee is sent out, with the order to sting Telepinus on the hands and feet to wake him, if she finds him. And so it happens. The sleep of Telepinus may have been death-like, like that of Ulysses in Book XIII of the Odyssey. Dirges were also sung for Telepinus, but he was not dead, only asleep in a wood. He raged madly when he was violently awakened, and had to be calmed down by magical charms. The bee had prepared wax as a remedy, and honey was also part of the soothing-potion:

"As honey is sweet and cream is mild, so shall Telepinus' heart be sweet and mild", we read on the Hittite tablets.

It is no longer difficult for us to imagine a pre-Greek myth about a god of nature who is not very friendly towards men. This is typical of mythic beings who were originally spirits of the nature, products of the vision of primitive peasant cunning, which fancied that it recognized itself in the processes of nature. Ulysses was such a being, and he did not quite lose his regal connexion with the fertility of the soil. In Book XIX of the Odyssey, Ulysses describes, nonsensically if one does not know his background, how a good king influences the course of nature. He addresses Penelope and refers to himself when he says in Book XIX, 110–14:

"... by virtue of whose equity and good governance
the masses prosper and the dark earth abounds
with wheat or barley and the trees bow down with fruit
and the ewes lamb infallibly and the seas yield fish."

Another character who in part represents the earlier, primordial Ulysses is his father Laertes (Plate 113). His name has no parallels in Greece, but resembles on the one hand the Etruscan name Lars, which every schoolboy knows from Macaulay's "Lars Porsena of Clusium", — and on the other hand the place-name Laerte in Asia Minor. The story of the king's giving up his palace and lordship in favour of his son, and retiring to his vineyard and orchard, is not in keeping with the customs of the kings of Mycenae, as described by Homer elsewhere. It would never have occurred to Nestor and Menelaus (Plates 18 and 22). But neither does it prove that the idea was at work here, that the own fertility lends fertility to nature, and that the King must die when he grows weak.

Old Laertes appears to have become again a sort of spirit of vegetation in the Odyssey, as he prowls around his vineyard (Plate 114), sleeping in the dust by the fire along with the servants only in winter, sleeping outside on the fallen leaves in summer and autumn, unwashed and unkempt, while his fig-trees and vines, his olives and pears and beds of plants appear all the better tended. Homer gives us to understand that the extremely strange condition of Laertes is due to grief for his son. He undoubtedly knows the story of the feigned madness of Ulysses, a variant and heightening of the motif of his sleep. In Book XXIV Agamemnon appears to allude to it in the underworld, when he speaks of the trouble it cost him and Menelaus to break down Ulysses' resistance to the idea of making war on Troy. It was not a story that Homer could use. But it showed Ulysses bound up with the earth like Laertes. He was ploughing like a farmer with a pointed cap on his head as a sign of madness, using a horse yoked to an ox. The wily Palamedes, who is mentioned neither here nor elsewhere by Homer, took the little child Telemachus from his cradle and set him down in the furrow before the plough. Ulysses then stopped appearing to be mad. The craftiness of the artisan had got the better of the craftiness of the peasant. From then on Ulysses hated Palamedes and took a cruel revenge on him — once more a story which did not suit Homer's purposes. The name of Ulysses' son and heir can mean "he who fights afar" or "he who stays far from the fight",

and Homer took it in the latter sense when he made Ulysses cry out in the Iliad (Book IV, 354) that even the father of Telemachus will be seen in the front line of battle.

PENELOPE AND THE WOMEN SURROUNDING ULYSSES

What lies behind this negative trait, the unwarlike character of the royal house of Ithaca, is the link with nature. Another archaic trait is the importance of the woman in Ulysses' family. It is not only Penelope (Plates 9, 26, 105, and 112) who stands out and whom Homer made the mythic example of wife's faithfulness to husband, but Ulysses' mother also. Penelope's background is also probably to be sought in the ancient myth. Her name can be understood as "she who tears out threads"[3] and this may have been her way at one time, in a sense different from that given by Homer. Here she refuses to choose between her importunate suitors before she has finished weaving Laertes' shroud — while he is still alive. Each night she unravels what she has woven by day, till after four years her "loyal deceit" is unmasked. The figure who tears out the threads and does so continually can also be the goddess of the underworld, so that Penelope may have migrated from the mythic sphere into human affairs. If so, the

238

reason why ducks are called *penelopes* in Greek is that they were thought, as in India, to be examples of wifely faithfulness in the animal kingdom. But it is also possible that some great goddess of pre-Homeric myth appeared for preference in the form of a duck and that Ulysses was originally linked with her. These backgrounds remain mere possibilities. We are on firm of ground with Anticleia, the mother of Ulysses in pre-Homeric and post-Homeric myth.

Her importance in the Odyssey is purely that of a human being, and it is at least as great as that of Laertes. Homer had placed the encounter with her in the underworld. If even the grief of Laertes as he longed for his son had been extraordinary, his mother had to die of it. And yet Ulysses had to meet her again. The situation is interpreted as follows by Karl Reinhardt:[4] "There was no more room at home, between Eurycleia and Penelope, for meeting the mother. We need the whole deep range of feelings shown by the dead mother as well as by the living son, if the story of her death from grief is not to remain an empty formula. Who but this poet could have let her die this way? How very different is the implication of the 'three times' that comes in twice here, if it is compared with its use in the battle-scenes of the Iliad! And how the desire of the living, to weep its fill with the dead becomes part of a new and mightier whole, different even in tone! What a recall of elements of the former heroic style, now serving a display of intimacy! If one eliminates the underworld-scene from the Odyssey, one eliminates the mother — and that from a poem whose author is never better than when describing encounters!"

It is not to be supposed that Homer gave the same rôle to Anticleia as she had in the sphere of mythology, where, as the daughter of the master-thief and robber of Parnassus, Autolycus, she linked up Ulysses with him. As a mythic being, Ulysses could also have originated from the earth or the water without any mortal mother, as Greek mythology narrated of the "first men". These were semi-divine beings, who were often very closely associated with a great goddess. Alalcomeneus, for instance, rose from the waters of Lake Cephisus in Boeotia, and was closely linked with Athene: he is said to have reared the goddess after she was born. He was at any rate called after her, because she was invoked in Boeotia as Alalcomene, "the guardian goddess who wards off harm", and was specially revered in the city of Alalcomenae. We are not very far from Ulysses here. He was given — certainly not by Homer, but in a pre-Homeric genealogy — a mother called Anticleia, whose name tells us nothing. But according to one tradition, she gave birth to him at the shrine of Alalcomene, the Boeotian Alalcomeneum, as the ward of Athene. According to another tradition, she bore Ulysses during a shower of rain, on the side of Mount Neriton in Ithaca, having been surprised by her birthpangs while travelling. Other primordial beings were also born in this way. On Ithaca too a city called Alalcomenae testified to the worship of Alalcomene. It was said to have been a foundation of the city of the same name in Boeotia. A tradition linking up with says that Alcomeneus (another way of writing Alalcomeneus) was another name for Ulysses. All this was once correct, in different variants of the myth: Ulysses was born on

Ithaca and in Boeotia, in the wilds of nature or at a shrine of Athene, he sprang from the primal earth or he was son of a mortal mother. Anticleia linked Ulysses with Mount Neriton and with Boeotia, with his guardian goddess and, as has been said, with Autolycus, the master-thief.

ULYSSES' FATHER SISYPHUS THE KING OF KNAVES?

Autolycus is taken by Homer to be the maternal grandfather of Ulysses. A paternal grandfather is mentioned only to provide a name for Laertes' father and assure him of descent from Zeus, as befitted a king. With the "lone wolf", the most natural translation of the eloquent name Autolycus, a whole world is conjured up, which forms the world of the picaresque novel, the romance of the rogue, in literature. Its atmosphere takes us back to pre-Homeric times, just as the sea-farers' tales do with theirs, and it displays features of ancient mythological themes, not yet refined by the nobler epic song. The stories told about Autolycus give us this atmosphere. It remains always the same, even if a given story, or indeed most of the stories, are actually post-Homeric. The rôle played in them by Anticleia is a passive one, and she appears quite different from Penelope, which may however well point to pre-Homeric times. We must recall the whole story, for the sake of the atmosphere.[5]

Autolycus was the son of Hermes, out of the latter's union with a bride of Apollo, Chione the "snow-maiden". He had taken the place of his elder brother by night, in a nook of Mount Parnassus, often covered with snow for long periods. This trick of Hermes gave birth to Autolycus, who revered his father above all other gods. From his father he received the gift of being a skilful thief and a cunning perjuror. Homer only speaks of Autolycus' gifts, not of Hermes being his father, and so proposes no definite genealogical link by which Ulysses would be associated with Autolycus' guardian deity, Hermes. When Autolycus had the gift of making everything that he touched with his hand invisible, of turning black beasts into white and white ones into black, of taking the horns from horned cattle and putting them on hornless beasts — so many tricks of early pastoral life —, this was a gift from *his own* Hermes. In the Odyssey Hermes appears as the messenger of the gods (Plate 29) and the escort of souls. When he helps against Circe's magic, it is surely on orders from above. The only reason why his mission from Olympus is not mentioned there is because Ulysses is the narrator. It is significant that he invokes the protection of Hermes when he is a wanderer and a beggar, in the house of the swineherd Eumaeus, where he is closest to the world of the picaresque novel.

In Autolycus' time, when the arch-rogue Sisyphus was king in Acrocorinth, — it must have been the time of the "first men", a sparse population of primal beings like Alalcomeneus — the flocks of the two rogues grazed on the wide pastures between Mount Parnassus and the Isthmus of Corinth. Autolycus could never be caught when he committed a theft. Sisyphus could only see that his flocks were growing smaller and those of Autolycus bigger. He finally thought of the following ruse. He was one of the first who had mastered the art of writing; so he cut the initials of his name under the hooves of his cattle. But Autolycus was able to change them, because he could change anything in a beast. Then Sisyphus poured lead into the grooves in the hooves, in the form of letters which formed the sentence "Autolycus stole me" in the tracks of the cattle. It was a battle of wits which anticipated printing. Autolycus admired the victor so much that he became friends with him and gave him hospitality. It was thought worthy of the most uninhibited picaresque romance that he should even offer his daughter to Sisyphus, so that she could give birth to the craftiest of men. Thus Anticleia became the mother of Ulysses. Laertes wooed her and won her, when she was already pregnant by Sisyphus.

We do not know whether the story of Autolycus had reached this picaresque climax by the time of Homer. But nothing could have been more repugnant to him than to let Sisyphus, who had tried to trick even the gods, and succeeded for a while, play the same rôle in the marriage of Laertes and Anticleia as Zeus did with Amphitryon and Alcmene. We read on the contrary in the Odyssey of the famous punishment of Sisyphus, in Book XI, where Ulysses tells of his journey to the underworld:

"Another whom I saw in torment was Sisyphus,
wrestling with a giant stone.
He would thrust with hands and feet,

working it towards the crest of his ridge
but when he was almost at the top,
it would twist back irresistibly and roll itself
down again to the level, the shameless stone.
Once more he would go push and heave at it,
with sweat pouring down his limbs,
and a dust cloud mantling higher than his head"
(Book XI, 593–600).

Homer used Autolycus to cast the odium of knavery entirely on the grandfather and his ilk. In the name of Ulysses, the Greek Odysseus, which sounds like a short form of *odyssomenos,* "the hated", he heard overtones of the hatred of mankind for the cunning. He describes in Book XIX how the child Odysseus is given his name. Autolycus had come to Ithaca just after his grandson was born. It is not as much as hinted that he came *in order to* see what had come of the marriage of Anticleia, of her union with Laertes — or with . . .? Homer certainly does not mean us to think of Sisyphus! The nurse Eurycleia places the child on his grandfather's knees and suggests a name:

"Autolycus, invent a name
for this your dear daughter's son —
a child much prayed for" (Book XIX, 403–4).

Thus his name is to be "the much prayed for". Autolycus answers:

"Son-in-law and daughter, name him as I shall say.
Forasmuch as I come here a hated one
by many dwellers upon earth, women as well as men,
so call him Odysseus for the odiousness"

(Book XIX, 406–9).

Homer's Ulysses, Odysseus, is "the hated one" — but
hated unjustly. How he suffered, the hated man, while he
was the one they longed for at home! Did not even the
gods hate him? Or at least must it not appear so? Athene
affirms it. She takes the place of Alalcomene in the
Odyssey, as Homer, the great master of the play upon
words, gives us to understand by a verbal echo in
Book XIII, 318–19. There Ulysses, using the verb
corresponding to the name Alalcomene, reproaches the
goddess:

"Since that day I have not set eyes on you,
o daughter of Zeus, nor been aware of you
within my ship to *ward off harm*."

And in the first book, where the goddess reproaches Zeus
for the hard fate that has befallen Ulysses, she ends her
speech by asking Zeus how it is that he still "hates"
Odysseus.

THE ULYSSES OF THE ILIAD

Ulysses was detested in the Epic Cycle and in Greek
tragedy, and hateful was the Ulixes of Virgil. It would
certainly not have been so, if the cunning in the kernel
of the hero had not been intrinsically linked with the
menace it offered. The proof of its fascination and of its
powerful effects has been given most recently in Kazantzakis' *Odyssia*, with its Dysseus, the corsair. Homer
knew how to disclose a different sort of fascination in *his*
Ulysses from the first moment that he appears in the
Iliad. We may trace here an ascending line. Ulysses was
known to the poet like a living human being, no phantom,
but a man of flesh and blood, that very king of Ithaca
who was drawn so unwillingly into the Trojan War and
of whom so many strange stories were told, who had
even a goddess to protect him, who was often described
as no friend of men, but rather a great hater and much
hated, but who was not really so, but . . . we shall learn
to know him better!

His name is first mentioned incidentally in the quarrel
between Achilles, the young doomed demi-god, and
Agamemnon, the great king. His name appears among
the names of other kings who have to beware of Agamemnon's might, if he chose to display it. It appears also
incidentally among those capable of leading the embassy
to the insulted priest of Apollo, to placate him and his
god. The embassy is then in fact led by Ulysses, "the man
of great wisdom". He is honoured by this title when he
first appears in person in Homer. At the altar, he addresses

a few necessary words to the priest whose daughter he has brought back. The important thing was the return of the girl, not the speech. Later, the situation of the Greeks becomes precarious, when Agamemnon tests them to see how ready they are to return back home. The experiment turns out badly and all stream towards the ships. The goddesses who are hostile to Troy have to intervene, and Hera sends Pallas Athene. Ulysses, "the man that can match Zeus in prudence", is watching the scene, thoroughly embittered. The goddess, who is herself "the daughter of prudence" — the *metis* which constantly recurs in the epithets attached to Ulysses, — the prudence of "Zeus the giver of wisdom", comes to Ulysses and advises him of what is to be done. He sets quickly to work and restores order. His counterpart is the hateful and spiteful Thersites, who is always ready to fan the flames of discord. The common beggar Irus plays a similar rôle in the Odyssey. Ulysses *has* something to do with this inferior class of men, but Homer makes it clear that he acts on a higher level. He breaks in on the scene, belabours Thersites with his royal staff, makes a prudent and conciliatory speech and saves the situation.

Only then does Homer provide the occasion for a fuller description of Ulysses. King Priam of Troy is standing with Helen on a bastion of one of the gates of the beleaguered city, surveying the enemy. "Who is the man", he asks, "smaller by a head than Agamemnon, but with broader shoulders, like a ram with a thick fleece among the sheep?" Helen names him: he has grown up on Ithaca, he is known for his inventive mind and many wiles. The wise Antenor can describe him even more closely: how

he came with Menelaus to Troy to demand the return of Helen, Menelaus the taller of the two, but when they were sitting down, Ulysses the more impressive and dignified. When he rose to speak, he stood silent for a while, staring at the ground, his hand clutching his staff, like a simple, ignorant man overcome by suppressed anger. Then his voice rang out, deep-chested and strong, and his word lashed out like a storm of hail. Soon after this, we hear him rebuking Agamemnon sharply, when the king addresses him as though he were the notoriously detested Ulysses, with the words "master of villainous tricks, bent only on gain" (Book IV, 339). Agamemnon takes the rebuke in good part, because he knows that Ulysses is really kind at heart! He only advances to kill in the battle when a beloved comrade has been slain beside him and his anger has been aroused. His intention of attacking great heroes remains in the planning stage, and it is almost an accident when a Trojan is actually killed by him. And when he has started to flee along with the rest, not even the voice of Diomedes can call him back to battle.

Ulysses is surely once more in his element when he is with the embassy to Achilles, whose return to the battle is infinitely more important than his own. The first speech to soften Achilles is delivered by Ulysses. It says nothing that does not correspond to the truth, and one would expect Achilles to answer with a straight-forward yes or no. In spite of this, he storms at Ulysses in a way that is quite unintelligible if his words are really addressed to the man standing before him, and not to the detested Ulysses whom he still envisages: "I hate like the gates of hell a man with one thought in his heart and another on his lips! And now I tell you what seems best to me ..." (Book IX, 314).[6] Autolycus could of course have been hated like the gates of hell. Achilles had addressed Ulysses as the "offspring of Zeus", which he was through his grandfather, but also as the "man of many wiles", and also shows his distate for him by being more gracious to the two other envoys. Homer shows that even his Ulysses is still under a cloud, in the opinion of others, though not of the poet, who knows better. Homer was such a master of his art that he could bring this out with regard to a character not of his own creation, but to whom he had given a sort of re-birth.

The mastery of Homer is missing in the next section, Book X. Tradition has it that it existed independently of the Iliad for a long time — probably because it filled a gap in the subject matter, without being the work of the master. Homer had set the stage for the dreadful night, but it was still possible for a singer to skip the scene. A gap left by Homer remains a very significant fact. The author who tried to fill the gap was intent on saving the honour of Ulysses, who had ignored, or perhaps not heard, the rallying-cry of Diomedes when in full flight to the ships along with the other Greeks. So Ulysses is seen to volunteer very earnestly for the night adventure along with Diomedes and the author introduces the scene by calling him twice "the daring Ulysses". In Homer, too, he was "brave and daring" but up to this he had no special heroic feats to his credit.

With exaggerated courtesy Diomedes accepts him as his companion in the deed of murder. "We find it rather unpleasant", writes Karl Reinhardt in his posthumous book on the Iliad. "Compared with other fights, it lacks heroic fury and hatred, it is ennobled by no grand passion. The two mighty warriors have such an advantage over the miserable Dolon that the heroic element suffers ... The murder, to be sure, has its dangers. We should like to see Athene helping her favourites against something better than sleeping wretches."[7] Their intimate connexion with Athene is portrayed over-emphatically by a series of invocations to the goddess, who is further called "goddess of the spoils" to indicate a matter of fact connexion with what is afoot. The miserable Dolon had been sent out to spy for the Trojans. Captured by the two Greeks, he was promised his life at once by Ulysses, in return for full information about the Trojans. He agreed, and gave all the necessary information and more, and was still killed by Diomedes, cruelly, for the sake of cruelty. Thirteen of Dolon's comrades are then killed in their sleep, but Ulysses only helps by piling the bodies out of the way, so that the horses they mean to make off with will not shy at the corpses. It is not a very honourable service, but it is still perhaps a way to save the honour of Ulysses. There are paintings which go back to a different version in another epic, depicting Ulysses himself as "first murderer", beginning on Dolon. If this is the oldest form of the story, Homer omitted the night scene, to escape a dilemma: he would have had to show Ulysses either as cruel or undignified.

There was no need to save Ulysses' honour, according to Homer. He attained his glory and retained his dignity when catastrophe befell the Greeks. It was all inevitable.

Along with the vain heroic efforts of Agamemnon, those of Ulysses are sung, and finally his wounding. And what greater tribute could be paid to Ulysses than that the darkest hour of the war for the Greeks should be signalled again and again by the words: "Diomedes is wounded, and Ulysses and Agamemnon?" Ever since Achilles has withdrawn from the battle, these are the three greatest names among the Greeks, and the moral greatness of Ulysses is displayed to even greater advantage, when he restrains the great king from ordering re-embarkment. His name is mentioned for the last time in the Iliad, after the athletic contests, in which he distinguished himself. In a wrestling-match with *one* Ajax, he at least makes a draw of it, by using a clever grip against a stronger opponent. Against the other Ajax, he wins the prize in the race with the help of Athene, who causes his opponent to slip on some cow-dung and fall. The beaten runner cries out: "My foot is injured, thanks to the goddess who has never ceased to watch over Ulysses like a mother!" The spectators laugh, which proves that after all they did not think badly of the victory of the king of Ithaca. So we take farewell of "godlike" Ulysses in the Iliad, and we meet him again ten years later, willing to die, if first he could have even one glimpse of the smoke of Ithaca.

TEN YEARS LATER

To describe how the kings who fought against Troy were living in times of peace ten years later, was a conception of genius, which could not have occurred to any ordinary epic singer. For what was happening in Pylos and in Sparta, when the son of Ulysses went there to look for news of his father? Nothing for a singer who wished to sing of deeds rather than paint *life!* And now comes a poet to sing of situations in times of peace. It is very unlikely that any singer had undertaken this before Homer! This is the innovation which strikes us as so modern — as if the great age of the modern novel had already dawned. The Odyssey is like a novel in the way it developes its story. It does not try to revive the tension of the heroes' struggles — a life which provides a heightening of one's own existence, but a very one-sided and barren stimulus. It makes us enter into past history, to *enjoy life*. We see it as it once was in Pylos with Nestor (Plate 18), in Sparta with Menelaus and the lovely Helen (Plate 22), daughter of Zeus, or as it might have been, with the Phaeacians. We see life tense and exciting even on the little island of Ithaca — tense and exciting for us, who can survey it all with the eyes of the poet and the gods — when the man whom some longed for and some hated had arrived unknown and gradually revealed himself. It is not just hearing news, not just listening to picturesque tales: it is a way of sharing life as if some magic had made this possible.

The Odyssey's own special magic lies between the charm of the fairy-tale and the spell of the great novel, which bewitches the reader by initiating him into the existence of other men. No magic radiates from the Iliad. It rather breaks a spell, in so far as bringing everything down to the level of man means the removal of a spell. Charm or spell border on the lie, though it is happiness and blessing to have one's existence thus enlarged. The joy that they bring with them, even when they serve a lie, is reserved in the Iliad to the gods: Zeus, the king of the gods, is bewitched, deceived and distracted by them. Hera, the queen of the gods, bewitches him, to help the Greeks in their hour of need when Diomedes, Ulysses, and Agamemnon have been wounded. But she distrusts her own strength, and uses the power of the goddess of love to work a spell. She borrows Aphrodite's "embroidered leather belt" and wears it at her bosom. For it is not the cincture which one looses, but a glittering magic belt that provokes the desire of the man. So she comes to Zeus, who is watching the battle for Troy from the top of Mount Ida and bewitches him to make love. He surrounds himself and Hera with golden clouds. Grass and flowers spring up from the earth, to make a couch for the loving pair. The magic is complete.

To be bewitched is basically an aphrodisiacal experience, and the natural magic of love existed before any magic was "made". The heroes of the Iliad experience no great bewitchment with the women they take as booty and when, by grace and favour of Aphrodite, a man finds happiness with some semi-divine woman, like Paris with Helen, Homer does not let us forget the misery that accompanies even this charm. Helen is full of shame and self-reproach, as she stands on the bastion and points out the Greek princes to Priam. She resists the goddess when she comes to lead her back to Paris. Aphrodite makes the terrible threat that she will abandon her, and Helen is forced to yield to the goddess. If we translate exactly the word which Homer uses for Aphrodite, "daimon", this is what the poet says: "The god who was her destiny led her on."

We enter the action of the Odyssey from on high, from the assembly of the gods (Plate 6), where we have learnt everything: where Ulysses is detained, why he may not return home. Poseidon (Plates 5 and 34), the god of the seas, is angry with him because he blinded Polyphemus, the son of the god (Plates 57 and 60). We also learn what will happen now. To be in a position to know all that may suit a magician like Prospero but not the ordinary man. Yet the epic poets, and after them the authors of our great novels for centuries, automatically claimed such a situation for themselves and their readers. The epic singers recounted what they had heard, and if they knew still more, it was the inspiration of the Muse, not their own magic powers or omniscience! With Homer, the gods become visible, and we do not feel we are believing a sorcerer, but we are not allowing him the right to tell us what only a god could know, as though this claim were obvious. We are believing his *vision*. If we do not, his work falls to pieces. It splits up into what is credible and what is incredible or at least hopelessly antiquated.

But his poetry is one and indivisible. It is no more antiquated than the storm conjured up by Prospero's wand. It is just as fresh and effective. We are of course in a very special situation when we accompany a goddess from Mount Olympus to Ithaca, but this corresponds precisely to the opening situation of the Odyssey, the region between the fairy-tale and the great novel. We are there to join Telemachus, Ulysses's son who has grown up in his father's absence, and to stay with him for the four songs which are devoted to Telemachus, making him the hero of this novel. These are the "Telemachia" which allows the Odyssey to begin with a journey and introduces us to a world long vanished in Homer's day, before we set out on our travels with the wandering Ulysses.

The meaning of the Telemachia is given with the young man's journey itself. It begins when he is stirred to action, after having looked on hopelessly and passively while his mother's importunate suitors took over his father's house and consumed his inheritance; and it makes a man of him. This aspect of the Telemachia, the pedagogical one, has always been recognized. It was brought out by "Les aventures de Télémaque", the edifying novel which it inspired Bishop Fénelon to write in the French classical era, and by Karl Reinhardt in our own day, who called it the "aristia", the finest feats, of Athene, and characterized this epic within an epic as follows: "It begins with the fact that Athene can no longer bear to look at the misery of her hero. But what does she do? With all her various apparitions, her instructive counsels and providential interventions, all she accomplishes is that those who should meet find themselves farther than ever from each other! Telemachus' journey was not only useless, but it brought a new and dire peril upon the house of Ulysses. But what looks like the malice of fortune's whims is used by the wisdom of the goddess to bring father and son together, not just in the flesh, but inwardly and spiritually, when the son is ripe enough for the meeting with his father. He can only find so happily when he has travelled and sought, when, with the help of the goddess, he has experienced an 'awakening', something that does not begin without self-distrust and the question — Am I too like that?"[8]

But the journey is a journey into that glorious vanished world, whose kings waged the unhappy war against Troy. It is now ten years later, when happiness may be said to have returned to the palaces, though not to all. The land of the Phaeacians, where Ulysses was cast ashore, was indeed a still happier place. It lay quite close to the seats of the gods, who showed themselves manifestly to the Phaeacians, feasted with them at the sacrificial banquets, sat beside them on their couches and did not conceal themselves when a traveller met them on the way. Help comes unexpectedly from a family friend, someone never seen or hardly known; the friend is suddenly seen no more a bird rises into the sky and — that was undoubtedly a "god" in Homer's times, what we might call "a divine event". Sappho, the great visionary among the Greek poets after Homer, still had the feeling that the goddesses she invoked were close to her — the feeling Ulysses must have had as Athene appeared, in the second book of the Iliad. The youth Telemachus was not capable of such a feeling, but seeing the bird fly up, he sensed the divine event. The "divine events" staged by Athene place him in a situation between that of the Phaeacians and that of the ordinary world. The magic surrounding the journey of the son is a lighter, more natural one — very different from the more perilous, serious, and far graver magic which weighs on the voyages of the father.

The presence of Athene — which we are allowed to recognize from the start — took the form of two friends of his father, Mentes and Mentor, and accompanied Telemachus with its cool, clear, luminous atmosphere till he reached Pylos. There Nestor sees the bird fly up, and recognizes what a blessed guest has been brought to his door. But what a happy moment of recognition for one who knows the old man from the Iliad and finds him still so loquacious (Plates 11 and 18)! And what happiness for us, if we have ever been to Pylos and have seen the foundations of the Mycenaean palace and the landscape around it! The atmosphere changes in the narrative of Homer and becomes more like the warm brightness which today bathes the countryside. There is a breath of the aphrodisiacal too, though nothing erotic takes place. Telemachus finds the king and his followers on the wonderful strand, on account of which Homer calls the place "sandy Pylos". They offer there a great sacrifice to Poseidon: the people divide up into nine sections of nine times five hundred men, and slaughter nine times nine black steers. This ceremony, with its memorable figures based on the number nine, which corresponds in fact to a group of place-names on clay tablets from Pylos, can well have run a similar course in the same place in Mycenaean times.[9]

In the Homeric description two elements in particular seem to go back to traditional memories. One is the gleaming white banks of stone, dripping with oil, before the door, which have not been found by the excavators, and the other is Telemachus' bath. This took place the next day, between the sacrifice and the banquet in honour of the guest. The sacrificial meal was still going on when Telemachus was led back to the palace for the bath. Maid-servants are to help Telemachus at his bath in the palace of Menelaus, when he comes to Sparta. Heroes are always bathed by women. Here at Pylos this ceremony is performed by the youngest of the king's daughters, the beautiful Polycaste. Ulysses refuses to allow himself to be washed by the Phaeacien maidens, or even to bathe in their presence, since he supposes they are not slaves, but friends of the princess. In the palace of Pylos the bath-room (Plate 20) served another purpose besides washing. It was used for ecstatic hours of a luxurious cult of life. The excavators were surprised to find a double container for wine-jars built into the room with the bath, and in the bath itself a broken drinking-vessel.

This reality makes Homer's description pale by comparison, though the use of bath may still fit it very well. Homer's picture seems like geometric art compared to Mycenaean though he also conveys the impression of an idealized reminiscence. There are many reasons for thinking that epic poetry was being chanted at the time when such palaces were still standing. One proof of this is the way in which the archaeological discoveries seem to corroborate Homer. He is giving *his* picture of life in those earlier days, not of life in his own time, when he says that Telemachus was attended by a princess and left the bath-room "with the body of an immortal". Descriptions in prose, giving the names and adjectives for the works of art, could not have survived long enough for Homer to have drawn this magic from them. But epic diction preserved something of them.

Carried by Nestor's horses over the mountain pass of the Taygetus range (Plate 21), Telemachus finds a double wedding going on in the palace of Menelaus. The royal house is bathed in a warmer glow of love ever since Helen has returned to it. How different now is Homer's description of the semi-divine woman! When she stood on the bastions of Troy, she had seemed to be the victim of a demonic force powerless against the might of the goddess. Now she still calls herself shameless, as she looks back on those days, but she appears like a second Aphrodite. As she enters the lofty hall, Homer compares her with the virgin goddess Artemis because the effect she still has on all is like that of the maidenly goddess. But if we had a vase-painting of her entrance, showing her surrounded by titled maidservants carrying a chair, a carpet, a silver basket, and a golden spindle, we should hardly doubt that it depicted the goddess of love herself! When men are weeping for Ulysses, she like an enchantress puts something in their wine that restores their gaiety. She weeps with them, but as she tells of Ulysses, she gives a glimpse of the unpredictability of her real character, her dangerous aphrodisiacal nature. She had been acquainted with a sly and bold Ulysses. She had only had a distant view of him from the bastion, but she was able to recognize him when he slipped into Troy disguised as a beggar (Plate 23), to prepare his stratagem of bringing in the wooden horse. Helen took him in and bathed him, because the maidservants were not to see the hidden beauty of the hero,

and then he entrusted to her the plan of the Greeks. She already had a change of heart, and Ulysses's story of the Trojans massacred as he sallied out filled her with joy. Still, when the horse was already inside the city, she put the Greek princes shut up within it to the test. She called out to each hero, using the voice of his wife, playing with the lives of the men in a senseless game. Ulysses had prevented them from breaking out too soon.

All this is Homer's supplement to his Iliad. How the Greeks broke out of the wooden horse (Plates 24 and 48) and captured Troy is sung by Demodocus among the Phaeacians. The mood which is generally recognized to be that of the Odyssey appears in the next morning. Menelaus, coming like a god from the arms of Helen, finds Telemachus in the porch where he has slept, sits down beside him and tells of his adventure on the island of Pharos off Egypt. There he had succeeded in capturing the crafty sea-god Proteus among his sea-calves, with the help of his daughter, a kindly sea-goddess, and so learned all that had happened at sea to the Greeks on their homeward way. And thus Telemachus also learns from Menelaus that his father is living with the nymph Calypso on her distant island, sad of heart and against his will, since he has lost his ship and his companions. Now the son can return home. But he can no longer do so without peril. This journey makes him worthy of his father, but the reason is just this: that he too begins to hover between life and death. The suitors are lying in wait for him behind a little island off Ithaca (Plate 27), intent upon murdering him. They will fail, no doubt, but the menace is part of the authentic atmosphere of the Odyssey.

OUR ULYSSES

We meet Ulysses for the first time in the Odyssey on the island of Calypso. He has been brought as low as a hero can be, short of death. Year after year he sits and gazes out to sea and lets his tears flow (Plate 30). He is surrounded by magic that can bewitch him no more, since the nymph no longer pleases him. No magic is aphrodisiac enough when the woman only wants love, like a soporific for her nightly sleep, and the man is bored and sated with it. It reads as naturally as our great novels, and we have the same initiation into the suffering of another existence, even of a divine one. Since Calypso is a real goddess and Homer's vision expanded the world around him to take in the gods and the mythic figures of menace and bewitchment, in all of which destruction lurked.

Not even a goddess, not even if she was the secure haven after all the perils that beset Ulysses, could satisfy him, because that was not his own choice. He wished for his own island, his own haven, his own couch with the wife that he had wooed. Here we have our Ulysses. It is not a matter of a ship-wrecked sailor who has found a lovely and devoted mistress on an exotic island. It is a myth depicting man. The Ulysses image shows man in full possession of his spirit and personality, faced with the numberless masks of death, all of which he penetrates. So too the Penelope image shows us woman, likewise in full possession of her spirit and personality, loyal to what she has chosen. The myth of these two is what makes and fills the Odyssey for us, while the original myth of Calypso is given by Homer in such a meagre form that it is hard to grasp its full meaning.

CALYPSO

Who was Calypso? The sea with its coasts and islands formed a special world for the Greeks, and they fixed its various aspects in the forms of goddesses with transparent names, or again, dissolved them into whole crowds of nymphs. One of these aspects was Calypso, the sheltering goddess of the cave. But her kindly protection was only a ruse. The rescue was only apparent, she really aimed at the destruction of the ships borne along by the stormy waves. Homer calls her "the cunning" and thought of her as "bent on destruction"[10], much more than her father Atlas, the mountain god in the far west who supported the sky. Homer probably also thought of her as having the high gift, like the sea-god Proteus, not Atlas watching from on high, of knowing all the depths of the sea. The secrets of the water were just as treacherous as the cave of the lonely goddess who dwelt at the navel of the seas. This must be far to the west, as the "Atlantic" origin of Calypso indicates: Atlas was therefore her father. The place must have been far beyond any distances that could be given in terms of days of travel, if "navel" means the central point of the sea, just as "the navel of the earth", as at Delphi, meant the centre of the world. For the sea was so wide that it stretched from the west to the east, and the sun travelled it along his nightly way, longer or shorter, from evening to morning. The isle of Calypso did not lie in perpetual darkness. It had its days and nights, but it certainly lay near the last points where such changes still occurred. Hence one vase-painting portrays Calypso holding out a bowl to the serpent which guards the apple-tree of the Hesperides, with its golden apples of immortality, the fruits of the night. Calypso could also have made Ulysses immortal. We must likewise consider that "navel" could mean not only the centre of a surface, of earth or sea, but also the point of juncture of the higher and the lower spheres of the world.[11] In Eleusis the surface of the earth could have been linked to the depths of the earth by the navel, and at Calypso's home, the surface to the depths of the sea.

Paradoxically, this navel was a central point — on the rim. Strange too is the Homeric description of Calypso's cave. Everything around it was bewitching, but the singing birds had not flown so far, and so they could not give life to such trees as are actually found in north Africa, by the Atlas mountain. Homer only gives the names of birds of prey, of the land and of the sea. There is a vine laden with grapes, springs flowing in four directions, thus indicating here a central point of the world, and blossoms springing luxuriantly from the ground. It is all so beautiful that Hermes, the messenger of the gods, stands still in amazement. We sense the loneliness that overcame not only Ulysses but Calypso according to Homer. She is indeed a great goddess, ruling at the edge and at the centre. But still she is only an unhappy woman, or, if we keep to the mythological expression, a nymph neglected by all the gods. "You have had no habit of visiting me", she tells Hermes (Plate 29), seeming to suspect that his visits to Circe had been more frequent. She reproaches the Olympian gods with being intolerant when a goddess chooses a mortal man as husband. And

it is only orders from above that make her an unambiguous benefactor of Ulysses. Then she helps him to build his raft (Plate 32).

So Ulysses leaves the brink behind him — the brink of immortality, the brink of death? It is the brink of *life* orientated in another direction. He sails on his raft (Plate 33), a favourable wind in its sail, for eighteen days. The time given is that which a sailing-ship takes from the Atlantic gates of the Mediterranean to a line drawn from north to south from the Ionian Isles. But just as the isle of Calypso did not lie on the geographical Atlantic Ocean, but on one that opened out on the mythic world, so too the Mediterranean of Ulysses. The brink is everywhere, all over the whole sea — the brink of abysses. Hovering always over an abyss: that was the voyage of Ulysses, not only back from Calypso, to Scheria, the land of the Phaeacians, but right from the start, from Troy to Calypso.

The Iliad was Homer's poem about the heroic life,[12] a life contrasted with a single, ultimate death which was its opposite pole. The Odyssey is his poem of a life penetrated by a death which is continually and everywhere present. The world of the Odyssey is that world of life in suspense, which touches death as closely as the front of a tapestry its back. It is a world with backgrounds and undergrounds, yawning chasms behind and beneath it, which are as much part of it as it is itself. Ulysses is poised above them continually. The sea, ambiguous beyond all else, from which one day death is to come for Ulysses, though not in the Odyssey, is the primary place of the abysses where men hover between life and death. It is the place where many men are in that situation and not only Ulysses. Countless Greeks, who had listened to the Odyssey, and to earlier songs and tales of the king of Ithaca who only reached home ten years after the fall of Troy, knew the situation from their own experience. They were the Greeks who had sailed to found their colonies in the east, on the shores of the Aegean and the Black Sea, and in the west, in Italy, France, and Spain. To be drawn to the unknown, even when it is deadly to experience the terrors of its mortal perils: this is the experience of the explorer and the colonist. Homer may have met with it, on the scene of the Odyssey, in such a way that a well-known coast or island, close at hand and safe, could have appeared to him at the same time as something dangerous and unattainable.

THE PHAEACIANS

That Ulysses reached the "navel of the seas", the point of the sea most distant from all directions, is to be attributed no doubt to the stories and songs which had their origin in Ithaca. By the introduction of the Phaeacians, a mythical race who took over the rôle of Hermes,[13] the escort and guide of souls, distance could be abolished. For Homer, the Phaeacians are no longer what their name meant, "the dark people". They are rather the swiftest and surest sailors, who freely bring all travellers home, though in other respects their behaviour towards men is not very friendly! Or more correctly: they once brought everyone home, but in Homer they bring home only those who have been cast up on their coasts. This restriction was made, perhaps earlier than Homer, in the stories of seafarers who no longer paid attention to the simple, original meaning of the name — though the meaning lay close to the surface, as close as death is in every moment of life, not just at sea, but everywhere. Death is always far and near, and so are the Phaeacians of Homer, who hide their darkness behind a brightness that is still in a way obscure. For it seems to be close at hand, perhaps on an island not far from Ithaca. But in reality this brightness can be found no more. It has been removed to a distance that can be only covered in dreams.

As Ulysses is swimming towards it, the island of the Phaeacians appears to him to be like a shield in the sea. This is an indication of its contours which would fit countless other islands. But its name, Scheria, defines it more closely. It means "the one that links up". It would have this name, if it were one of a row of islands that linked up as it were with another. This is not spoken of in the Odyssey, but Ulysses can invent the fictitious story that he travels on foot before he is escorted home by the Phaeacians from their country to the friendly Thesproti on the mainland, and from them to Dodona, the oracle of Zeus in Epirus. This was easily done from Corcyra, the present-day Corfu. The Philhellene scholar and archaeologist Friedrich Thiersch and many others saw in Corfu the land of the Phaeacians (Plates 36, 37, 40, and 43). "All the scenery attests the accuracy of the Homeric landscape" was the impression of an English traveller.[14] Thiersch wrote in 1830: "We find everything there: the situation of the city of the Phaeacians, the river where Ulysses landed and where Nausicaa washed her laundry, the double harbour, and in front of one of them, now sifted up, a rock like a ship, which could have occasioned the well-known legend in the epic."[15] Fifty years later Ferdinand Gregorovius wrote: "It gave the impression of a paradise floating over Elysian coasts, a soft airy idyll by the sea, still wrought in the grand style. I thought I really stood on one of the islands of the blessed and breathed the divine air of bliss. Perhaps it was only the magic of Homer's poetry that made this picture of an island seem even more beautiful than the coasts of Sicily."[16]

Just as in the case of Ithaca Homer had here too turned an island into a mythic image. He had paid no attention to exactness, and yet he had somehow described the true island of Ulysses. In the same way he transformed this great island into the mythic land of the Phaeacians. The guiding line of the narrative in Book XIII makes it clear that he abandons his own lofty view of the gods, no miracle-workers in his eyes, in favour of the beliefs of the Corcyrans, the Corfiotes of his day. The Phaeacians have brought Ulysses home, like a dead man on a ghost-ship, and set him ashore, out of the dangers of the sea. Then Poseidon learns of the rescue of the man whom he had refused to release from his realm of perpetual menace — the menace of death at sea. In that realm not even Athene could help Ulysses, but only a kindly goddess of the sea, Leucothea, whose veil sustained the swimmer for

two days and two nights in the water. The Phaeacians broke for him the spell of the power of Poseidon. In Book XIII they must expiate this.

Poseidon wishes to destroy the ship of the Phaeacians on its way home and prevent them from ever again flouting his will be rescuing a man. A great mountain is to surround and lie upon their city. The destruction of the ship would have been in the style of Homer. How often had such things happened already! But Zeus proposes that the ship should be turned into a rock, which is what happens: a miracle, a lowering of the Homeric level. Why? Only because the Corcyrans of Homer's day were already pointing to a rock shaped like a ship off their coast. The idea of a mountain inside which the Phaeacians are to disappear is also un-Homeric; so much so, that Homer cannot bring himself to describe the miraculous process. He leaves the Phaeacians trying to placate Poseidon with a sacrifice. There was probably a story in existence which told how the characteristic two-peaked mountain, from which Corfu later took its name, hid the Phaeacians. Homer may have heard the story on the island itself, like the story of the ship changed into rock. Homer also perpetuates a way of speaking that could only have been in use among the earliest colonists of Corcyra, the Eretrians from Euboea.[17] The Corinthians only came in the eighth century B.C., following the Eretrians. Now Homer makes the Phaeacians speak of Euboea as the land most distant from them. Only colonists coming from there could do this, in memory of their ancient homeland.

The tradition that Corcyra once belonged to those friends of the gods, the Phaeacians, seems to be as old as the first Greek colonization of the island, in the ninth century B.C. by the Eretrians. It was maintained by the colonists from Corinth and all through antiquity. There was even a shrine of Alcinous, king of the Phaeacians, in classical times, which is — at least partly — due to Homer. He undoubtedly came to Corcyra, to give songs of the Phaeacians firm footing. We cannot picture him in his old age as anything but a great composer of a novel in song. He made Scheria out of Corcyra and moved it further than Ithaca into the region of the mythic, and in another sense. For a long time the Phaeacians do not know whether Ulysses came to them from the east or from the west. And where did he come from? Troy was in the east, the island of Calypso the daughter of Atlas was in the west. The coasts and islands where death had menaced him and where he had lost all his companions lay in the wide ocean — as though there were no mainland north of Epirus — of which Calypso guarded the navel. If that central point was likewise the "edge", then the Phaeacians ruled the other edge. They were a marginal people, between gods, giants, and Cyclopes on the one hand, and men on the other, with faults and virtues that made them a higher type of Greek, living in a country in which the luxurient aspects of Corfu can be recognized. Corcyra has another aspect, which menaces sailors with death, its steep, towering west coast, which resembles the "White Rock" along which Hermes led the souls of the suitors to the asphodel meadows of the underworld, in the last book of the Odyssey. When compared with this, the side of the island facing the mainland seems to be the aspect of Corcyra that offers life. It seems as though made for the Phaeacians, a superior sort of Greece with Hades in the background.

To be with the Phaeacians was for Ulysses almost to be already at home. It was no doubt his last and greatest temptation, not quite without an aphrodisiacal magic. But what a contrast to the worn-out magic of Calypso or the imperious magic of Circe! The only thing that seems non-Greek about the Phaeacians is the calm, decisive power of the queen Arete (whose name means "the prayed-to"), compared to that of king Alcinous. The place held by the lady of the house is more important than that of Ulysses's mother or wife, but it is still not matriarchal. It is against the matriarchal order of things that Arete should be the niece of her husband the king. So too Persephone was the niece and wife of Hades. A superior way of Greek life among the Phaeacians borders on the matriarchal but does not enter it. On the margin of the Greek way of being showing it on a higher level, stands Nausicaa, the king's daughter, radiating *her* magic. If he married her, as all expected, Ulysses would be inserted into the royal family and would one day become through her — this too a matriarchal trait — king of the Phaeacians. This was one element of the seduction which Ulysses withstood. But the mightiest, and the one with the most direct impact, is still the special magic of this maiden, an element stemming basically from Aphrodite, but also from Artemis in the brilliance of its fascination. Ulysses' attitude in face of Nausicaa's charm forms a climax in the poetry of Homer. Ulysses says he wonders whether he is in the presence of a mortal maiden or the virgin goddess herself, and this is no pure flattery. It is an expression of that knowledge of gods and men which is proper to Homer in the Odyssey.

The moment when he was tempted to become the husband of Nausicaa and king among the Phaeacians was a climax in the life of Ulysses, just before the abysmal depths he was to plump when he reached Ithaca. When he seized the greatest discus and threw it farthest, he anticipated in a way his shots with the bow, the definitive climax in Ithaca. When he is telling before Alcinous the story of his voyage from Troy to Calypso, he is looking back from his high point of vantage on a series of throughs and crests which gave his voyages over the length and breath of the seas a third dimension in depth. They were no longer the surface travel of a sailor's, but plunges into depths and chasms that took him down to the underworld. Combined into a narrative told in one night, they form a sixth of the whole epic. Ulysses travels about, first with twelve ships, then with one, in a descending spiral. After he has visited the world of the dead, he is robbed of his closest companions by death. We must follow both lines, that of his travels and that of his gradual isolation, till he is stripped of all but his naked existence with Calypso. Together they compose what we have earlier called 'being poised over abysses'.

FROM TROY TO CALYPSO

At the first landing-place on their travels, among the Ciconians in Thrace, almost opposite Troy, Ulysses and his companions were still a band of impudent raiders, and apart from Ulysses, fickle and careless enough to turn to carousing at the first opportunity. "Appetites" is what they are — governed by forces that Ulysses does not underestimate. But these companions are only there so to speak, to be themselves and to let it be seen, by contrast, what kind of a man Ulysses is. They serve to describe what he is not, for he is the man whose spirit must suffer for the unreasonable ways of others. They have to pay for it too, because six of them fall at once from each ship under the onslaught of the Ciconians. The journey proceeds, southwards, to a land where the voyagers taste the intoxicating delights procured by eating a flower which Homer calls the lotos (Plate 53 and 54). The sailors who eat it have to be dragged back to the ships by force, because they think no more of going home. From the very start home and life and a conscious existence, the only one worthy of a human being, are all linked up. Ulysses knows better than any of his companions what suffering of the spirit is. It is not only hunger.

The school where Ulysses learned to understand his new situation, so different from that of a hero of the Iliad, was the cave of the Cyclops Polyphemus. The winds that carried him away from the land of the lotos-eaters did not actually drive him ashore there, with his twelve ships. He could have sailed by the land of the Cyclopes, these dangerous giants with a single eye in their forehead (Plate 57). On a little off-shore island he found enough goats to feed his crew. But he was curious, he hoped to be honoured by presents and he was full of his position as a great man at home and among his countrymen at Troy. So he was enticed to land, and found himself faced with a strange death in this strange and savage country. It was the way he had to learn that he really was what he gave himself out to be, in a moment of inspiration that is precisely: "Nobody". Only, no doubt, he always possessed the source from which his inspiration came: his spirit. And this strange death, at the hands of a gigantic cannibal, in a cave reeking of cheese and the milk and dung of sheep and goats — what a chance it offered too, for the resounding triumph of the inventive spirit! But till it reached the stage where the Cyclops had made himself drunk with the wine brought by Ulysses and so could be blinded (Plates 59 and 60), the companions were being devoured two by two (Plate 58). And at the very end, as he was escaping from the maw of death with a few companions (Plates 61 and 62), boastfulness led Ulysses to commit the blunder of calling back his name to Polyphemus, so that the blinded giant was able to complain to his father Poseidon who from that time on never ceased to rage against Ulysses.

Ulysses had learned his lesson, but his men never did. Sailing from the land of the Cyclopes, they were driven ashore on the island of Aeolus (Plates 64 and 65), the god of the winds, who gave them the contrary winds, shut up in a wine-skin, to take along with them. While Ulysses slept, with Ithaca already in sight on the horizon,

his companions let them loose, and all the ships were driven back by the winds and carried to the Laestrygonians (Plate 66), cannibal giants as big as mountains, with still greater riches in flocks than Polyphemus. There already Ulysses was prudent enough to remain on watch with his ship, in the rear-guard. He managed in this way to escape with his crew, and no one else. The survivors were still able to console each other by saying: "We do not come to the land of shades before the day that destiny has set!" But still they reached the land of shades in spite of man's destiny. They had to reach the realm of death, not only of strange death caused by ogres and Sirens, Scylla and Charybdis, but of the common death of all mortals. Without this the Odyssey would not be the poetry of humanity which it is.

When Ulysses learned from Circe that he must visit the realm of the dead, "his loving heart gave way". He sat on the couch which the goddess and enchantress shared with him, and rolled to and fro weeping, such were the depths of sorrow to which he was brought. Ulysses had gained Circe's bed, his companions only their pig-sties. The last ship left had made its way from the Laestrygonians to the island of Aeaea, "the eastern isle" where Circe dwelt, the daughter of the sun. Perhaps this meaning, of "eastern", had been forgotten, when Aeaea was placed in the west, which happened in the early archaic period, even before Hesiod, and identified with the promontory on the Tyrrhenian Sea now called Monte Circeo (Plate 67)? Homer gives up indicating the direction east or west, after he has told how Ulysses almost reached Ithaca from the island of Aeolus, with the west wind behind him, and was then driven back and carried away further to the Laestrygonians. He thought of Calypso as dwelling on the western rim, and he may have thought of Circe on the eastern: but the important thing was that whatever direction it took, the way from her isle led to the all-encircling Ocean and to the sunless heavens under which the Cimmerians dwelt in perpetual mists. And from Circe too one could reach the underworld! First Ulysses and his companions (changed back to human form after having been changed into swine) spent a whole year with the daughter of the sun. She transformed men into wild beasts (Plates 69, 70, and 71) — only the companions of Ulysses were turned into swine — but Ulysses had been made proof against this crude magic by the plant *moly* (Plate 73), which Hermes had shown him. But had he really been defended by the *moly*? The tales told before Homer undoubtedly said so. But Homer gives no indication that the counter-charm has been used, for instance, in the magic drink offered by Circe. Instead, as I translate it, the goddess says to Ulysses (Plate 75): "How firmly seated must be your indomitable spirit!"[18] The word "spirit" *noos,* an older word than *pneuma* in this sense, is used as in the case of the soothsayer Teiresias, to whom the queen of the underworld had granted the possession of his mind, even among the dead (X, 494).

To meet the blind prophet Teiresias, so that he can foretell Ulysses his destiny, and so that we too can learn that wanderings on the mainland await him, and death from the sea, after his home-coming, the journey must be made to the farthest limits, to that border of the underworld (Plate 76) where the smell of sacrificial blood can at once attract all the dead. The whole world of spirits streams to the offerer: Ulysses is in Hades, though he offers his sacrifice only in a grove dedicated to the queen of the underworld (Plate 78). Teiresias (Plate 81), however, is only one reason for the journey to Hades. There are also the encounters: with his mother Anticleia, and with the heroes of the Iliad (Plate 80), Agamemnon, Aias and Achilles. The most typical examples of punishment, like Sisyphus and Tantalus, fixed images among the streaming world of ghosts, must also be seen, when one has gone so far. But why the endless stream of mothers of heroes, which crowds out everything else? "It seems that a concept of humanity is first formed in face of death" says Karl Reinhardt,[19] very correctly. "At any rate, this is the first poem that sings of humanity, and that not merely because of the multitudes it evokes . . . With the train of heroines, their hero sons also pass by, a whole procession of illustrious and unhappy destinies." But this does not tell everything about this poem of humanity, the Odyssey. It is not just heroines who pass by, women who thanks to gods and men had heroes for sons. They are mothers. Ulysses has pressed on to the mothers, to the root of humanity, down to which — or up to which — Goethe brings his Faust. So Ulysses goes back to Circe, who has become his divine counsellor after being a baneful sorceress, like the nymph Egeria in the Roman saga of King Numa.

Following her counsel, Ulysses now goes on in greater personal security — into utter isolation. The song of the Sirens (Plate 83) which for all others is a musical death, can be heard by Ulysses, bound to the mast (Plate 84), while his companions, their ears stopped by wax, refuse to unloose him. They obey him between Scylla and Charybdis, in the straits between the visible and the invisible monster, though six of them must fall victim to the six dogs' jaws of Scylla (Plates 86–92), when they choose the lesser evil: Charybdis would have swallowed up the whole ship. On Thrinacria, the island of the Sun-god, where his three hundred and fifty oxen, and as many sheep, were grazing, obedience and loyalty come to an end (Plates 93 and 94). After a month of contrary winds from south and east, during which they had nothing to eat but the birds they could bring down and the fish they could catch, the Ulysses' men raid the cattle, which were, after all, very manifest symbols of the days of the year, the days of man's life. To pay for it, they are all deprived of *their* day, the day of home-coming. Such is the will of the Sun-god, Helios. As the ship sails on, Zeus destroys it. Ulysses alone can save himself, on two beams tied together — and comes to Calypso.

THE TURN OF THE YEAR IN ITHACA

After the night taken up by the story, another day goes by, with the sacrificial banquet and the song of Demodocus, for the Phaeacians who bring travellers home are sailors of the night. The next day Ulysses wakes up on Ithaca (Plates 7 and 96). Athene welcomes him (Plate 98) and disguises him, reveals his homeland and gives him directions. What happens then is already outside the realm of magic — except that the goddess changes Ulysses into a beggar (Plate 102) by magic (which is only the materializing of his actual condition and may even occasionally be forgotten), or ends the transformation (which is not a miracle), gives light to the father and the son for their secret work by night, and terrifies the avengers of the suitors during the battle by a cry which commands peace. All this, and the signs noted and interpreted by the seer Theoclymenus (introduced unnoticed for the occasion), is quite natural for a poet and for a world where vision like Homer's is natural, since it does not dissolve the natural order. In spite of everything, we have the irresistible impression that we are reading a novel in the songs about the happenings on Ithaca. Their length — half the epic — and the absence of great warlike deeds or seafaring adventures, forces us finally to take the same attitude as when reading a great novel. Ulysses appears definitely as the first hero of a novel, Ithaca as the final scene of a novel which starts the novels in literature.

We see everything at the nadir. Ulysses is at the lowest point of his fortunes, an old beggar, the guest of the swineherd at first (Plate 101), not of the palace. And the souls of those who remained true to him have also hit bottom. All this is palpable, and it is the decisive reason for treating this final episode as the first example of great novel-writing. We are dismayed to see that even the most loyal people, like the swineherd or Penelope, no longer believe that Ulysses will ever come back. Ulysses may tell the most persuasive falsehoods to say that he is already close at hand. He can swear, on the second last day of the year, that he will be there on the last. All he does is to make himself suspect as a deceiver. Only the aged nurse Eurycleia, who feels his scar, ceases to doubt (Plates 106 and 107). He is surrounded by hardened disbelief, which is rather characteristic in a sacred story about the re-appearance of a god no longer believed in. In addition there is the disbelief of Telemachus, who has been brought back safe by Athene after a journey beset by menaces. Ulysses discloses himself to him in the swineherd's hut, but Telemachus will not believe in his mother. He does not trust Penelope. Her apparent coquetry towards the suitors, indeed her passivity itself, was enough to make the son deeply jealous and secretly disturbed. Penelope behaves like someone walking in her sleep — while wide awake. She does not consciously believe, not even in her great and unmistakable dream, but unconsciously she still acts in such a way that all she does, seemingly moved by womanly moods and unpredictability, is for the benefit of Ulysses. It seems as though she had agreed with him upon a secret plan, which will assure him of victory over the suitors. Athene works in her — but how naturally!

At this point in the story, nature, too, has reached the lowest depths and finds itself at a turning-point. Storm and rain make the dark night terrible (XIV, 457). There can be no doubt that it is winter. The day on which Ulysses, after the crude humiliation in his own palace, receives his heavy bow and reveals himself as the archer returned home to take vengeance (Plate 108), was the day of the winter solstice in Ithaca, and also the first day of the month after the new moon, a feast of the divine archer Apollo. Apart from this we know nothing of the calendar of Ithaca about 800 B.C. But the careful details given by Homer make it clear that Ulysses' home-coming took place on such a last and first day, a day of a change in the moon as well as the sun, such as only happened every eight years. Is the Odyssey, then, not a novel, but a humanized nature-myth, in which Ulysses has taken the place of the pre-Homeric Apollo, who is in a way the same as the sun and is linked in a brotherly way with the moon? At any rate, the word "but" is incorrect; myth and novel are not mutually exclusive. The novel, where we meet it in its later prose form, in Hellenistic times, from the first century B.C. on, shows close contact with sacred stories, and betrays its mythic origin.[20]

If the story of Ulysses' home-coming on Ithaca was humanized nature-myth, this does not in the least prevent us from seeing the Odyssey as the primordial novel, becoming in its second half even a great and authentic novel. But what was Homer's achievement? Was it that he showed here the human element of an already existing god, as elsewhere he brought out the human traits of the gods whom he called "eternal"? Or was it the other way round, so that in Ulysses' victory on Ithaca he enabled the man of *noos*, of spirit, to reach his goal as a second Apollo? The latter seems to be true. Homer takes particular care to explain the merciless vengeance which Ulysses takes on his wife's suitors (Plates 109, 110, and 111) and the unfaithful servants, girls and men, and which was certainly a stable element in the narrative tradition on Ithaca. He explains it in such a way that no shadow is cast upon his hero. If he had been in Homer's eyes just another hero like the figures of Greek mythology, or indeed a god disguised, this explanation would not have been necessary. As it is, Athene works unceasingly to provoke the suitors and the disloyal members of the household to treat Ulysses more and more insultingly, with the avowed purpose, as the poet says, of making them merit a cruel punishment.

WAS THE ODYSSEY EVER FINISHED?

The question arises, in the case of a great work which was composed in the form of separate songs and was stored up in the poet's memory as he worked upon it: was it ever finished? There can be no question of its having been given its final form in the shape of a manuscript finished by the poet. Even if the songs were meanwhile written down, as aids to memory, the work, on account of its purpose — which was to be heard, not read, to be sung, not learned silently — could only be further polished as it was sung. In singing it, it was possible to smooth out the unevennesses and discrepancies as they came to light, though perhaps this could only be at best an approximation to perfection. It is not surprising that the Odyssey never achieved this perfection.

We must rather suppose that neither the Iliad nor the Odyssey had been finally rounded off when Homer left them to the school of singers which according to tradition he had founded on the island of Chios. This is no doubt the solution of the Homeric question. In the Iliad there was also the gap which was later filled by the feeble song of the murder of the miserable Dolon. Nothing seems to be missing in the Odyssey of Homer, but much in it points to a stage where a part was composed and was not yet fully or finally adapted to the whole, which was still in the making.[21] Such would be the poem of the dead in the last book. Hermes arrives at the realm of the dead with the souls of the suitors, like a flock of bats. The soul of Agamemnon is just describing to the soul of Achilles the great funeral rites which had been accorded to Achilles, the greatest hero of the Iliad. It is a supplement to the Iliad, like others which Homer has inserted into the Odyssey — but how late it comes now, after the scenes described in the song of the journey to the underworld! Then the soul of one of the suitors tells of all that had happened — to the glory of Ulysses — in the palace of Ithaca. But the description is not exactly that of the Odyssey. It is a summary sketch, which Homer wanted to give *before* his portrayal of the scene. At the end of the Odyssey he obviously took up a dirge composed earlier, leaving dissonances such as a poet can permit himself and does in fact, without meaning to. A later comer could allow himself far less licence.

Ulysses has reached his goal. He has come "to himself", he is at home. The place and the image for his having "come to himself" is the bed which he has constructed for himself and Penelope from a living olive-tree, there where the tree has its roots. It is a secret known only to himself and Penelope. He seeks and finds his father in the vineyard. The old man marches out with him like a youth to give battle to the relatives of the suitors. It is Athene's second to last piece of magic. Her last is to command and make peace. This would make the Odyssey a finished work. But it is not quite that, and it is not so everywhere. It is a poem on which each of us, each in his own way, can go on working, as if it were a novel which is still too short. And we *can* use pictures to try to go on "working" on the Odyssey and enjoying it in a way which is as contemporary as it is ancient!

NOTES BY C. KERÉNYI

[1] In his book *The Singer of Tales* (Harvard University Press, 1960), p. 150; a work which fulfills the late Milman Parry's purpose and uses his principles.

[2] Cf. Stanley Casson, "How Homer wrote the Odyssey" in *Antiquity* 16 (1942), pp. 71–84.

[3] Paul Kretschmer, "Penelope" in *Anzeiger der Akademie Wien* (1945), pp. 80ff.

[4] Karl Reinhardt, "Die Abenteuer der Odyssee" in *Tradition und Geist* (Göttingen 1960), p. 106.

[5] Cf. my book *The Heroes of the Greeks* (London 1959, New York 1960), p. 77.

[6] Following W. B. Stanford's interpretation.

[7] Karl Reinhardt, *Die Ilias und ihr Dichter* (Göttingen 1961), p. 250.

[8] Karl Reinhardt, *Tradition und Geist* (Göttingen 1960), p. 44.

[9] For the following see my *Griechische Miniaturen* (Zürich 1957), pp. 102ff.

[10] This reading of Od. I, 52 is attested, while what follows is my conjecture.

[11] Cf. my *Mysterien von Eleusis* (Zürich 1962), p. 88 (after G. Widengreen).

[12] For the following see "Korfu und die Odyssee" in my *Apollon* (Düsseldorf, 3rd ed., 1953), pp. 118ff.

[13] Friedrich Gottlieb Welcker, *Die Homerischen Phäaken und die Insel der Seligen*. Kleine Schriften II (1845), pp. 1ff.

[14] Quoted by Welcker.

[15] Quoted by Welcker.

[16] Ferdinand Gregorovius, *Korfu. Eine Ionische Idylle* (1881).

[17] Od. VII, 321, "Let them be further than Euboea".

[18] Od. X, 329; cf. my *Religion of the Greeks and Romans* (London 1962), p. 148.

[19] Karl Reinhardt, *Tradition und Geist* (Göttingen 1960), p. 107.

[20] Cf. my *Griechisch-orientalische Romanliteratur in religionsgeschichtlicher Beleuchtung* (Darmstadt, 2nd ed., 1962).

[21] G. D. Kirk, *The Songs of Homer* (Cambridge 1962), p. 228ff.

The following abbreviations are used frequently in the Index:
Cat. — Catalogue number;
Inv. — Inventory number;
Lit. — Literature;
pl. — Plate number;
c. — circa.
In page references, for example, p. 1300,2; p. 33,173; p. 1177,48, or plate references, for example, pl. 43,2; pl. 53,148, the first number indicates the page, while the number immediately following the comma refers to the catalogue number. References are made according to style and practice of the individual sources referenced.

1. HEAD OF ATHENE. Statue of Parian marble. From the Palazzo Mattei, Rome, later in the Fesch collection. Acquired by Louis XVIII. Roman copy of a Greek original (Athena Agoraia?) from the second half of the 4th cent. B.C. Height: 7 ft. 6 in. — Paris, Louvre, Inv. 530.

Lit.: W. Fröhner, *Notice de la Sculpture Antique du Musée Impérial du Louvre* I (Paris 1869), No. 121. — Charles Picard, *Manuel de la Sculpture* IV, 2, 1 (Paris 1963), p. 368. — Giulio Emanuele Rizzo, *Prassitele* (Milano 1932), p. 118, pl. 143.

PICTORIAL AND LITERARY INDEX

BY

CORNELIA KERÉNYI

2. ULYSSES. Bronze statuette. Roman period. Height: 4 ft. 7 in. — Paris, Bibliothèque Nationale, Inv. 809.

Lit.: Ernest Babelon – J.-Adrien Blanchet, *Cat. des bronzes antiques de la Bibliothèque Nationale* (Paris 1895), p. 349, 809. — Heinrich Heydemann, *Pariser Antiken* (1887), p. 69, 11.

5. POSEIDON. Bronze statue, from the sea at Cape Artemisium, found without the arms, 1926; the arms found 1928. Second quarter of the 5th cent. B.C. Height: 6 ft. 10 in. — Athens, National Museum, Inv. 15161.

Lit.: Charles Picard, *Manuel de la Sculpture* II, 1 (Paris 1939), pp. 63 ff., p. 14 and 14 *bis*. — Reinhard Lullies – Max Hirmer, *Griechische Plastik* (Munich 1960), pp. 58 ff., pl. 130–2.

3. OLYMPUS. A mountainous mass of many peaks, seen from the sea. The highest elevation in Greece, Mt Olympus (9568 feet) forms the border between Thessaly and Macedonia. It was regarded in antiquity as the dwelling-place of the gods.

6. MISSION OF ATHENE. Cameo from the Becken collection, presented to the Bibliothèque Nationale in 1846. Roman period. Size: 1.3 × 1.2 in. — Paris, Bibliothèque Nationale, Inv. 3.

Lit.: Ernest Babelon, *Le Cabinet des Médailles et Antiques* (Paris 1924), p. 167, 3.

4. ZEUS ENTHRONED. Bronze statuette from Mt Lycaeum in Arcadia, probably Zeus Lycaeus. Corinthian, second half of the 6th cent. B.C. Height: 4 in. — Athens, National Museum, Inv. 13209.

Lit.: K. Kourouniotis, *Archaiologiké Ephemerís* 24 (1904), pp. 185 ff. Fig. 12–14. — V. Stais, *Marbres et Bronzes du Musée National* (Athens, 1909–10), p. 314. — Ernst Langlotz, *Frühgriechische Bildhauerschulen* (Nuremberg 1927), p. 80, pl. 41 b.

7. ITHACA. View from the coast road near Stavros. The harbour in the Odyssey was in the bay, and the market-place was on the mountain-ridge. As late as the first cent. B.C., Ulysses was worshipped as a hero in a small cave on the shore of the headland.

8. GREEK SINGERS. Clay statuette from the geometric period. Found in 1924 in the Arcades/Crete. Height: 3 in. — Iraklion, Archaeological Museum, Inv. 8104.

13. PRIAM. Limestone relief from the frieze on the west wall of the Heroon at Gjölbaschi-Trysa (Lycia). First decades of the 4th cent. B.C. Height: c. 4 ft.; length: c. 20 ft. — Vienna, Kunsthistorisches Museum.

Lit.: Otto Benndorf, *Das Heroon von Gjölbaschi-Trysa* (Vienna 1889), pl. 12. — Fritz Eichler, *Die Reliefs des Heroons von Gjölbaschi-Trysa* (Vienna 1950).

9. PENELOPE AND TELEMACHUS. Attic red-figured skyphos of the Penelope-painter, from Chiusi, Central Italy. About 440 B.C. Height: 8 in.; diameter: 10 in. — Chiusi, Museo Nazionale, Inv. 1831.

Lit.: Doro Levi, *Il Museo Civico di Chiusi* (Rome 1935), p. 115, fig. 63a–63b. — J. D. Beazley, *Attic Red-figured Vase-Painters* (Oxford 1963), II, p. 1300,2. — Ernst Buschor in Adolf Furtwängler – Karl Reichhold, *Griechische Vasenmalerei* III (Munich 1900), p. 124, pl. 142.

10. PYLOS. Entrance to the bay of Navarino on the west coast of the Peloponnese. About a mile from the coast are the ruins of the palace of King Nestor, from Mycenaean times.

14. THE CAPTURE OF TROY. Limestone relief from the frieze on the west wall of the Heroon at Gjölbaschi-Trysa (Lycia). First decades of the 4th cent. B.C. Height: c. 4 ft.; length: c. 20 ft. — Vienna, Kunsthistorisches Museum.

Lit.: Otto Benndorf, *Das Heroon von Gjölbaschi-Trysa* (Vienna 1889). — Fritz Eichler, *Die Reliefs des Heroons von Gjölbaschi-Trysa* (Vienna 1950).

11. TELEMACHUS AND NESTOR. Red-figured bowl from Lower Italy, 4th cent. B.C. Acquired in Naples in 1849. Height: 20 in. — Berlin, Staatliche Museen (Charlottenburg), Inv. (of the Antiquarium) 3289.

Lit.: Adolf Furtwängler, *Beschreibung der Vasensammlung im Antiquarium* (Berlin 1885), p. 922, 3289.

15. THE THRONE-HALL IN CNOSSOS. The benches and throne of alabaster, flooring of limestone flags. The frescoes partially restored. Excavated by the English archaeologist Sir Arthur Evans (1851–1941). The frescoes are from the latter part of the 15th cent. B.C. Height of throne with foot-rest: 4 ft. 10 in.

Lit.: Friedrich Matz, *Kreta und frühes Griechenland* (Baden-Baden 1962), p. 120, fig. 29. — Georg Karo, *Greifen am Thron* (Baden-Baden 1959), p. 8, pl. 3. — Spyridon Marinatos – Max Hirmer, *Kreta und das mykenische Hellas* (Munich 1959), p. 78, pl. 33. — Arthur Evans, *The Palace of Minos* IV, 2 (London 1935), pp. 901 ff.

12. WARRIORS AT TROY. Limestone relief from the frieze on the west wall of the Heroon at Gjölbaschi-Trysa (Lycia). First decades of the 4th cent. B.C. Height: c. 4 ft.; length: c. 20 ft. — Vienna, Kunsthistorisches Museum.

Lit.: Otto Benndorf, *Das Heroon von Gjölbaschi-Trysa* (Vienna 1889), pl. 13. — Fritz Eichler, *Die Reliefs des Heroons von Gjölbaschi-Trysa* (Vienna 1950).

16. MYCENAE, citadel wall and Lion Gate, second half of the 14th cent. B.C. Discovered by the German archaeologist Heinrich Schliemann, in 1876/7.

Lit.: A. J. B. Wace, *Mycenae* (Princeton, N. Jersey 1949), p. 22. — Spyridon Marinatos – Max Hirmer, *Kreta und das mykenische Hellas* (Munich 1959), p. 104, pl. 141. — Friedrich Matz, *Kreta, Mykene, Troja* (Stuttgart 1956), pp. 109 ff., pl. 79.

17. AGAMEMNON. Gold mask from Tomb V, Mycenae. 16th cent. B.C. Excavated by Heinrich Schliemann. Height: 10 in. — Athens, National Museum, Inv. 624.

Lit.: Georg Karo, *Die Schachtgräber von Mykenai*, 2 vols (Munich 1930–3), fig. in text p. 18. — Spyridon Marinatos – Max Hirmer, *Kreta und das mykenische Hellas* (Munich 1959), p. 115, pl. 162. — Friedrich Matz, *Kreta, Mykene, Troja* (Stuttgart 1956), p. 272, pl. 87.

18. NESTOR. Attic red-figured vase, like a kantharos, by the Eretria-painter, from Vulci. Last quarter of the 5th cent. B.C. Formerly in the Basseggio collection, Rome. Height (without handle): 3 in. — Paris, Bibliothèque Nationale, Inv. 851 (Luynes collection 732).

Lit.: A. De Ridder, *Cat. des Vases peints de la Bibliothèque Nationale* (Paris 1901), p. 501, 851. — J. D. Beazley, *Attic Red-figured Vase-Painters* II (Oxford 1963), p. 1251, 41. — Joseph Clark Hoppin, *A Handbook of Attic Red-figured Vases* I (Cambridge 1919), p. 298.

19. BULL WITH GOLDEN HORNS. A rhyton of silver and gold from Tomb IV in Mycenae. 16th cent. B.C. Height: 12 in. — Athens, National Museum, Inv. 384.

Lit.: Helmuth T. Bossert, *Altkreta* (Berlin 1937), p. 22, pl. 96. — Spyridon Marinatos – Max Hirmer, *Kreta und das mykenische Hellas* (Munich 1959), p. 117, pl. 175. — Friedrich Matz, *Kreta und frühes Griechenland* (Baden-Baden 1962), p. 172.

20. KING NESTOR'S BATH. Clay, about 1200 B.C. Excavated in the palace of Pylos in 1955 by the American archaeologist Carl W. Blegen. Length: *c.* 5 ft. 10 in.; width: *c.* 2 ft. 4 in.

Lit.: Carl W. Blegen, *American Journal of Archaeology* 60 (1956), p. 100, pl. 47, fig. 20–21.

21. VIEW TOWARDS SPARTA. Telemachus must have looked from the top of this pass onto the plain of Lacedaemonia. The pass forms the boundary between Messenia and Lacedaemonia, as is proved by an ancient boundary stone found on the site.

22. MENELAUS AND HELEN. Etruscan bronze mirror, 4th cent. B.C. Height: 10.5 in.; diameter: 6.7 in. — London, British Museum, Cat. 712 (Towneley Collection).

Lit.: H. B. Walters, *Cat. of the Bronzes in the British Museum* (London 1899), p. 120, 712. — Eduard Gerhard, *Etruskische Spiegel* II (Berlin 1843–97), pl. 201, III, p. 194.

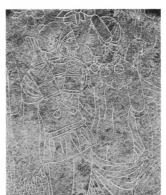

23. ULYSSES CREEPING. Marble statue from Rome, found in 1885. An archaizing Roman work of about A.D. 50. Height: 2 ft. 1 in.; length: 3 ft. 8 in. — Boston, Mrs Stewart Gardner Museum.

Lit.: R. Lanciani, *Notizie degli Scavi* (1885), p. 341. — V. Poulsen, *Acta Archaeologica* 25 (1954), pp. 301 ff.

24. TROJAN HORSE. Wall painting from Pompeii, from the cubiculum of House IX, 7, 16. First half of the first cent. A.D. Height: 1 ft. 3 in.; length: 1 ft. 3.5 in. — Naples, Museo Nazionale, Inv. 9040.

Lit.: Wilhelm Klein, *Jahreshefte des österreichischen archäologischen Institutes* 19/20 (1919), p. 284, fig. 184. — C. M. Dawson, *Romano-Campanian Landscape Painting* (New Haven 1944), p. 86, 13, pl. 5. — Karl Schefold, *Die Wände Pompejis* (Berlin 1957), p. 268.

25. PROVISION JAR in the cellar of the royal palace of Cnossos. 15th century B.C. Height: *c.* 5 ft. 4 in.

Lit.: Arthur Evans, *The Palace of Minos* IV (London 1921–36), pp. 630 ff. — Spyridon Marinatos – Max Hirmer, *Kreta und das mykenische Hellas* (Munich 1959), p. 78, pl. 41.

26. PENELOPE MOURNING. Terracotta relief. Roman period. Height: 10 in.; length: 10.5 in. — London, British Museum, Cat. D 609 (Towneley Collection).

Lit.: H. B. Walters, *Cat. of the Terracottas in the British Museum* (London 1903), p. 403,609.

27. THE ISLAND OF ASTERIS, where the suitors lay in wait for Telemachus in the strait between Ithaca and Cephalonia, seen from Ithaca. The island is now called Dascalion.

28. "HIGH-THRONED DAWN that brings daylight to both gods and men." It is the signal very often in the Odyssey for a change of scene or the start of a new episode.

29. HERMES. Bronze statuette from Mt Lycaeum (Arcadia). Beginning of the 5th cent. B.C. Height (without base): 5 in. — Athens, National Museum, Inv. 13219.

Lit.: K. Kourouniotis, *Archaiologiké Ephemerís* 24 (1904), pp. 196 ff., pl. 9. — V. Stais, *Marbres et Bronzes du Musée National* (Athens 1909–10), p. 317,13219.

30. ULYSSES MOURNING. Gem of light-brown sardonyx. Roman, 3rd to 2nd cent. B.C. Size: 0.9 in. × 0.7 in. — Berlin, Staatliche Museen (Museumsinsel), Inv. (of the Antiquarium) 1378.

Lit.: Adolf Furtwängler, *Beschreibung der geschnittenen Steine im Antiquarium* (Berlin 1896), p. 82, pl. 15.

31. THE SEA COAST. Day after day Ulysses sat eyeing the fruitless sea.

32. ULYSSES AND CALYPSO. Red-figured Ralpis (type of hydria) from Paestum, S. Italy. Last quarter of the 5th cent. B.C. Height: *c.* 20 in. — Naples, Museo Nazionale, Cat. 2899.

Lit.: Heinrich Heydemann, *Die Vasensammlungen des Museo Nazionale* (Berlin 1872), No. 2899. — Festa, *Rendiconti dell' Acc. dei Lincei* 21 (1912), pp. 383 ff.

33. ULYSSES' RAFT. Boeotian cotula (cup) from Thebes, acquired in 1892. About 440–420 B.C. Height: 6 in. — Oxford, Ashmolean Museum, Cat. 262.

Lit.: Percy Gardner, *Cat. of the Greek Vases in the Ashmolean Museum* (Oxford 1893), No. 262, pl. 26. — Roman Stiglitz, *Jahreshefte des österreichischen archäologischen Institutes* 44 (1959), pp. 123 f.

34. POSEIDON. Bronze statuette, second half of the 2nd cent. B.C. Height (to the fingers of the left hand): 12.2 in. — Munich, Antikensammlung, Loeb Collection No. 15.

Lit.: Johannes Sieveking, *Die Bronzen der Sammlung Loeb* (Munich 1913), pp. 41 ff., pl. 17–18. — Charles Picard, *Manuel de la Sculpture* IV, 2 (Paris 1963), pp. 509 f., fig. 208.

35. STORM AT SEA. Poseidon, the sea-god, shows his anger towards Ulysses by bringing a furious gale that buffets him for two days and two nights off the Phaeacian coast.

40. THE RIVER POOLS where Nausicaa took her linen to wash. The stream rises on the plain of Ropas and flows down through a mountain valley to reach the sea in the bay of Ermonais.

36. PHAEACIAN COAST. The island of Corfu, the ancient Scheria, was already regarded in antiquity as the country of the Phaeacians. The bay of Ermonais in the foreground, which is the only sandy beach on the whole west coast of Corfu where a river flows into the sea, corresponds exactly to Homer's description of Ulysses' landing-place.

37. OLIVE TREE. Groves of olive-trees are still to be seen a little inland from the shore of Ermonais. Here Ulysses lay down to sleep.

41. ULYSSES AND ATHENE at the meeting with Nausicaa. Attic red-figured amphora by the Nausicaa-painter, from Vulci. About 450–440 B.C. Height: 20 in. — Munich, Museum antiker Kleinkunst, Inv. 2322.

Lit.: Friedrich Hauser, *Jahreshefte des österreichischen archäologischen Institutes* 8 (1905), p. 27. — J. D. Beazley, *Attic Red-figured Vase-Painters* II (Oxford 1963), p. 1107,2. — Reinhard Lullies, *Corpus Vasorum Antiquorum Munich* 5, pp. 9–11, pl. 213.

38. ATHENE. Bronze statuette from Aetolia, of provincial workmanship, from the 5th cent. B.C. Height: 8 in. — Paris, Louvre, Cat. 173.

Lit.: A. De Ridder, *Les Bronzes antiques du Louvre* I (Paris 1913), p. 33,173, pl. 18.

42. FLEEING MAIDEN. Attic red-figured amphora by the Nausicaa-painter, from Vulci. About 450–440 B.C. Height: 20 in. — Munich, Museum antiker Kleinkunst, Inv. 2322.

Lit.: Friedrich Hauser, *Jahreshefte des österreichischen archäologischen Institutes* 9 (1905), p. 27. — J. D. Beazley, *Attic Red-figured Vase-Painters* II (Oxford 1963), p. 1107,2. — Reinhard Lullies, *Corpus Vasorum Antiquorum Munich* 5, pp. 9–11, fig. 213.

39. LAUNDRESS, Attic red-figured pyxis by the vase-painter Aison of Athens. Last quarter of the 5th. cent. B.C. Height: 1.4 in., diameter: 5.5 in. — Boston, Museum of Fine Arts, Inv. 04.18.

Lit.: Friedrich Hauser, *Jahreshefte des österreichischen archäologischen Institutes* 8 (1905), p. 18, pl. 1. — J. D. Beazley, *Attic Red-figured Vase-Painters* II (Oxford 1963), p. 1177,48.

43. THE GROVE OF ATHENE, a little before the double inlet of Paleocastrizza, on the road from Ermonais through the plain of Ropas.

44. THE PHAEACIANS' BANQUET in honour of Ulysses. Attic red-figured bowl. Second quarter of the 5th. cent. B.C. Since 1814 in the Kunsthistorisches Museum, Vienna. Height: 18 in.; width: 17 in. — Vienna, Kunsthistorisches Museum, Inv. 824.

Lit.: Fritz Eichler, *Corpus Vasorum Antiquorum Vienna, Kunsthistorisches Museum* 2, p. 27, pl. 89.

45. YOUNG ACHAEANS AT THE ATHLETIC CONTESTS. Relief in Pentelic marble from a square pedestal. Found 1922 in a wall at the Dipylon, Athens. Probably part of the base of a statue. 510–500 B.C. Height: 12.8 in.; length: 32 in. — Athens, National Museum, Inv. 3476.

Lit.: Charles Picard, *Manuel de la Sculpture* I (Paris 1935), pp. 628 ff. — Reinhard Lullies – Max Hirmer, *Griechische Plastik* (Munich 1960), p. 48, pl. 62–65.

46. ULYSSES WITH SPEAR. Bronze relief from Hexamila (Thracian Chersonnese), found in 1876. Roman period. Height: 35 in. — London, British Museum, Cat. 1443.

Lit.: H. B. Walters, *Cat. of the Bronzes in the British Museum* (London 1899), p. 236,1443.

47. GREEK SINGERS. Bronze statuette from the geometric period. Height: 2.15 in. — Iraklion, Archaeological Museum, Inv. 2064.

48. TROJAN HORSE. Depicted on the neck of an earthenware amphora with reliefs, from Mykonos, found in 1961. First half of the 7th cent. B.C. Height: 4 ft. — Mykonos, Museum.

Lit.: Georges Daux, *Bulletin de Correspondence Hellénique* 86 (1962), p. 854, fig. 16, pl. 29. — Hans Walter, *Athen. Mitt.* 77 (1962), p. 196. — Karl Schefold, *Frühgriechische Sagenbilder* (Munich 1964), pl. 34.

49. ULYSSES AS CHARIOTEER. Small bronze plate from the foot of an Etruscan cist from Chiusi. Sixth cent. B.C. Presented to the king by the French archaeologist and collector of antiques, Count Caylus (1692–1765). Height: 3 in. — Paris, Bibliothèque Nationale, Inv. 810.

Lit.: Ernest Babelon – J.-Adrien Blanchet, *Cat. des Bronzes antiques de la Bibliothèque Nationale* (Paris 1895), p. 349,810.

50. HEAD OF ULYSSES. Fragment of a marble statue from the cave of Tiberius in Sperlonga, middle of the first cent. B.C. (?) Height: 26 in. — Sperlonga, Museum.

Lit.: Giulio Jacopi, *I ritrovamenti dell'antro cosiddetto "di Tiberio" a Sperlonga* (Rome 1958), fig. 10. — Giulio Jacopi, *L'antro di Tiberio a Sperlonga* (Rome 1963), fig. 23, 24, 55–57.

51. GREEK SHIP. Limestone relief from the frieze on the west wall of the Heroon of Gjölbaschi-Trysa (Lycia). First decades of the 4th cent. B.C. Height: 45–46 in.; length: 36 ft. — Vienna, Kunsthistorisches Museum.

Lit.: Otto Benndorf, *Das Heroon von Gjölbaschi-Trysa* (Vienna 1889), pl. 9. — Fritz Eichler, *Die Reliefs des Heroons von Gjölbschi-Trysa* (Vienna 1950).

52. "ROSY-FINGERED DAWN". Sunrise greets the Achaean ships, waiting for favourable weather to bring them around the Peloponnese.

53. THE PALM TREES OF THE LOTOS-EATERS. The island of Djerba off the coast of Tunis was already regarded in ancient times as the dwelling-place of the Lotos-eaters of the legend.

58. POLYPHEMUS EATING. Bronze statuette, Roman period. Height: 3.6 in. — Paris, Bibliothèque Nationale, Inv. 812 (Oppermann Collection).

Lit.: Ernest Babelon – J.-Adrien Blanchet, *Cat. des Bronzes antiques,* p. 350,812.

54. FRUIT IN A BOWL. Terracotta pomegranates, lotos-fruit, figs, almonds and a sort of cucumber. Ulysses was compelled to use force to drag three of his travel-weary companions from this rich fare. Found 1864 in Cameiros, Rhodos. Archaic period. Height: 2 in.; diameter: 4 in. — London, British Museum, Cat. B 313.

Lit.: H. B. Walters, *Cat. of the Terracottas* p. 123, B 313.

59. ULYSSES HANDS POLYPHEMUS THE SLEEPING-DRAUGHT, relief on a fragment of a sarcophagus of Grecian marble. Roman period. Before 1796 in the museum at Portici. Height: 39 in.; width: 22.5 in. — Naples, Museo Nazionale, Inv. 6580.

Lit.: Carl Robert, *Die Antiken Sarkophagreliefs* II (Berlin 1890), p. 159, pl. 53,148. — Arnoldo Ruesch, *Guida del Museo Nazionale* (Naples 1908), p. 175,620. — Wilhelm H. Roscher, *Mythologisches Lexikon* III, 2, col. 2704, fig. 3.

55. THE HARBOUR OF THE CYCLOPES. A small bay at the foot of Mt Posillipo, invisible from the landward side.

60. THE BLINDING OF POLYPHEMUS. Early Attic amphora from Eleusis, found in 1954. Second quarter of the 7th cent. B.C. Height: 4 ft. 4 in. — Eleusis, Museum.

Lit.: G. E. Mylonas, Ὁ πρωτοαττικὸς ἀμφορεὺς τῆς Ἐλευσῖνος (Athens 1957). — Karl Schefold, *Frühgriechische Sagenbilder* (Munich 1964), p. 32, pl. 16, pl. 1.

56. SMOKE HOLE or fumarole in the mud of the crater of Solfatara, one of the extinct volcanoes of the Phlegraean Fields near Pozzuoli. Such a sight perhaps inspired the myth of the one-eyed giants.

57. HEAD OF POLYPHEMUS. Terracotta fragment from Smyrna. Hellenistic period. Height: 2 in. — Paris, Louvre, Inv. CA 1003.

61. ULYSSES' ESCAPE UNDER THE RAM. Black-figured convex lekythos by the "Ambush-painter", from Girgenti. Last decade of the 6th cent. B.C. Height: *c.* 10.5 in. — Munich, Antiken-sammlung, Inv. 1885 (J. 755).

Lit.: Jane E. Harrison, *Journal of Hellenic Studies* 4 (1883), table, p. 259, No. 4. — Emilie Haspels, *Attic Black-figured Lekythoi* (Paris 1936), p. 61.

62. The Route from the Island of the Cyclopes. The little island of Nisida can be seen from the many caves of Mt Posillipo, most of which were made or enlarged in the time of Augustus. The rocks which Polyphemus threw after Ulysses' ship are in the water in the foreground.

63. Oarsmen. Attic red-figured stamnos by the Siren-painter, from Vulci. First quarter of the 5th cent. b.c. Height: 14 in. — London, British Museum, Cat. E 440 (Canino Collection 829).

Lit.: C. H. Smith, *Cat. of the Greek and Etruscan Vases in the British Museum* III (London 1896), p. 268, E 440. — *Corpus Vasorum Antiquorum British Museum* III, Ic, pl. 20, Ic, p. 8. — J. D. Beazley, *Attic Red-figured Vase-Painters* I (Oxford 1963), p. 289,1.

64. The Island of Aeolus. The island of Stromboli, one of the Lipari group, was regarded in antiquity as the seat of Aeolus, the lord of the winds. The volcano on the island, 3038 feet high, is still active.

65. Aeolus' Wall of Fire. On the northwestern slope of the vulcano on Stromboli, the petrified lava-flow falls very steeply into the sea. It was the gold-bronze coloration of the wall which the ancients recognized as Aeolus' famed wall of fire.

66. The Cliffs of the Laestrygonian Coast. At Cape Bonifacio, the southern point of the island of Corsica, the coast rises sharply in steep fissured cliffs. The strait of Bonifacio which divides Corsica from Sardinia, is one of the seven great channels of the Mediterranean.

67. Circe's Island. Monte Circeo on the Gulf of Gaeta, now joined to the mainland by a change in the ocean bed, was already regarded in antiquity as the home of the goddess Circe.

68. The Magic Wood. This wood lies at the foot of the northern slope of Mt Circe, about half a mile from the ancient landing-place at Torre Paola.

69. Circe Offers Ulysses the Magic Potion. Attic black-figured lekythos by the Athene-painter, from Eretria on the island of Euboea. First quarter of the 5th cent. b.c. Height: 11.4 in. — Athens, National Museum, Inv. 1133.

Lit.: Eugénie Sellers, *Journal of Hellenic Studies* 13 (1892), pp. 7 ff. — Emilie Haspels, *Attic Black-figured Lekythoi* (Paris 1936), p. 256,49, pl. 45,6.

70. Companion of Ulysses, Changed into a Pig. Attic red-figured lekythos from Eretria, Euboea. 485–475 b.c. Height: 7.3 in. — Athens, National Museum, Inv. 9685.

Lit.: J. D. Beazley, *Attic Red-figured Vase-Painters* I (Oxford 1963), p. 693,1. — Julius Ziehen, in: *Festschrift Overbeck* (Leipzig 1893), pp. 120 ff.

71. COMPANION OF ULYSSES, CHANGED INTO A PIG. Fragment of a funeral urn in alabaster. Found in the necropolis of Volterra. Etruscan. Height: 11.4 in.; width: 11.4 in. — Volterra, Museo Etrusco Guarnacci, Inv. 606.

72. CIRCE'S GROVE. On the way from the Magic Wood (Plate 68) to San Felice Circeo at the edge of the now dry Pontine Marshes.

73. THE MAGIC PLANT, which the god Hermes gave to Ulysses, grows abundantly in Circe's grove. Bérard designates the plant as Atriplex halimus. All plants of the garlic family were regarded in antiquity as possessing magical healing powers.

74. ULYSSES THREATENING CIRCE. Etruscan sarcophagus relief from Torre S. Severo, found in 1912. Of pepper-tree wood. From the end of the 4th cent. B.C., probably an imitation of a Greek painting of the 5th cent. B.C. Height (with lid): 37 in.; length: 31.5 in. — Orvieto, Museo dell'Opera del Duomo.

Lit.: Edoardo Galli, *Monumenti antichi pubblicati dall' Accademia dei Lincei* 24,1 (1916), pp. 19 ff. — Pericle Ducati – G. Q. Giglioli, *Arte etrusca Scultura* (Rome–Milan 1927), p. 45, fig. 51. — Reinhard Herbig, *Die jüngeretruskischen Steinsarkophage* (Berlin 1952), p. 40, No. 73.

75. ULYSSES AND CIRCE. Etruscan bronze mirror. 4th cent. B.C. Formerly in the Fejervary-Pulsky collection. Diameter: 6 in. — London, British Museum, Cat. 724.

Lit.: H. B. Walters, *Cat. of the Bronzes in the British Museum* (London 1899), p. 124,724. — Eduard Gerhard, *Etruskische Spiegel* IV (Berlin 1843–97), p. 77, pl. 417.

76. LAKE AVERNUS. A water-filled crater north of Pozzuoli, was regarded in antiquity as the dwelling-place of the Cimmerians (Odyssey, Book XI), and as an entrance to the underworld. There are several caves and grottoes on the southern shore, one of which is called the "Cave of the Sibyl". Under Augustus, a canal was cut to join the lake to the Gulf of Pozzuoli.

77. SACRIFICIAL RAMS. Attic red-figured rhyton from Capua, second third of the 5th cent. B.C. Height: 9 in.; diameter: 3.3 in. — London, British Museum, Cat. 800.

Lit.: C. H. Smith, *Cat. of the Vases* III, p. 379, E 800. — *Corpus Vasorum Antiquorum, British Museum* III, Ic, p. 9, pl. 43,2. — J. D. Beazley, *Attic Red-figured Vase-Painters* I (Oxford 1963), p. 766,12.

78. ULYSSES SACRIFICING. Etruscan sarcophagus relief from Torre S. Severo, found in 1912. Of pepper-tree wood. From the end of the 4th cent. B.C., probably an imitation of a Greek painting of the 5th cent. B.C. Height (with lid): 37 in.; length: 31.5 in. — Orvieto, Museo dell'Opera del Duomo.

Lit.: Edoardo Galli, *Monumenti antichi pubblicati dall' Accademia dei Lincei* 24,1 (1916), pp. 19 ff. — Pericle Ducati – C. Q. Gigioli, *Arte etrusca Scultura* (Rome–Milan 1927), p. 45, fig. 51. — Reinhard Herbig, *Die jüngeretruskischen Steinsarkophage* (Berlin 1952), p. 40, No. 73.

79. ULYSSES AND ELPENOR. Attic red-figured pelike by the Lykaon-painter. Third quarter of the 5th cent. B.C. Height: 18.6 in. — Boston, Museum of Fine Arts, 34.79.

Lit.: J. D. Beazley, *Attic Vase-Paintings in the Museum of Fine Arts* II (Boston 1931–64), p. 86. — Ernst Buschor, *Griechische Vasen* (Munich 1940), p. 209, fig. 227.

80. WARRIORS AT TROY. Attic red-figured cup by the Euergides-painter, from Vulci. Last quarter of the 6th cent. B.C. Height: 4.5 in.; diameter: 12.6 in. — London, British Museum, Cat. E 20 (Canino Collection).

Lit.: C. H. Smith, *Cat. of the Vases* III, p. 55, E 20. — J. D. Beazley, *Attic Red-figured Vase-painters* I (Oxford 1963), p. 90,35. — J. D. Beazley, *Journal of Hellenic Studies* 33 (1913), pp. 347 ff.

81. ULYSSES AND TEIRESIAS. South Italian red-figured bowl, from the Barone collection. End of the 5th cent. B.C. Height (without base): 18.8 in., diameter (at top): 18.8 in. — Paris, Bibliothèque Nationale, Inv. 422 (Luynes 731).

Lit.: A. De Ridder, *Cat. des Vases peints*, p. 312, 422.

82. "ROSY-FINGERED DAWN" heralding fine sailing for the Achaeans on the next stage of their voyage.

83. SIREN. Attic red-figured stamnos by the Siren-painter, from Vulci. First quarter of the 5th cent. B.C. Height: 14.1 in. — London, British Museum, Cat. E 440 (Canino Collection 829).

Lit.: C. H. Smith, *Cat. of the Greek and Etruscan Vases in the British Museum* III (London 1896), p. 268, E 440. — *Corpus Vasorum Antiquorum, British Museum* III, Ic, pl. 20, Ic, p. 8. — J. D. Beazley, *Attic Red-figured Vase-Painters* I (Oxford 1963), p. 289,1.

84. ULYSSES' SHIP. Campana terracotta relief (much restored and painted over). 2nd cent. A.D., probably from the time of Hadrian. Height: 13 in.; length: 16.1 in. — Paris, Louvre, Inv. 747.

Lit.: H. von Rohden – H. Winnefeld, *Architektonische römische Tonreliefs der Kaiserzeit* (Stuttgart 1911), p. 111, pl. 132. — Franz Müller, *Die antiken Odysseeillustrationen* (Berlin 1913), p. 44.

85. THE ISLANDS OF THE SIRENS. The Isole li Galli in the Gulf of Sorrento.

86. SCYLLA. Handle of a bronze mirror, from a work-shop at Tarentum. 4th cent. B.C. Height: 7.1 in. — Paris, Louvre, Inv. 1686.

Lit.: A. De Ridder, *Les Bronzes antiques du Louvre* II, p. 43, pl. 76. — Erich Pernice, *Jahrbuch des deutschen archäologischen Instituts,* pp. 95 f., fig. 8.

87. SCYLLA'S ROCK guards the Straits of Messina, the narrow channel dividing Italy from Sicily. It is opposite Punta del Faro, the eastern tip of Sicily.

88. STEERSMAN. Fragment of a group in marble from the Cave of Tiberius in Sperlonga, found in 1957. Middle of the first cent. B.C. (?) Height: 7 ft. 2 in.; length: 9 ft. 10 in. — Sperlonga, Museum.

Lit.: Giulio Jacopi, *I ritrovamenti dell'antro cosiddetto "di Tiberio" a Sperlonga* (Rome 1958), fig. 15. — Giulio Jacopi, *L'antro di Tiberio a Sperlonga* (Rome 1963), fig. 48–51.

89. SCYLLA. Earthenware decoration on a late Italian vase. Height (of the whole vase): 15 in.; length: 12 in. — Boston, Museum of Fine Arts, Inv. 99.541.

Lit.: Arthur Fairbanks, *Greek Gods and Heroes* (Boston 1915), p. 29, fig. 20.

90. SCYLLA'S TAIL. Fragment of a group in marble from the Cave of Tiberius in Sperlonga, found in 1957. Middle of the first cent. B.C. (?) — Sperlonga, Museum.

Lit.: Giulio Jacopi, *L'antro di Tiberio a Sperlonga* (Rome 1963), fig. 38.

91. HAND OF SCYLLA. Fragment of a group in marble from the Cave of Tiberius in Sperlonga, found in 1957. Middle of the first cent. B.C. (?) Height: 8 in.; length: 13.7 in. — Sperlonga, Museum.

Lit.: Giulio Jacopi, *I ritrovamenti dell' antro cosiddetto "di Tiberio" a Sperlonga* (Rome 1958), fig. 6, 16. — Giulio Jacopi, *L'antro di Tiberio a Sperlonga* (Rome 1963), fig. 38.

92. SCYLLA AND A SHIP. Decorative relief on a Roman bronze cup from Boscoreale near Pompeii. Acquired in 1897. First cent. A.D. Diameter: 10.7 in. — London, British Museum, Cat. 2882.

Lit.: H. B. Walters, *Cat. of the Bronzes in the British Museum* (London 1899), p. 162,882. — A. Pasqui, *Monumenti antichi pubblicati dall'Accademia dei Lincei* 7 (1897), p. 514, fig. 75.

93. THE OXEN OF THE SUN. Caeretan Hydria from Italy, about 550 B.C. Height: 16.8 in. — Paris, Louvre, Inv. E 702.

Lit.: N. Plaoutine, *Corpus Vasorum Antiquorum,* Louvre III F., p. 9, pl. 8,3.

94. ONE OF ULYSSES' COMPANIONS in despair over the slaughter of the sacred cattle. Bronze statuette from the Acropolis in Athens, found in 1836. 6th cent. B.C. Height: 3.7 in. — Paris, Bibliothèque Nationale, Inv. 811 (Oppermann Collection).

Lit.: Ernest Babelon – J.-Adrien Blanchet, *Cat. des Bronzes antiques de la Bibliothèque Nationale* (Paris 1895), p. 350,811. — H. G. Niemeyer in *Antike Plastik,* Fasc. III, 1, pl. 31 a.

95. CHARYBDIS. There are several whirlpools in the Straits of Messina, which can produce dangerous cross-currents, especially when the wind sets up a strong flow through the straits. The legend of Scylla and Charybdis grew up about these whirlpools. The picture shows the view towards Sicily, with the rock of Scylla.

96. THE BAY OF PHORKYS on the east coast of Ithaca. The ship of the Phaeacians carrying the sleeping Ulysses landed here. The crest of Mt Neriton rises in the background.

97. HEAD OF ULYSSES. Bronze statuette, Roman period (detail of No. 2). Height: 4.7 in. — Paris, Bibliothèque Nationale, Inv. 809.

Lit.: Ernest Babelon – J.-Adrien Blanchet, *Cat. des Bronzes antiques de la Bibliothèque Nationale* (Paris 1895), p. 349,809. — Heinrich Heydemann, *Pariser Antiken* (1887), p. 69,11.

98. ATHENE. Marble statue from Crete. End of the 5th cent. B.C. Height: 4 ft. 6 in. — Paris, Louvre, Inv. 847.

Lit.: *Encyclopédie Photographique* III (Paris), p. 181. — Charles Picard, *Manuel de la Sculpture* II, 2, p. 550, fig. 225. — E. Reisch, *Jahreshefte des österreichischen archäologischen Instituts* 1 (1898), pp. 72 ff., fig. 35.

99. CAVE OF THE NYMPHS. On Ithaca, about a mile and a half from Ulysses' landing-place on the Bay of Phorkys there is a cave with stalactites, the Cave of the Nymphs, where Ulysses hid the presents given him by the Phaeacians. The entry is narrow, but there is an opening in the roof, "the entrance of the gods".

100. THE PLATEAU OF MARATHIA, in the south of Ithaca, supposed to be the place where Eumaeus, Ulysses' faithful swineherd, kept his herds.

101. EUMAEUS. Melian terracotta relief (detail) showing the return of Ulysses. 460–450 B.C. Height: 7 in. — New York, Metropolitan Museum, Fletcher Fund, 1930, Inv. 30.11.9.

Lit.: Gisela Richter, *Handbook of the Greek Collection* (Cambridge 1953), pp. 79 ff., pl. 62 a. — Paul Jacobsthal, *Die melischen Reliefs* (Berlin 1931), p. 68, pl. 88. — Franz Müller, *Die antiken Odysseeillustrationen* (Berlin 1913), p. 83, fig. 7.

102. ULYSSES. Bronze statuette from Roman imperial times. Height: 25.5 in.; badly damaged. — Vienna, Kunsthistorisches Museum, Inv. VI–476.

Lit.: Salomon Reinach, *Répertoire de la statuaire grecque et romaine* II (Paris 1897), p. 40, No. 8. — E. Sacken – Sr. Kenner, *Die Sammlungen des Münz- und Antikencabinets* (Vienna 1866), p. 318, No. 1262. — E. Sacken, *Die antiken Bronzen des Münz- und Antikencabinets in Wien* (Vienna 1871), p. 106, pl. 35–36.

103. THE BAY OF TELEMACHUS, where Ulysses' son landed secretly, to escape the ambush of the suitors. It is south of the plateau of Marathia, in the bay of Port St Andrew.

104. THE SUITORS' BANQUET. Alabaster funeral urn. Found in the necropolis of Volterra. Etruscan. Height (without lid): 18.5 in.; width: 30.8 in. — Volterra, Museo Etrusco Guarnacci, Inv. 514.

Lit.: Heinrich Brunn – Gustav Körte, *I rilievi delle urne etrusche* III (Rome 1870), pp. 238 ff., 2a. — E. Fiumi, *Studi Etruschi* 25 (1957), p. 395.

105. PENELOPE. Melian terracotta relief (detail) showing the washing of Ulysses' feet. 460–450 B.C. Height: 7.7 in. — New York, The Metropolitan Museum of Art, Fletcher Fund, 1925, Inv. 25.78.26.

Lit.: Gisela Richter, *Handbook of the Greek Collection* (Cambridge 1953), p. 80, pl. 62 d. — Paul Jacobsthal, *Die melischen Reliefs* (Berlin 1931), p. 71, pl. 95.

106. THE WASHING OF ULYSSES' FEET. Attic red-figured skyphos by the Penelope-painter, from Chiusi. About 440 B.C. Height: 8 in.; diameter: 9.8 in. — Chiusi, Museo Nazionale, Inv. 1831.

Lit. Doro Levi, *Il Museo Civico di Chiusi* (Rome 1935), p. 115, fig. 63a–63b. — J. D. Beazley, *Attic Red-figured Vase-Painters* II (Oxford 1963), p. 1300,2. — Ernst Buschor in Adolf Furtwängler–Karl Reichhold, *Griechische Vasenmalerei* III (Munich 1900 ff.), p. 124, pl. 142.

107. ULYSSES RECOGNIZED BY EURYCLEIA. Campana terracotta relief, probably from Tusculum. First quarter of the first cent. A.D. — Rome, Museo delle Terme, Inv. 901.

Lit.: R. Paribeni, *Le Terme di Diocleziano e il Museo Nazionale Romano* (Rome 1932), p. 281, No. 901. — H. von Rohden – H. Winnefeld, *Römische Tonreliefs,* p. 252, pl. 28.

108. ULYSSES AS ARCHER. Attic red-figured skyphos by the Penelope-painter, from Tarquinia. About 450–440 B.C. Height: 7.7 in.; diameter: 9 in. — Berlin, Staatliche Museen (Charlottenburg), Inv. 2588 (2522).

Lit.: Adolf Furtwängler, *Beschreibung der Vasensammlung im Antiquarium* II (Berlin 1885), p. 729, 2588. — Adolf Furtwängler – Karl Reichhold, *Griechische Vasenmalerei* (Munich 1900), p. 138,2. — J. D. Beazley, *Attic Red-figured Vase-Painters* II (Oxford 1963), p. 1300,1.

109. THE SLAYING OF THE SUITORS. Limestone relief from the frieze on the west wall of the Heroon of Gjölbaschi-Trysa (Lycia). First decades of the 4th cent. B.C. Height: *c.* 3 ft. 8 in.; length: 25 ft. — Vienna, Kunsthistorisches Museum.

Lit.: Otto Benndorf, *Das Heroon von Gjölbaschi-Trysa* (Vienna 1889), pl. 7. — Fritz Eichler, *Die Reliefs des Heroons von Gjölbaschi-Trysa* (Vienna 1950).

110. THE FIGHT WITH THE SUITORS. Funeral urn of alabaster. Etruscan, 3rd to 2nd cent. B.C. Length: 30.8 in. — Chiusi, Museo Nazionale, Inv. 529.

Lit.: Heinrich Brunn – Gustav Körte, *I rilievi delle urne etrusche* I (Rome 1870), p. 128, pl. 98,7. — Doro Levi, *Il Museo Civico di Chiusi* (Rome 1935), p. 42. — Jürgen Thimme, *Studi Etruschi* 25 (1957), p. 146, pl. 21.

111. SUITOR WITH TABLE. Limestone relief from the frieze on the south wall of the Heroon of Gjölbaschi-Trysa (Lycia). First decades of the 4th cent. B.C. Height: *c.* 3 ft. 8 in.; length: 25 feet. — Vienna, Kunsthistorisches Museum.

Lit.: Otto Benndorf, *Das Heroon von Gjölbaschi-Trysa* (Vienna 1889), pl. 8. — Fritz Eichler, *Die Reliefs des Heroons von Gjölbaschi-Trysa* (Vienna 1950).

112. ULYSSES AND PENELOPE. Melian terracotta relief, 460–450 B.C. Height: 7.3 in.; length: 5.7 in. — Paris, Louvre, Inv. 212.

Lit.: Paul Jacobsthal, *Die melischen Reliefs* (Berlin 1931), p. 69, pl. 89.

113. LAERTES. Melian terracotta relief (detail), showing the return of Ulysses, 460–450 B.C. Height: 7.4 in. — New York, The Metropolitan Museum of Art, Fletcher Fund, 1925. Inv. 30.11.9.

Lit.: Gisela Richter, *Handbook of the Greek Collection* (Cambridge 1953), pp. 79 ff., pl. 62 a. — Paul Jacobsthal, *Die melischen Reliefs* (Berlin 1931), p. 68, pl. 88. — Franz Müller, *Die antiken Odysseeillustrationen* (Berlin 1913), p. 83, fig. 7.

114. LAERTES' VINEYARD. In the north-west of Ithaca, near Exoge and the Bay of Aphalais. It is in the most fertile part of the island, the area of which is four square miles.

115. ZEUS THE THUNDERER. Bronze statuette from Dodona, by a Peloponnesian master. About 470 B.C. Height: 5.3 in. — Berlin, Staatliche Museen (Charlottenburg), Inv. 10561.

Lit.: A. Greifenhagen, *Antike Kunstwerke* (Berlin 1960), p. 4, pl. 12. — Ernst Langlotz, *Frühgriechische Bildhauerschulen,* p. 69, pl. 37.